Books of Merit

The Island of Canada

For Colin
a fine man and
a fine officer.
In warm respect
yours aye
Vic Suthren

VICTOR SUTHREN

THE
ISLAND
of
CANADA

How Three Oceans Shaped

Our Nation

THOMAS ALLEN PUBLISHERS

TORONTO

Library and Archives Canada Cataloguing in Publication

Suthren, Victor, 1942–
    The island of Canada : how three oceans shaped our nation /
Victor Suthren

Includes bibliographical references and index.

ISBN 978-0-88762-406-3

1. Canada—Discovery and exploration. 2. Shipping—Canada—History.
3. Canada—History, Naval. I. Title.

FC179.S88 2009   971   C2009-902512-4

Editor: Patrick Crean
Cover image: Lowell Georgia/Veer

Published by Thomas Allen Publishers,
a division of Thomas Allen & Son Limited,
145 Front Street East, Suite 209,
Toronto, Ontario M5A 1E3 Canada

www.thomas-allen.com

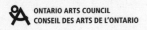

ONTARIO ARTS COUNCIL
CONSEIL DES ARTS DE L'ONTARIO

Canada Council
for the Arts

The publisher gratefully acknowledges the support of
The Ontario Arts Council for its publishing program.

We acknowledge the support of the Canada Council for the Arts, which
last year invested $20.1 million in writing and publishing throughout Canada.

We acknowledge the Government of Ontario through the
Ontario Media Development Corporation's Ontario Book Initiative.

We acknowledge the financial support of the Government of Canada
through the Book Publishing Industry Development Program (BPIDP)
for our publishing activities.

13 12 11 10 09   1 2 3 4 5

Printed and bound in Canada

For Lindsay

CONTENTS

THE ISLAND OF CANADA

A NATION SHAPED BY WATER, AND NEVER FAR FROM IT

JONES SOUND
Devon Island
75°W   60°W
LANCASTER SOUND
SOMERSET IS.
GULF OF BOOTHIA
BAFFIN BAY
GREENLAND
Baffin Island
Melville Peninsula
FOXE BASIN
Southampton Island
FOXE CHANNEL
CHESTERFIELD INLET
HUDSON STRAIT
DAVIS STRAIT
Ungava Bay
ATLANTIC OCEAN
HUDSON BAY
Labrador
Belcher Is.
JAMES BAY
Charlton Is.
STRAIT OF BELLE ISLE
LAKE NIPIGON
Saguenay River
Anticosti Is.
GULF OF SAINT LAWRENCE
Newfoundland
CABOT STRAIT
Prince Edward Island
Cape Breton Island
LAKE SUPERIOR
GEORGIAN BAY
Ottawa River
Richelieu River
NORTHUMBERLAND STR.
Nova Scotia
BAY OF FUNDY
LAKE MICHIGAN
LAKE HURON
LAKE ERIE
LAKE CHAMPLAIN
LAKE ST. CLAIR
LAKE ONTARIO

Introduction

CANADA is an island, for all that it occupies almost half a continent and turns its gaze inward or toward its huge, vibrant neighbour to the south. When the midsummer sun rises out of the cold North Atlantic and warms the first evergreen, rockbound shores, it will not cease bestowing its warmth on Canadian coastlines until twenty hours later. It will have shone down on the longest coastline in the world, fronting three oceans, and the world's largest lake system. Of the immensity of that scene few Canadians are aware, just as they are largely ignorant of the turbulent, colourful history of Canadian experiences on and beside the sea. That history has shaped and defined Canada as much as any stroke of a legislative pen or the blood-soaked carnage of distant battlefields. It has made Canada an island of perceptions, values and commitments, and has helped shape a unique national character. This is a story of the sea and Canada, and of the making of that island.

There is no nation with a greater physical connection to the sea than Canada, and yet there are few people with such a stunning wealth of seacoast who are as unaware, or unknowing, of that connection as Canadians. Perhaps because of the forbidding nature of Canada's oceanfronts, or the often bitter experiences of immigrants who crossed cold seas in grim voyages of endurance to build new lives here, the population of Canada has largely turned its back on the oceans, leaving them to be admired but misunderstood backdrops for urban development on one coast, and a cold, overfished and unloved wasteland for communities that cling like barnacles to the other coast. Perhaps the icy lethality of the northern seas leads the mind and heart to turn away from them, toward a self-preoccupation and myopia conditioned by the difficulties of survival in a climate, until recently, deadly for half the year. It is nonetheless extraordinary that a nation so dependent on the sea for its modern survival as a political and economic entity should remain so ignorant of the sea's impact in shaping Canada as a society, and of its importance for the future.

Perhaps it is naive to look for a rhapsodic love affair with the sea in the Canadian psyche. For the immigrant, maritime memories might principally have been of a hellish voyage of seasickness, creating a mindset of avoidance that sent new arrivals plunging inland on arrival. On Canada's east coast, the immigrant arrived into dark, smoky, grimy seaports that worked with a tight-lipped grimness to wrest a living from the sea. There was nothing of the comparatively benign face that showed itself to a settler of the Carolinas or Virginia, where the principal hazard was one's fellow man. In Canada's West, the towering beauty of the forested shore was as often shrouded in mist and drifting sheets of rain through the long grey winter, and again the seas that washed those beautiful, ironbound shores were as unforgiving as those of the East. To the north, vast sheets of ice and a demanding climate of near-continuous winter made the sea a murderous waste unless, by means of an ancient Arctic culture, a living could be torn from its grasp. Even the shining waters of the Great Lakes could turn in a moment into ship-killing hells of wind and sea as terrible as any tempest on the open ocean. The seas of Canada were places to keep a level head and hold few illusions, lest those illusions lead to disaster and death.

Canadians, new and old, have not been shaped in a world that saw the sea and seafaring in the benign terms of more southerly climes. Even though most major Canadian cities were either built on the sea or had navigable access to it, the people by and large turned their backs on the cold, grey waters—if they could—and gave their hearts elsewhere. Canada has no thriving deep-sea merchant marine to any real extent, its navy has no emotional flagship, unlike Britain and the United States, and only once in its history has a Canadian effort on the sea won the affection and interest of the common men and women on the street: the transcendent career of the Nova Scotia schooner *Bluenose*, queen of the now-vanished Atlantic fishing fleet. Canadians instead made practical adjustments to the sea, accommodating to it because they had to, using it for commercial highways, ruthlessly harvested fishing grounds and, notoriously, sewage outflows. With their cultural hearts and minds drawn from, and taking inspiration from, warmer climes, Canadians have yet to embrace fully the history, the realities, the responsibilities and ultimately the immense possibilities of their northern ocean heritage.

This book is intended as an overview of that heritage for the general reader, seeking to portray it as a broad and understandable panorama for those who may never have access to deeper scholarship on the various aspects of the scene. Each of the many parts of the story of Canada and the sea is like an iceberg, with far more hidden than is visible. It is hoped that this book touches with accuracy on at least those visible parts so that there can be awareness of the great mass yet hidden. There is no newly discovered information here; many of these stories will be familiar. What may be new for the reader will be to see them drawn into an interlocking vista that brings understanding of what the cold northern seas have meant to Canada, and what they can still mean.

The physical scale of the theatre in which the drama of Canada's relationship with the sea has been played, and will be played, is startling in its immensity. Canada's land mass is the world's second largest, 3,854,083 square miles in an area and with a coastline of 36,358 miles, excluding the many islands off those coasts. With those islands added, Canada's coastline soars to a staggering 151,492 miles, making it the longest in the world. More ocean water washes Canada than any other nation in the world.

On Canada's west coast, a spectacular place of deep fjords, large offshore islands and snowcapped mountain ranges looming inland, the mild Kuroshiro Current brings warm water eastward across the arc of the North Pacific and washes a coastline of 14,226 miles, a distance three times the length of the transcontinental border between Canada and the United States. On the east coast, with parts of its evergreen, iron shore touched by the equatorial waters of the Gulf Stream moving north and the frigidity of the southward Labrador Current, the coastline runs to an indented, harshly beautiful 6,960 miles. To the north, the Beaufort Sea, Arctic Ocean, Hudson Bay and Davis Strait waters wash against some of the most stark and forbidding shores on earth, and some of the most hostile. The sea ice of the Arctic archipelago until recently has been almost land-like between October and June, open only here and there in clear patches called polynyas. Out of this vast icefield, and fed as well by ice from fading Greenland glaciers, the Arctic has been sending icebergs on the Labrador Current into the waters of the Grand Banks and Newfoundland, over an area more than half the size of Europe.

Inland, the 1,200 miles of the great St. Lawrence River system lead into the Great Lakes, the world's largest freshwater lake system, with an area of over 95,000 square miles on Lakes Superior, Michigan, Huron, Erie and Ontario. Twenty percent of the world's surface fresh water is held in these glittering, cold inland seas, remnants of meltwater seas from departed glaciers: a volume of some 5,500 cubic miles. The huge inland mass of Canada drains in five major directions into the seas and the Great Lakes: to Hudson Bay, to the Pacific, to the Arctic, to the Atlantic and—by interlocking river systems—to the Gulf of Mexico by the Mississippi River. Fully 60 percent of this rainwater flows north, however, creating or leaving behind almost 291,000 square miles of freshwater lakes and rivers. If sheer statistics are any guide, Canada is the most astonishingly aquatic of nations.

The use that Canadians have made of all this water as, to begin with, a means of transportation has been limited by climate, geographical hindrances such as shallows, rapids and difficult tidal flows, and the tendency in the twentieth and twenty-first centuries for internal trade to rely more and more on highways, trucking and the rail system. The goods that Canada does carry on its navigable waterways tend to be bulk cargoes such as grain, ore, coal and salt. There are, broadly speaking, three types of shipping in Canada: "ocean" shipping, in which fully a third of what Canada makes is exported, with a third going out through Vancouver and two-thirds through east coast ports; "inland," for the most part the bulk cargo carriers of the Great Lakes, added to by numbers of "salties," or foreign-flag freighters using the St. Lawrence Seaway system to get into the Great Lakes; and "coastal" shipping on both coasts and in the Arctic. This last comprises small, general-purpose freighters carrying the goods and services of everyday life, and the ferry systems linking islands and communities to each other and the mainland. Of Canada's leading urban centres, only Calgary and Edmonton lack direct access to the sea. Montreal and Toronto are seaports by virtue of the Seaway, and Vancouver fronts directly on the sea. The majority of the Canadian population lives within a few kilometres of a navigable shipping channel, in the continuous corridor of settlement and cityscape that runs from Quebec City in the northeast to Windsor in the southwest.

The other great traditional activity in Canadian waters since before the coming of the Europeans has been the fishery, and no activity has revealed both the rich resources of those waters and their misuse as the fishery has. On the Atlantic coast there are six formerly plentiful fishing areas: two parts of the Grand Banks themselves, St. Pierre, Banquerau, Sable Island and Georges Bank. In these prime areas, and inshore, the fishery once produced a bounty of Atlantic salmon, capelin, mackerel, scallop, flounder, turbot, hake, redfish, haddock, pollock, herring, plaice—and the once-inexhaustible mainstay, cod. But five hundred years of thoughtless plundering have brought to an end a half-understood resource once thought to be limitless. The east coast fishery has recovered somewhat through fishing less valuable species, and by pursuing lobster and shrimp. But the days of the fishery as an economic powerhouse for the region ended as the twenty-first century opened, its demise

marked by the tombstones of the great offshore oil-drilling platforms that have become the modern hope for eastern communities
in their lonely sea-edge vigil of survival.

Canada now confronts a future of uncertainty and accelerated
change that will affect its relationship with the sea almost as funda-
mentally as has the entire last millennium. The vast North, with its
trackless coastline, is moving from a silent, icebound land only challenged successfully by hardy Inuit into a navigable new world of
opportunity and also of challenges, whether territorial, environmental or political. With a population of barely more than 30 million, Canada faces a teeming, warming world in which avaricious
and determined nations with ten times Canada's population will
compete in building intensity for dwindling resources of which
Canada is a major last citadel of availability. Trade on the world's
oceans continues to grow and become more complex, as does competition between those who wish to preserve what is left of the
world's fisheries and those whose blinkered cultural or corporate
biases have them bent on plundering the oceans for short-term gain
until the fish are truly extinguished. The North–South dichotomy
between an urbanized, consuming elite and the teeming, angry
masses outside that privileged camp will increase in severity; and in
every aspect of national survival, from the maintenance of national
sovereignty to the rescue of an abused and plundered environment,
Canada will need to know what it is doing on its oceans and waters,
and what it will do in the future.

The legacy of Canadians at sea has been one of gritty resolution,
courage and a capacity to overcome the most daunting of challenges. That legacy may well be lost if Canadians remain ignorant
of it, and of the lessons it gives for the looming future toward which
Canada hurtles. Those lessons will be ignored at the country's great
and lasting peril.

In the preparation of this book I owe a lasting debt of gratitude
to Patrick Crean of Thomas Allen Publishers, who believed in the
worth of the story and an attempt to write it, and whose unstinting

encouragement, and the wise editing of John Sweet, made it possible. I am grateful to the staff of the libraries of the University of Ottawa, Carleton University, the University of Toronto and McGill University, and the National Archives of Canada, for their help, and to the library staff of the Stewart Museum, Montreal, and the Maritime Museum of British Columbia, Victoria, for the patient assistance they provided. My wife, Lindsay, provided thoughtful and astute advice on the manuscript as well as inexhaustible patience as it was being written, for which I am deeply grateful.

Having the preparation more of a novelist than a scholar, I have tried to touch on the most salient points of the story of Canada's relationship to the sea in the hope of capturing at least part of the drama of that grand story, and telling it in a popular way. The story lends itself to being painted in plain and simple colours, spare and powerful; Canada's future on her waters can equally be one of bold and powerful imagery, if the will is there to pursue it.

Victor Suthren
Merrickville, Ontario

1

The Pre-European Period

Many thousands of years ago, a great skin boat emerged slowly out of the cold North Pacific mist, lifting over the long grey swells as the fur-clad men and women it carried plied their long paddles in unison. In the middle of the boat, with children huddled in furs around her, a white-haired old woman sang a strange, rhythmic chant to which the paddlers kept time. The paddlers had strong, bronze faces, lined now with fatigue and worry, and they shook back black hair damp with sweat to look out at the empty ocean stretching away into the fog. Their last encampment was days in the past, and the water and seal meat in the skin bags was almost gone. Then a young man in the bow suddenly paused in his paddling and squinted ahead. The fog was lifting, and he could see a long line of surf breaking against a dark shore, above which a sunlit rampart of towering mountains gleamed in glacial whiteness. The young man turned and called back to the others, and there was a cry of relief and thanks. He beamed, knowing he would always carry the honour of having seen the new land first. It was the moment of the human discovery of North America—and of Canada.

IFTY THOUSAND YEARS before that boat's voyage, the physical shape of the enormous land mass of North and South America had become that of the present day. But lying between that distant time and the modern era were one or more ice ages in which huge sheets of glacial ice, much like those found today in Greenland and Antarctica, covered

North America as far down as the middle of the continent. From the evidence that has been found, no human foot had yet trod the Americas. The expansion of the human species out of its African homeland and into two great migratory thrusts, one westward toward Europe, the other eastward toward the Pacific, had not yet reached the American world behind its barrier of the Atlantic and Pacific oceans.

Then, sometime between 40,000 and 12,000 years ago, at the time of a great ice age, the eastward wanderings of humankind did reach the western hemisphere. The actual date is still under question by archaeologists, but the most widely held theory until recently has been that the sea levels were considerably lower world-wide due to the retention of water in the continental glaciers, and that an easily walkable land bridge existed between Siberia and Alaska, where the waters of the Bering Strait now roll. With sea levels down by an estimated 325 feet, the land bridge, which archae-ologists have named Beringia, could have been as much as six hun-dred miles wide. This land may have had a climate and appearance similar to Canada's Arctic today, and been the home of herds of muskoxen, horses, bison and mammoths, in sufficient numbers to lure family groups or bands of neolithic Asian hunter-gatherer nomads across to the empty lands of North America. From what can be determined archaeologically, these first arrivals in North America were biologically modern men and women. No evidence has been found to date to indicate that other types of humanoids lived in the Americas prior to or contemporary with modern humans, as Neanderthal populations appear to have done with Cro-Magnon (modern) man in Europe.

The largest mass of the North American glacier of some 12,000 years ago was the Laurentide Ice Sheet, which covered two-thirds of Canada. A second major glacial massif covered the Rocky and Coastal ranges of mountains. But for various climatological and physical reasons, an ice-free corridor, running from the moun-tains of Alaska to the edge of the great ice sheets in Montana and Wyoming, opened just after the peak of the glaciation, and remained open. This corridor was a place of harsh conditions similar to mountain tundra landscapes today, swept by powerful storms, an unforested, rock-strewn waste dotted with lakes of meltwater and bisected by rivers originating at the faces of the slowly retreating ice mass. An easy passage southward through this corridor would not have been possible much before 10,000 BCE, yet the principal theory until recent times was that the peopling of the Americas took place down this corridor, with the Asian nomads working their way south and spreading within a few millennia to the farthest ends of South America, astonishingly only then turning eastward, so that Labrador became the last place in North America to be inhabited. For the land mass of Canada, the slow retreat of the ice and the change from barren, ice-scraped tundra to boreal forest took place between 10,000 and 5,000 years ago—when agriculture was already under way in the Middle East—and the Canadian climate did not approach its current norms until about 1,500 years ago. In the land migration theory, the ancestral populations of Canada's First Nations passed down the ice-free corridor into what is now the continental United States, only returning northward into what would be eastern Canada as the glaciers slowly retreated.

The culture of these foundation populations is referred to by the term Clovis, after the New Mexico town where characteristic fluted stone arrowheads were found that seem to have been a common feature of early North American settlement. They place the probable time of the land corridor arrival at approximately 12,000 years ago. Recently, however, archaeological discoveries at Monte Verde, Chile, revealed evidence of human habitation that may predate the Clovis culture, dating as far back as 15,000 BCE, when the ice-free corridor did not exist. This has led to a rethinking of how ice age mankind reached North America, and the answer has been to look to the sea.

If, 15,000 years ago, the central land mass of North America was impenetrable, sealed under a three-mile-high cap of unending ice, the southern coastline of Beringia might well have been suitable to support a human population that adapted to a maritime environment in ways similar to the Inuit of today. With the use of hide-covered watercraft resembling the Inuit kayak and larger umiak, a sea-edge culture could have existed, supporting itself by fishing and the hunting of sea mammals, as the Aleuts would do millennia later. It has been suggested there was southward migration by sea of these people along North America's western coastline, moving with such rapidity that by 12,000 years ago, when the ice-free corridor finally opened, humankind had already settled the coasts of North, Central and South America as far south as Chile, making possible the Monte Verde site. The settlement pattern would then have seen coastal communities spreading inland to the east, joined by the later arrivals down the ice-free corridor as it opened, allowing human activity to reach Nova Scotia by 10,000 years ago, well before the full disappearance of the glaciers.

The archaeological record of this stunning 12,000-mile voyage from Siberia to Tierra del Fuego is scant, because the coastal lands where the settlements or campsites of this maritime culture would have been located have been flooded by the return of the sea after glaciers melted. Yet most archaeologists now feel it is likely that the initial settlement of the Americas was in fact accomplished by this seaborne passage along the coast of the glaciated continent to the open lands below the ice sheets, perhaps 13,000 to 15,000 years ago.

On the British Columbia coast, the moderation of the climate gradually turned grey, icebound fjords into the forested paradise of waterfalls and lush greenery that is the Canadian west coast of today. The population of that coast and of its innumerable inlets and islands, the ancestors of the Tsimshian, Haida, Nootka, Coast Salish and other peoples, developed a rich and thriving society based on a fruitful interaction with the sea. Their economy relied on fishing and hunting, pursuing marine mammals such as seals and whales, as well as halibut, seabird eggs, shellfish and herring. As the forests grew into towering stands of evergreens, the coastal peoples developed an ocean-going capability with the production of log canoes well over sixty-five feet in length. These allowed not only aggressive whaling and sealing far offshore, but also the establishment of an extensive trading network along the coast and with inland people. In contrast with the more austere societies in the winter-bound interior of the continent, the bounty of nature allowed the coastal peoples of western Canada to experience a flowering of art and the development of a culture that had as its basis a mythical and metaphysical relationship with the sea.

The wave of human migration moved from its western beginnings into eastern Canada as, far to the south, it reached the limits of the land at Tierra del Fuego. The lowered sea levels of the glacial period meant that Prince Edward Island was part of the mainland, and into this region First Nations groups left evidence of passage as early as 10,600 years ago. With the sea as their primary focus, the movements and encampments of these coastal people appear to have had a pattern similar to that of

Group of Esquimaux, by George F. Lyon *C 127967*

northern bands within historical times, who were hunter-gatherers of marine life in the summer, and who moved inland during the winter to pursue herds of caribou, establishing camps in the forested interior out of reach of the savage winter ocean gales. One might imagine Canada at the close of the last great glaciation period as a huge horseshoe-shaped area of tundra-like land fringing the remains of a retreating glacier, and marked by a great inland sea that would in time shrink to become the Great Lakes. Within this land mass one would find, on the west coast, hardy bands and family groups of neolithic hunters effectively surviving as skin-clad pursuers of sea mammals, rapidly developing a highly complex and seagoing culture based on log canoes; and, on the east coast, a migrating, coast-to-inland society that likely took to the sea in boats similar to the historical Inuit umiak, but who were unable for climatic reasons to develop as artistically complex a society as their west coast cousins.

Yet as these ancestors of Canada's "Indian" First Nations spread across from one coast to the other in the millennia following the glacial retreat, there are tantalizing suggestions of sea-edge migrations on the east coast, along the edge of the North Atlantic glacier wall, that may have rivalled the Beringian quest southward down the Pacific coast. Excavations along the east coast of North America have found evidence of complex sea-hunter societies, almost as developed as those of the west coast, as far south as Maine. After the discovery of evidence of neolithic humanity in Canada's Maritime provinces, dated to around 10,000 BCE, there is a three-thousand-year blank in the archaeological record, which archaeologists refer to as the Great Hiatus, in which no firm evidence of human habitation can be found. The traces resume around 7000 BCE, when sea levels had stabilized after the glacial retreat. Some archaeologists have argued that a culture they refer to as the "red paint" culture—one using red ochre for many purposes, particularly burial—left sufficient traces in coastal North America and coastal northern Europe to suggest a circum-Atlantic maritime culture of sea people extending from the glacial edge in Europe right around the Iceland–Greenland arc to coastal Canada and New England. This would parallel the coasting theory of primary North American settlement by southward voyages from Beringia along the west coast. The theory of the "red paint" culture is based principally on the shape and nature of hilltop burial tombs, and the use of red ochre on the bodies they held, all dating to approximately 7,500 years ago. Most archaeologists and paleohistorians disagree with the concept of such a transatlantic culture, but the shreds of "evidence" continue to stir occasional debate.

More certain was the prevalence in eastern Canada of what is termed the Maritime Archaic culture, which appears to have been the common mode of human existence in what are now the Atlantic provinces from 7,500 years ago, at the end of the Great Hiatus, to about 3,000 years ago. This culture, which was apparently shared by the inhabitants of coastal Labrador, Newfoundland's west coast, Cape Breton and mainland Nova Scotia, was marked by common designs in tools and campsites, and a lifestyle heavily dependent on the hunting of sea mammals. Little is known of the seafaring abilities of this culture; nor do we know whether, like their cousins in distant British Columbia, they set off in large canoes to hunt whales and seals at sea. The lack of resources such as the west coast's cedar trees suggests not, as skin-covered boats—the Maritime Archaic culture's most probable large vessel, rather than dugouts—cannot be built beyond a certain size and remain sufficiently strong for seafaring. Whaling and sealing were more likely carried out much as they were in historical Inuit fashion, the latter on the ice floes, the former an inshore process using many small boats. The image is open to much conjecture. But there are some intriguing similarities between the Maritime Archaic people and the culture of their western cousins, and one of them, albeit on a smaller scale, was the presence of great artistic skill in the carving of bone and stone into meaningful representations. The killer whale was carved in stone, often with great fidelity, and in a manner that suggests it was a totemic or spiritual emblem used, as it was on the other coast, to admire or solicit the hunting and killing power of the killer whale in the pursuit of seals.

The Maritime Archaic culture did not persist in the northern portions of the Maritime provinces, however. About 4,000 years ago a very different northern people, whom archaeologists refer to as "paleoeskimos" or more properly *Tuniit*, spread eastward from Alaska and pushed down the Atlantic seaboard, displacing the Maritime Archaic culture so completely that no trace of the latter is found in Newfoundland or the mainland after 3,500 years ago. With a culture very close to that of the historical Inuit, the Tuniit were part of a third wave of settlement into North America. The first had been the two-stage arrival of what some anthropologists refer to as the Amerindian people, the voyagers along the edge of Beringia and the ice sheets who descended the west coast, and who made a second movement by land down the ice-free corridor that opened at the end of the glacial period.

The second wave had been the arrival of a newer Amerindian group, known as the *Na-Dene*, who not only came to occupy areas of northwestern Canada but penetrated far to the south, to the deserts of Arizona and New Mexico. The third wave had been the great Inuit migrations across the top of Canada from west to east, led by the Tuniit, who penetrated down Labrador to supplant the Maritime Archaic people, only to be themselves supplanted by a later Inuit group known as the *Thule* people. These latter had reached the northern tip of Newfoundland by about 1000 CE, where they were fated to meet the astonished Norse in the role of "skraelings," and thereby close the circle of the great human migration to the west and east out of Africa that had begun tens of thousands of years earlier.

The Thule people themselves retreated northward, to vanish or be absorbed into yet another Inuit population, that of today, by about the end of the Norse Greenland experiment. That had collapsed around 1400 CE, beset by pirates, plague and a rapidly cooling climate. The southern shores of Labrador, coastal Newfoundland and mainland Nova Scotia were now the home of a fairly generic culture of hunter-gatherers of Amerindian origin that would be in place when the major European age of contact opened. Tribal groups such as the Mi'kmaq, the Maliseet and the reclusive Beothuk lived in a manner not unlike that of the vanished Maritime Archaic people. In winter they were dependent upon inland encampments that allowed the stalking and trapping of game deep in protective woods, and in summer they moved to the seacoast to harvest shellfish, fish from shore or canoes with net, weir or spear for mackerel and cod, and pursue the more ambitious hunting of seals and small whales from larger bark and dugout canoes. Their behaviour was echoed by the Iroquoian people of the upper St. Lawrence, normally farmers of corn, squash and beans, but who were known to travel down into the widening mouth of the Gulf as far as modern Gaspé, there to hunt small whales in the Atlantic manner from canoes. Such was the seaborne activity of eastern coastal people when happened upon again by Europeans at the beginning of the 1500s.

On the west coast, the lush physical resources at hand had given the Haida, the Nootka (or Nuu-chah-nulth) and other tribal groups incomparable possibilities for hunting and voyaging at sea, in the form of the huge seaworthy cedar canoes with which coastal peoples came to pursue seals, sea otters and whales as the forests recovered after the retreat of the glaciers and the great trees grew. Among the most capable whalers were the men of the Nootka nation, who carved and shaped extraordinary vessels as long as one of Columbus's ships from towering cedars, forming them into ocean-going canoes with only tools of stone, bone and fire joined to millennia-old knowledge.

Writing in 1975, the west coast historian Howard White provided a revealing view of this vanished technology, outlining how the great canoes were shaped, the rituals and beliefs that governed each step and procedure in their construction as much as did simple practicality, and the ways in which the paddlers created their equipment of harpoon, line, floats and other weapons from the natural resources about them. The whaling season on the British Columbia coast was typically from early May to the beginning of July, and was intended particularly to fit with the migratory patterns of the smaller whales that passed along the coast, whales sometimes no bigger than the canoes that pursued them. Rarely would a canoe attack a huge blue whale, but attacks were launched against grey whales, right and humpback whales, sperm whales and finbacks. On occasion a killer whale would be "struck" to demonstrate courage and prowess, and to obtain the delicacy of its meat.

As White relates, there was a complex ritual involved with the hunt, designed to ensure success and the safe return of the crews.

The principal figure of every whaling expedition was the chief, who served as harpooner on the lead canoe . . . The chief was considered the greatest whaler of the tribe and all whaling equipment belonged to him. The strictest rituals of preparation for the hunt were reserved for the chief and his wife, who were required to live separately and abstain from sexual contact for weeks prior to the whaling excursion.

The couple spent days in singing and praying to the whale before the canoes actually [departed], and rubbed each other's body vigorously with hemlock branches until the plant's needles had been torn off. With blood flowing freely from their scratches, they entered a special fresh-water bathing pool. Submerging and surfacing four times, the pair spouted water in imitation of the whale and moved in the direction that they wished the whale to follow after being harpooned. The wife repeatedly chanted a chorus of "this is the way the whale will act" as her husband sang to the unseen animal. The ritual reflected their great concern to have the whale stay close to the village after being struck. If it headed out to sea it might take days of laborious paddling to bring it back, or it might run out of range, taking the prized harpoon head with it.

A considerable amount of attention was paid to the need for sexual abstinence by all involved in the hunt, beginning with the chief and his wife. When the canoes finally sailed, the chief's wife had to isolate herself in her house and remain under a cedar bark covering until the canoes returned safely, after having ensured that the chief went off to sea wearing the required regalia of a bearskin robe, a ceremonial hat which the wife had woven, and a bundle of hemlock twigs tied to his forehead.

The hunt itself began with an early morning departure to allow as much daylight as possible in the hunting ground, usually a secluded bay or cove where whales might be resting during their migrations, although canoes were known to pursue whales out of sight of land. The lead canoe, carrying the harpooner, was sometimes accompanied by smaller canoes, which would help in the hunt or return quickly to shore with news of a successful strike so that the waiting villagers could pray and sing in support of the canoe crews. Paddling in unison, the eight to ten men comprising the core crew of the lead canoe would draw it swiftly up behind a resting whale on the surface. The harpooner would then strike home his weapon, traditionally behind the left flipper of the animal. The floats and line would be thrown over the side, and the canoe paddled swiftly astern to avoid the plunging flukes of the wounded animal. As the whale struggled to escape, preferably swimming toward rather than away from the village, the crew watched for a chance to close in for a killing blow with lances. Meanwhile, the harpooner/chief sang to the whale, calling it to head toward the village:

Fastening the harpoon point.
C 30205

> Whale, I have given you what you are wishing to get—my good harpoon. And now you have it! Please hold it with your strong hands and do not let go. Whale, turn toward the beach of Yahk-sis and you will be proud to see the young men come down to the fine sandy beach of my village at Yahksis to see you! And the young men will say to one another, "What a great whale he is! What a fat whale he is! What a strong whale he is!" And you, whale, will be proud of all that you hear them say of your great-ness. This is what you are wishing, and this is what you are try-ing to find from one end to the other of the world, every day you are travelling and spouting!

When the exhausted animal was at last brought to bay and killed with the final lance thrusts, additional floats were attached to the body to keep it from sinking, and a crewman would leap over the side and use a chisel to hack holes in the whale's upper and lower mouth so it could be sewn shut, to prevent it filling with water. Then the great prize would be towed back to the village beach. The arrival was the occasion for much religious and traditional cere-mony, beginning with a song of praise to the whale from assembled tribal members, followed by offerings made by the chief's wife. A choice cut of the whale's meat was displayed on a rack outside the chief's house. For days thereafter, celebratory singing and chanting went on in front of the beached carcass, as preparations were made to cut it up. Blubber was boiled in wooden boxes, and the resultant oil was stored in bags made from the whale's bladder and stomach, while the meat was cut, dried and then stored in cedar boxes as food for the time ahead. The effort to dismantle so enormous a hunting prize took several days, and traditionally on the fifth day after the hunt a feast was given, at which the chief and his wife handed out cuts of blubber to the community while accepting none themselves, a precaution against losing luck for future whale hunts.

The scene of the Nootka whale hunt, and the culture of the men and women who carried it out, represents in microcosm a scene that could have been played innumerable times as Asian hunter-gatherers moved into the lands of Canada as the glaciers revealed them, on all its coasts. It was a hardy, self-reliant culture that would not have been unfamiliar to Europeans of 5,000 years ago, who had since left the neolithic world behind as more advanced societies in warmer climes affected them with tools and knowledge. Those tools and that knowledge, and a mixture of curiosity and greed, led them finally to expand out from their European home to enter the world of the North American peoples. Within a few hundred years of that contact, a North American sea-edge culture that had lasted in various forms for perhaps 15,000 years vanished forever.

Ironically, it has been the most recently settled lands and waters of Canada that have retained fragments of that ancient sea-edge culture into modern times, and allowed a glimpse of its nature: the Canadian Arctic, and the Inuit who have called it home. Subject now to climatic change to an unprecedented degree, the Arctic once offered a challenging yet abundant larder of life's necessities to human populations able to adapt to its severe world. Until recent years the Arctic Ocean was frozen from shoreline to shoreline in winter, providing a three-feet-thick expanse of ice that could be travelled over and hunted upon. As the Danish Arctic adventurer

Peter Freuchen wrote over half a century ago, the historical Inuit did not view this harsh world with dislike:

> Although the Eskimo live in a world where even the smallest deviation from the usual—as, for instance, a change in the trek of the seals—can spell catastrophe, a world where danger and death are daily companions, they think it is a beautiful world. They pity those who live far to the south, where there is no ice to drive a dogsled on, and where it is too hot for comfort.

The animal life of the Arctic was abundant when the ice and climate could be relied upon, and it provided the basis of the material culture of the Inuit in pre-European times, at least until the coming of the whalers into the Arctic and the introduction of European trade goods, weapons and foodstuffs in the nineteenth century. Beyond seabirds, sea mammals were the cornerstone of survival: walruses, seals and whales teemed in the frigid waters, and on the endless ice or the barren lands that edged it the Inuit hunter could pursue the muskox and caribou, as well as smaller animals such as the Arctic hare and fox—and be wary of *Nanook*, the polar bear, who was as likely to pursue and eat the hunter as be the prey. From these creatures the Inuit obtained not only blubber and meat for food, but skins to make clothing, bedding, summer tents, and the skin-covered kayak and umiak watercraft. Animal bones were shaped, along with stone, into tools and weapons of astonishing utility and efficient design. Virtually nothing went to waste in the adaptation of the Inuit to their Arctic environment through thousands of years of experience, trial and error, and the sustaining mindset of being at one with the world rather than in conflict with it.

Freuchen's first-hand observations on Inuit watercraft, seen before the technology of the twentieth century brought planked boats and outboard motors to the Arctic, reveal a seagoing technology little changed from that of the ice age mariners who first skirted the shores of Canada:

The [kayak] is also a skin boat, about fifteen feet long, very slender and round on the bottom. The kayakman wears a watertight garment of sealskin, and the manhole is covered with skin in which there is a wooden ring that closes tightly around the hunter's waist. The hunter's hood and sleeves are tight-fitting also, and neither man nor boat takes a drop of water. During a storm the kayakman must be able at will to turn his craft bottom side up and then make it turn up again. For if he sits upright and lets a breaker hit him, his spine may be broken. No, he throws his boat over and takes it on the bottom. Many kayakmen who are well practised in this sport prefer to hunt the seal in stormy weather with big waves, because they can get much nearer to the seal under cover of the waves.

A Fair Breeze   C 30193

The kayak is—or was—a man's boat. Women paddled the umiak, a "large, deep boat made of one or two layers of sealskin tightened over a framework of wood or whalebone." Freuchen found by personal experience that the Inuit women were no less seaman-like than the men:

The performance of these large skin boats is a delight. They float like giant birds on the waves and take no water except for a little spray from the waves. Even this could add up considerably if it were not for the escort of the kayaks. On a trip, the umiak is surrounded by kayaks, like a battleship surrounded by destroyers, and they take the impact of the waves.

On my first umiak trip I sat in the stern of the boat watching the kayakmen. But at length I couldn't sit idle while the women were working, so I insisted upon taking an oar, much to the amusement of both the men and the girls. A couple of hours of the pace set by the girls left me exhausted, and I had to hand the oar back to the embarrassed young woman who had been trying to teach me. The stamina of these girls was astonishing. When we reached our destination they had been rowing for thirteen hours, yet they attended the common merrymaking in the evening and danced for five hours.

The hunting of seals from kayaks involved the use of every possible ruse to approach the wary animals in the months when they would lie basking in the weak sun at the edge of the ice floe, and to be able to strike them with bow and arrow or line-tied lance. Some hunters set up a small screen on the foredeck of the kayak to create a confusing shape behind which they sank down as they drifted toward the seal. In winter, when the ice stretched to the horizon and seals came up to breathe through small holes in the ice, the Inuit hunter would often wait motionless for hours, bent over such a hole, ready to lunge at the animal with a barbed spear and line. For the pursuit of larger game, such as walruses or whales, not being equipped like the Nootka with great log canoes, the Inuit hunted from shore or with fleets of kayaks. And that hunt had its rules and traditions as well, developed over millennia. As Freuchen relates:

> We went walrus hunting on Saunders Island. Knud and I were in our rowboat with a couple of the men, and we acted as mother ship to four or five kayaks. Even with this unusually large number of hunters present, each man knew exactly which part of each walrus was his, for the old tradition decided it according to his participation in the killing of the beast. The one who was "lucky to get first harpoon" got the best parts, "second harpoons" next best, and so on . . . Even the hunters who came up after the demise of an animal would throw their weapons at it in a token gesture of their claims. Actually, we got plenty of walrus to go round . . . but the Eskimos insisted on upholding their rigorous code, and the flensing was done in the way that each man cut out his part.

What Freuchen had been privileged to observe was both a tech-nology and the social conventions related to the use of that technology, and these were living artifacts of the sea-edge, hunting culture that had sustained the men and women of Canada's Arctic for thou-sands of years. In his recording of it, there is no hint of an awareness that it was a culture about to face both a social and a technological assault from the south, and then a climatic transformation of that culture's historic environment into a troubling and unpredictable new form, all brought about by a wider world's technology-based culture, less in balance with the natural world than the Inuit way of life.

With the collapse of indigenous Inuit culture in the face of the arrival of southern technology, educational methods, religions and forms of communication, Canada as a nation is rapidly losing sight of how these most northerly of Canadians understood the origin and function of their world, the ideas that shaped their behaviour, and the cosmology that guided them and revealed the wisdom with which they viewed the natural world and the respect due it. In the following story collected by Freuchen, a folk tale presents a sub-tle message about the linkage between responsible human behav-iour and the capacity—or willingness—of the world to support human life:

There was once an orphan girl named Neqivik who lived in a big settlement by the coast. Nobody cared for her, and she had to fend for herself, and her clothes were poor and worn.

One time they decided to move the settlement, and the people tied their kayaks together, loaded their things on them, and prepared to leave. Neqivik came running down to the scree, she wanted to come along, but the people forbade her to come into the kayaks. And they told each other that if they left her she would starve to death, and they would be rid of her.

Then they sailed out, and the desperate Neqivik had no other choice than to jump into the water and swim after them. She became cold and tired, and she tried to pull herself up into one of the kayaks. But one of the people chopped her fingers off with his ax, and she sank back into the water. But so great was the evil now committed against her that she became the most powerful spirit there is. Her chopped-off fingers became seal and walrus and other animals, and that is how the game animals were created. She herself sank down to the bottom of the sea, from where she rules all the animals in water and on land. She sends them out to people when they have been good and obeyed all taboos. Jealously she watches for breaks of taboos or other things that can insult the souls of animals, and when people have been wicked she closes up the animals in the water basin in her house.

It is a simple but effective allegory. As the Arctic warms, and human society continues to insult the souls of the animals with whom we share the world, it is hard not to think that, far beneath the vanishing ice, Neqivik will indeed close up the bear, the walrus, the whales and the seals. And Canada will know why they have gone.

2

The
Legends

IN RECENT TIMES, books and television documentaries have appeared—musing more on the basis of imagination than on factual support—about European contacts with North America that preceded Columbus. Of these theories, only one has been substantiated by archaeological evidence. The Norse, expanding out of their Scandinavian homeland during a warm climatic period that lasted from approximately 800 CE to 1300 CE, were voyagers to the waters of Canada in exploits that are retained in stories of the era known as *sagas*. These voyages were confirmed, at least in part, by archaeological findings unearthed in 1961 at the northern tip of Newfoundland.

The story of alleged European contacts with Canada prior to the coming of the Norse begins four thousand years before the modern era, when a culture similar to the Maritime Archaic culture, and identified by the creation of large stone funereal structures, spread by sea from the Iberian peninsula to coastal France and on to the British Isles, including Ireland. The common culture this gave the seacoast lands of western Europe provides evidence of a regular and consistent seafaring, and disseminated a body of seamanship knowledge that persisted on the Atlantic coast as empires and cultures waxed and waned. The physical nature of the ships used by these people is unknown, but it is logical to assume that they were open craft propelled by oars and possibly one or more square sails, precursors of the Greek vessels of the classical age.

In the centuries prior to the establishment of the Roman Empire, the Greeks had emerged out of their mountain valley city-states to plant colonies throughout the Mediterranean and into the Black Sea by seaborne expeditions. There is evidence that they, and the Levantine voyagers of Phoenician civilization based in what is now Lebanon, may have brought their Mediterranean oared galleys regularly into the north, sailing out past Gibraltar to track north along the European coast to Britain. The tin mines of Cornwall early became a desired objective of these voyages.

Greek and Roman geographers referred, often in conflicting accounts, to the northern voyages of one Pytheas of Massalia, who reached Britain around the year 300 BCE and then sailed on farther north to an icebound land, which was given the name Ultima Thule. This lay to the north of Britain a distance of six days' sail, and a further day's sail brought Pytheas to a "congealed"—perhaps frozen—sea. Scholars have pondered the identity of Ultima Thule, seeing it as anywhere from the coast of Norway to the Orkney, Shetland or Faeroe islands, or even Iceland. The Greek historian Geminus quotes Pytheas:

The barbarians showed us the place where the sun goes to rest. It so happened at that time that the night in these regions was very short, in certain places of two hours' duration, in others of three, so that the sun rose once again only a short time after it had set.

What Pytheas's voyage, whether fact or fable, did illustrate was that navigation on the northwestern seaboard of Europe in the late Bronze and early Iron ages was apparently a reality. The Britain that the Roman Empire absorbed into its steely embrace just before the beginning of the Christian era was not an unknown outpost at the extremities of European civilization, but already a regular destination for coastal vessels trading for the tin of Cornwall or for other goods of the pan-European Celtic culture of which Britain was a part.

The integration of Britain and its economy into the imperial Roman state ensured a continuous navigation within the realms of the Empire, including the British Isles, but there is little evidence that Roman navigators, like the Greeks or Phoenicians before them, attempted systematic voyaging out of sight of land. When, after 400 CE, the Roman Empire withdrew its legions from Britain, it was the missionary energy of the surviving Christian Church in Ireland that maintained sea contact between that island and southern England, and by 500 CE it was maintaining such a link to mainland Europe and the disintegrating remnants of the western Roman Empire in sailing routes that seem to have survived the dark period of Roman collapse. By the time of the great easing of the climate that began around the year 800, the Irish churchmen, missionaries and hermit monks seeking subjugation of the body on some remote islet had not only maintained the navigation skills and sailing routes that might have collapsed altogether after the Roman departure, but had also quested northward and westward into the Western Ocean on voyages that became legend.

What appears to have happened is that bands of these Celtic monks, seeking closeness to God by means of self-exile on voyages of hardship, travelled to virtually every remote coast of the British Isles by the year 600, and thereafter sailed beyond, particularly to the north and west, in search of new opportunities for self-denial. Their hide-covered boats, built of ox-hides over a wooden frame due to a lack of indigenous timber, and likely driven by a simple square-sail rig supplemented by oars, were the ancestors of the existing Irish currach, and usually carried no more than ten men. In these frail craft the Irish reached the northern archipelagos of the Orkneys, the Shetlands and the Faeroes, and possibly much farther. The historic accounts of their voyages are found in a compilation of legends for which there has been so far little archaeological confirmation: the Imrama, which relates principally the story of Saint Brendan and his companions. The tale of Brendan's voyage into the Western Ocean, though fantastic in some respects and full of borrowings from other stories, provides sufficient evidence, when compared with later Norse traditions, to suggest that Irish monks did indeed reach and settle—if a community intent on punitive self-denial can be said to have settled anyplace—Iceland, having voyaged there some 250 miles from the Faeroe Islands to the east. Writers armed more with speculation than with facts have built on the success of the Irish in reaching Iceland to propose Irish contact with Canada by way of Greenland, but to date no evidence of monkish arrivals on the green coasts of Newfoundland or in the Gulf of St. Lawrence, either in document or in artifact, has surfaced to support the claim.

The possibility that voyagers from Irish or other cultures could have reached Canadian shores well before the accepted period of European contact has given rise to a virtual industry in speculative writing which has attempted to find proof of such contact in cultural similarities, biological evidence, hillside root cellars, mysterious inscriptions on rock faces, and in a very liberal interpretation of the surviving classical literature of those cultures. Certain adventurers, among them the Norwegian Thor Heyerdahl and the Irishman Tim Severin, have undertaken the construction of largely conjectural "replicas" of ancient vessels, and have demonstrated in such craft that transoceanic voyaging was technically feasible for many ancient cultures—that is, if the replicas accurately re-create the sailing technology of those times. Where such demonstrations fail to be convincing, other than as demonstrations of the participants' own courage and seamanship, is in the often bizarre cultural theories on which they are based. Heyerdahl demonstrated the physical possibility of Polynesia's settlement from the coast of South America by voyaging westbound on a balsa raft. Scholars were generally of the opinion that voyaging, if anything, went the other way, with the Polynesians slowly travelling up the wind corridor of the South Pacific from Samoa and Tahiti to Easter Island and, possibly, a South American landfall. Fired by similarities between Mesoamerican pyramids and Egyptian tomb building, Heyerdahl also attempted to show, by a voyage across the Atlantic to the Caribbean on a bizarre reed raft, that Egyptian contacts produced the pyramid architecture of the Mayan and Aztec cultures, an argument that does little justice to the indigenous abilities of the Maya and Aztecs themselves.

More relevant to Canada, and a far more convincing demonstration of a voyage that may actually have taken place, was the so-called Brendan Voyage of Irish writer and adventurer Tim Severin, who with several companions in 1977 successfully sailed a replica two-masted currach from Ireland to Newfoundland, following the land-hopping route by way of Iceland and Greenland. Severin had noted that the Norse sagas told of the Norse discovery on Iceland of evidence of the *papar*, the Norse term for the Irish monks. The notion that storm-tossed Irish monks were the first Europeans to set eyes even farther west, on Canada, remains without documentary or archaeological support. But Severin, unlike Heyerdahl, expanded rather than countered serious historical thought to show that an arrival of Irish monks on Canada's forested shores five hundred years after the birth of Christ *could* conceivably have taken place. And French claims of Christian-like ritual among Amerindians met on the shores of the Gulf of St. Lawrence in the early 1500s leave tantalizing suggestions of a story yet to be told.

More extreme suggestions for transatlantic or trans-Pacific contact with, or even settlement of, North America have followed in the wake of the Heyerdahl and Severin voyages, many motivated by semi-occult religious beliefs or fanciful interpretations of archaeological remains left by vanished North American Native cultures. Arguments have been made that the facial features of Olmec statuary in Mesoamerica give clear evidence of African contact with America, and more than one writer has claimed "proof" of contacts between America and the Greece or Rome of the classical era. Finds of coins, inscriptions and amphora-like wine containers have been used to claim Mediterranean contacts with the Americas, only to be later disproven as either local products, outright fabrications, or the likely transportation of Greek and Roman artifacts to the Americas by immigrants in historically modern times. One such "find" was of Roman coins in a disintegrating leather pouch in New Albany, Indiana, that mirrored other Roman coin finds in New England but which, like those instances, offered no archaeological contextual material to support a truly Roman origin.

The legends of contacts with America include imaginative interpretations of the relation by Aristotle of the discovery by North African Carthaginians, before the rise of Rome, of fair lands out beyond Gibraltar whose location was a closely guarded secret. A Spanish historian writing in the 1500s claimed the Carthaginian discovery to be no less than the West Indies, not the Canary Islands, as most historians had assumed. Stone root cellars found in New England have been used as "proof" of the presence of Irish monks, and a widely believed legend in Wales held that in 1170 the Welsh nobleman Madoc voyaged for some reason to the west, found an attractive land and returned there in 1174 with settlers, who became the source of fair hair, blue eyes and Welsh vocabulary among the Mandan tribe of the upper Mississippi. Colonial stone towers in New England have been used to argue the arrival of medieval knights in Rhode Island, and a Bronze Age runic script known as Ogham has been "identified" all over eastern North America, including an inscription near Peterborough, Ontario.

The list of such conjectural contacts is endless, and subject only to the imaginations and wishful thinking of the writers involved. But until about the year 1400, the only human voyagers known for a demonstrable certainty to have sailed the waters of Canada were members of Canada's First Nations—and the Norse.

The year 1400 becomes a watershed to a degree, because it was shortly after that date that two major contact efforts took place, the one still conjectural, the other much more a matter of historical probability. They included both Canada's west and east coasts.

In the west, both serious historians and popular writers with less rigorous standards for historical proof have been grappling with a persistent claim that Chinese seagoing junks may have visited the west coast of North America, including British Columbia, in the early 1400s. The argument has been put forward by controversial author Gavin Menzies that a fleet of enormous junks arrived off the west coast in 1421, during a period of overseas exploration by the Chinese court. That the sailing technology of the Chinese could have achieved a trans-Pacific voyage of such magnitude is not in doubt: the junk is a sturdy and weatherly design with a lattice-like sail rig that offers the capacity to ride out any sea with buoyancy and stability, and the ability to reduce sail area to contend with any wind conditions. Junk hulls are spacious and able to carry great quantities of stores, and the Chinese were excellent astronomers and understood the use of a compass. The east-flowing Japan Current in the North Pacific, and equatorial west-flowing currents in the trade wind belts, allowed for Asia–North America passages and returns, as Spanish galleons voyaging from the Philippines to Mexico were to demonstrate a century later. The argument is that Chinese historical records, such as the Shan Hai Jing compilations, detail the existence of an attractive land to the east of China named Fu-Sang. Believers in the Fu-Sang identity as the west coast of North America took comfort in the 1972 revelation of a supposedly authentic Chinese map, dated to 1418 CE, that, it is claimed, accurately depicts the west coast of North America and names it as Fu-Sang. Detractors challenge both the map's authenticity and the trans-Pacific thesis, suggesting that the land in question was in fact Japan.

Again, clear archaeological proof for a visit by Chinese explorers to British Columbia is not present. However, the tremendous exploratory period of the Chinese is a matter of record. Chinese fleets were sent off by the court to seek foreign shores in all the directions of the compass, and to determine if anything could be found there that would be of value to the Middle Kingdom, as the Chinese referred to themselves. Fleets of enormous multi-masted junks sailed southwestward through Indonesia and into the Indian Ocean, to India and possibly as far as Madagascar and East Africa. Intriguing discoveries of Chinese ship's bells and other artifacts have been made on the coast of Australia, and it is not beyond possibility that the fleets which sailed to the east did in fact achieve a trans-Pacific crossing and looked on the shores of modern-day British Columbia. The conclusive evidence is yet to be unearthed.

As for the impressive navigational achievements of the Chinese in this era, they came abruptly to an end when the imperial court assessed the findings of the returned fleets. The court concluded that China had no need or use for anything that had been found, and declared an end to oceanic exploration. Further seagoing navigation was banned, and the Chinese turned inward, leaving to history the record of their extraordinary and efficient voyaging. They also left the seas open for the coming of the next great exploratory thrust, that of the Europeans, whose questing across the North Atlantic would lead to the founding of modern Canada.

3

The Norse

The hunter was a small man, smaller than his brothers, but he had learned the ways of the old ones well, and now his wife and her aunt who lived with them wore boots of the finest sealskin. His wife boasted to the other wives that her husband was the best hunter in the village, and that her children ate the finest fat and never went hungry. Now he was paddling his kayak carefully around a rocky headland, his favourite lance balanced across the little boat, hoping that once round the headland he would see a small herd of walruses drawn up on the sunlit beach, and that he could lance a young one before the herd thundered and humped its way into the sea.

Then he froze in mid-paddle, staring in astonishment. Coming into the bay beyond the headland was the largest umiak he had ever seen, but oddly shaped, with a curved point like a lance on its prow. And a huge skin hung above the umiak, bellying gently against the wind. There were great paddles reaching out from the sides of the vessel, rowing slowly in unison. But it was the hunters aboard the umiak that astonished him the most. They were indeed men, but strange men, with skin as pale as winter snow, and great beards, more than his grandfather ever grew, some black, but some the colour of the island grass after the summer sun had been on it. The hunter dug in his double paddle and eased the kayak into the shelter of the headland. He would hide and watch the great umiak, for it was not clear to him whether these ghost creatures meant well or ill . . .

IF THERE IS UNCERTAINTY about most theories of early European transatlantic contact with Canada before the major discovery period, there is little doubt about one story. The Norse, expanding out of their Scandinavian homeland during the warm climatic period between 800 and 1300 CE, were confirmed voyagers to the waters of Canada in exploits that are retained in the sagas, and which are supported by archaeological evidence found at the northern tip of Newfoundland in 1961.

While the ancestors of the modern Danes and Swedes provided their share of the wandering freebooters, traders, pirates and outlaws who formed the ensemble of notorious rovers known as Vikings, it was principally the Norse whose westward explorations would bring them finally to the evergreen shores of North America. This great explosion of the Northmen, as fearful southerners called them, came when a growing population and the limits of arable land in the fjords and coastal valleys of Norway produced increasing numbers of landless men for whom seafaring for trade or plunder seemed the only possible way of life. Simultaneously, the climate of northern Europe underwent a precipitous warming that lessened the brutal risks of northern sea voyages. The Scandinavians had developed a unique boat and shipbuilding technology based on a graceful, double-ended hull design that made use of the plentiful timber supplies and capable ironworking available to them. The design utilized overlapping planks of wood in the hull, a pattern known as "lapstrake," which, when clenched and fastened to internal support frames and a long curved keel, created a flexible and speedy hull that sailed well under a simple wool and leather square sail, and also rowed swiftly when as many as twenty men seated themselves at the oars. The sail could be "braced," that is to say, swung at an angle from its usual crosswise position, and with the windward corner of the sail pressed tautly forward by means of a long bearing-out pole known as a *beitass*, the double-ended boat with its long keel could be sailed to windward, although less efficiently than the Arab lateen. Steering was accomplished with an oar affixed at the stern on the right side of the hull—the "steering board" side of the hull, later shortened to "starboard"—and crew and cargo alike were exposed to the elements in the open hull of the craft.

There were two major types of these "Viking" vessels. One was the long, slender, lethal-looking "snakeship" of popular tradition with a detachable dragon figurehead, a shallow-draft coastal vessel meant more for fighting than for voyaging. The square sail and the single mast on which it was set could be lowered and laid fore-and-aft in the middle of the ship, the men's shields could be hung out of the way on the gunwales, and with the oars pulled with a will, the Norse swept in these craft along the coasts of western Europe and the British Isles in a terrifying period of piracy and shore raiding that began in earnest in the 790s. Striking without warning, the snakeships left few communities untouched on the British and Irish coastlines, penetrated the Seine as far as Paris, and were known to have passed Gibraltar and entered the Mediterranean. In the east, at the same time, Swedes ventured into northern Russia, penetrating the river systems until, finally, astonished Greek residents of Constantinople were visited by the pale-eyed northerners, some of whom remained to become members of the emperor's bodyguard.

As the 800s opened, the Norse and Danes in the west slowly shifted from merely pursuing sack and plunder to establishing trade, and finally to actual settlement. As this pattern developed, a second and more useful Norse vessel came into its own. This was the *knorr*, of the same basic design as the snakeship, but an ocean-capable cargo ship rather than a fighting machine. Bulkier in the hull than the snakeship, the knorr could carry cargo, passengers and even animals in its capacious hull, and could be rowed and sailed in open-water conditions that would have swallowed up a slender, shallow-draft snakeship. Able to contain sufficient provisions for serious voyaging, the knorr carried the Norse and Danes outward to Ireland, Scotland, the Orkney, Shetland and Faeroe islands, and everywhere in coastal Britain, driven not only by population pressures at home but also by the upheaval resulting from King Harald's efforts to subjugate west Scandinavia to his rule. The dispersing Norse fleeing this fight in turn fought for and claimed new land in the British Isles, and held it against the counterattacks of the Celtic or Anglo-Saxon inhabitants.

In the 880s, however, the Vikings were handed severe defeats by the Bretons and elsewhere in France. When they shifted their focus to England, the armies of Alfred the Great halted them, while in Ireland the native chieftains were regaining the upper hand, as were the Welsh in Anglesey. Driven back on themselves, the Norse did one of two things. One was to put down the outlaw sword and build new lives and accommodations in the lands they had once plundered. England would have its Danelaw and France its Normandy. The other choice was to return to the sea and discover what new lands, what new homes, might lie over the warming ocean to the west. By 860, Norse-Danish *knerrir* had already been reaching Iceland on exploratory voyages, astonished to find there those pockets of Irish hermit monks, the *papar*, who soon disappeared to an unknown fate—perhaps farther west—within a few years of the Norse arrival.

The Norse rediscovery of Iceland meant there was a place where men could escape not only the diminishing opportunities in the now-aroused conquered shorelands of Britain and western Europe, but also the continuing juggernaut of Harald's ruthless pursuit of power in Norway. Many Norse could not accept Harald's insistence that they submit to him as feudal vassals or forfeit lands and rights. So they filled their knerrir with their goods and families, tools and livestock, and sailed for the refuge of Iceland, joined by men whose conquests in Britain were becoming too difficult to defend.

The Welsh historian Gwyn Jones, writing in 1964, gave a clear description of the level of seamanship this sort of ocean adventure required, and the unique suitability of the Norse to achieve it.

> The sea passages west over the open Atlantic demanded good ships and good men to sail them. Throughout the Viking age the Norwegians had both, and had them in plenty. They had the best ships of any European people . . . By sail, and when necessary by oar, [the knorr] could go anywhere, to the Atlantic Islands, to Iceland, Greenland, and the North American coast. The ocean-goers were sailed with immense courage and skill by men without compass or chart but inured to hardship and learned in the sea's ways. They sailed by latitude and the sun and stars, by landmarks and the flight of birds, by the evidence

of marine creatures and the colour of water, by rough or dead reckoning, by currents, driftwood and weed, by the feel of the wind, and when need be by guess and by God. They used the line to search the ocean's bottom. In a good day's sailing of 24 hours they could cover 120 miles and more.

Whether alerted to the existence of land to the west by the flights of seabirds, or simply having trusted to fate and their own intuition, the Norse found Iceland, and within fifty years of the first settlement, which took place around 870, several hundred families were established on the island, the climate of which was considerably more benign than it had been. Flourishing small farms were created in the valleys and at the heads of bays and inlets, and a sturdy pagan republic of sorts—marked by a general assembly called the Althing—produced a society that sheltered the homeless men ejected by King Harald's hegemony or the resistance of more southerly Europeans. Iceland became a western outpost of Europe nonetheless, more so than when it held only Irish monks intent on self-denial. A sea route now lay open, readily navigable to and from the islands north of Britain. It was only a matter of time, however, before the pressures and passions that had brought the Norse to Iceland would send them questing westward again. The story of that quest is related in the Norse manuscript known as the Groenlendinga Saga, contained in the Flateyjarbok, written at the end of the 1300s.

The westward voyaging did not take long to begin. The process of discovering Iceland itself, and the very inexact nature of marine navigation in the ninth and tenth centuries, meant that missed landfalls, deadly storms, and ships either swallowed by the sea or sailing hundreds of miles off course were a matter of fact. Around the year 900, a Norwegian with the resonant name of Gunnbjorn Ulf-Krakason sailed westward from Norway bound for the new settlement in Iceland, but was caught in a storm out of the northeast. It drove his knorr far past Iceland, and he was astonished after several days of running before the gale to see land ahead—rocky islets, and the mass of a much larger shore looming behind. Ulf-Krakason did not land, but turned when the gale abated and managed to find Iceland, where this new land and its outlying islands were promptly christened the Gunnbjarnarsker in his honour. The news of his discovery spread through the communities of farms and captured the imagination of a troublesome outlaw named Eirik the Red. Eirik had fled Norway after a feud with another family in which blood had been spilled, resulting in Eirik's banishment. He had proved no less a problem in Iceland, and, faced with a three-year exile from the island for more killing, he chose to sail west for Gunnbjarnarsker, toward what Gwyn Jones would call the "glimpsed cloud-hackles and ice-shirted mountains of Greenland."

Sailing from Iceland, Eirik and his crew faced an open sea passage of some 560 miles. The usual Norse custom, if sailing night and day, was to keep the position of the North Star at a constant altitude above the northern horizon, and thereby sail directly along a line of latitude. Norse technique was to lie-to with the sail lowered if there was no moon or starlight, so as not to run into land in the darkness, and by means of this general plan Eirik's knorr made the passage ahead of the sub-polar easterly wind, from Snaefellsnes at the extreme western end of Iceland to a landfall in Greenland approximately at the location of modern Angmagssalik, in just under four days. His first glimpse was of an iron, inhospitable coast of rock and mountains, with a white glacier gleaming inland. Turning left, or southwestward, Eirik sailed along the Greenland shore, threading his way through the offshore islands, until he rounded the southern tip of Greenland, the modern Cape Farewell. Here he turned northwestward into a region sheltered from the strength of the easterly wind, where he found fjords, bays and islands similar to his native Norway. The shorelines were rich in grasslands, stands of juniper, birch and willow, and a profusion of flowers and edible berry plants, all basking in a warm summer sun in a scene of heartwarming beauty. The Norse found evidence of human existence, likely of paleoeskimo origin—or of Irish monks—but the land was now empty.

Without knowing it, Eirik had chanced upon one of the two isolated places on the southwest coast of Greenland where human habitation was possible. Taking a particularly beautiful fjord for his own use, which became Eiriksfjord—the modern Tunugdliarfik—Eirik and his men built a settlement over the course of Eirik's three-year banishment, and then sailed triumphantly back to Iceland, laden with animal skins and walrus tusk ivory. So impressed was Eirik by what he had found, and anxious to convince other Icelanders to move there with him, that he named the new country Groenland, or Greenland.

His news fell on welcoming ears in Iceland. The colony had not yet recovered from a ten-year period of famine, and strife among the surviving farmers added to a general atmosphere of discontent and restlessness in which Eirik's return and news of the new land gripped the imaginations of many. Eirik prepared to return to Greenland in the summer of 986, and was astonished to find twenty-five ships laden with hopeful settlers and their goods ready to accompany him. The passage was not an easy one, with some ships turning back and others lost in fierce weather. But most of the sturdy knerrir made it through, the total of the survivors numbering some four hundred men, women and children. The Icelanders settled in two main areas. The eastern one, known as Eystribyggd, was located where Julianehaab now stands, and 375 miles to the northwest along the coast, the western settlement, or Vestribyggd, was established, about where the modern town of Godthaab sits. Few other sites in the narrow coastal plain allowed farming to any degree. But if traditional farming was a tenuous business, the rich hunting, sealing and even whaling available in the waters up the northwestern coast soon drew hunting parties far to the north, almost into the true Arctic. Very soon a pattern developed, with the basic farming pursuits of cattle raising and sheep herding being supplemented by extensive hunting of both sea mammals and caribou, as well as by fishing. This produced a sustainable and thriving little community, which only needed trade with other parts of the world to anchor its future.

The seagoing valour of the Norse soon led the Greenlanders to create a trading voyage pattern, not to hard-pressed Iceland, but to Norway itself. As Jones explains:

> Among the early settlers were men who owned their own ships and plied the seas as merchant-venturers. From Greenland they carried furs and hides, ropes and cables so strong that the heaving of three score men could not part them, with walrus and narwhal ivory . . . In addition [to these things and wool] the Greenlanders had seal oil and similar commodities for export. In return they needed . . . timber, iron for all purposes, made weapons, [wheat], clothes of continental style . . . malt, wine, and church vestments. [These could not] be obtained from Iceland. They came from Norway instead, and for a while came sufficiently. So long as this balance of trade could be maintained, in theory the life of [the Norse] in Greenland could go on forever. Like the [Inuit] they had hunting and fishing with all their products, and in addition animal husbandry to provide them with meat, milk and wool. They lived in a hard world, but a world filled with hope and promise, and time must have seemed their friend.

For the first few centuries, the Norse thrived in Greenland. But by the 1300s the settlement would be in decline, ravaged by the Black Death that came with the rats carried aboard the few ships that appeared, by the depredations of pirates, and by a cooling of the climate that ended the sunnier era of 1000 CE, ushering in the Little Ice Age, which lasted until the late 1700s. Of all this, however, there were few omens in the heady years of first settlement, and it was in the flush of those years that the Norse would reach westward again. The prows of the knerrir would now have Canada ahead of them.

A few weeks after Eirik's fleet sailed for Greenland in 986, another ship put out from Iceland, steering to the west in Eirik's track. This ship was steered by a young man named Bjarni Herjolfsson, an Icelander. Herjolfsson had been in Norway over the previous winter, collecting a cargo for Iceland, and had sailed home expecting to rejoin his father. On arrival in Iceland, however, he found that Herjolf had gone with Eirik's settlement fleet, and had sold his—and presumably Bjarni's—Icelandic possessions before departing. With his crew's agreement, Bjarni reprovisioned and set off in pursuit. On the voyage's third day, Herjolfsson's crew spotted Greenland's mountains before encountering fog and strong winds, which drove the knorr off to the south. When the fog cleared, Bjarni was astonished to find they were off a low, forested shore. After sailing for some time northward along that shore, Bjarni turned with a favourable wind to the northeast and managed to arrive safely in Greenland. Bjarni made little mention of his discovery—the land he saw had not seemed farmable—and contented himself with establishing himself in Greenland.

Fourteen years later, in 1000, the arrival of Christian missionaries and the death of the powerful King Olaf Tryggvason of Norway set in train social upheavals in both Iceland and Greenland, and for some reason Herjolfsson voyaged to Norway. During or just before this trip, he casually revealed to Eirik and his sons what he had seen to the west fourteen years earlier. If Bjarni Herjolfsson himself had been unmoved by the significance of what he had found, the story of his discovery raced like wildfire through the great halls of the farms of the western and eastern settlements. Most excited by the story was Leif, the son of Eirik, who had become a superb sailor, voyaging regularly between Greenland, the British Isles and Norway. Gathering an adventurous crew of thirty-five men, Leif bought Bjarni Herjolfsson's knorr and prepared to seek out these new lands. His father gave some thought to going on the voyage too, but fell off his horse on the way to the beach and injured himself. This would be Leif's voyage.

Eiriksson adopted a simple plan. Herjolfsson had sailed southwest from Iceland, then north along the new land, then eastward for Greenland. Eiriksson would sail west, retracing Herjolfsson's final leg in reverse, and then coast southward. The square sail of the knorr could be advanced on one side of the ship or the other, and the yard from which it was hung could be swung to allow the ship to tack against headwinds to a degree. Only a strong headwind dead out of the west would prevent the voyage, and in these high latitudes the prevailing winds were from the east.

The Groenlendinga Saga relates the voyage simply, as quoted in Jones:

> They prepared their ship, and when they were ready they sailed out to sea and came first to the country which Bjarni had seen last. They sailed to land, anchored, put out the boat and rowed ashore. From the shore to the glaciers was as one flat slab of stone, and the country did not appear attractive to them. Then Leif spoke, saying "Things have not gone for us as they did for Bjarni regarding this country, for we have been ashore here. I shall now give this country a name, and call it *Helluland*, Flatstone Land." After which they returned to the ship. They sailed on and found another land. They went in to land, anchored, put out the boat and went ashore. This country was low and wooded. Stretches of white sand spread out before them, and the coastline did not fall off sharply into the sea. Leif said, "We shall give this country a name fitting its appearance and call it *Markland*, Wood Land." Then they rowed straight away back to the ship.
>
> They sailed on over the sea for two days with a northeasterly wind again and came to a country and an island which lay north of the country . . . Then they returned to the ship and sailed into a sound between the island and the ness which projected from the country to the north. They steered west past the ness. It was now very shallow there at ebb tide. The ship went aground, and soon they had to look far to catch sight of the sea at all. But they were so eager to get ashore, and not wishing to wait until the sea once again lifted the ship, that they landed immediately . . .

Eiriksson and his crew found the conditions at this last landfall so attractive—"Neither the river nor the lake was lacking in salmon. They had never seen such large ones"—that they determined to overwinter at the site. Their experience was highlighted by the discovery of what the Groenlendinga Saga claimed were grapes, although the translation of the Old Norse word *vin* and its meaning have been subject to debate by scholars. The new land became Vinland.

The landfalls made by Leif have equally been subject to discussion, but most likely the stony Helluland was northern Labrador, or possibly Baffin Island. Markland, with its densely wooded shores and long white sandy beaches, describes a specific area of the coast of southern Labrador. As to Vinland, conjectural thinking before 1961 placed it anywhere from Newfoundland to New England, and even farther down the American coast. Then, in 1961, an extraordinary archaeological discovery was made by Helge Ingstad and his wife at L'Anse aux Meadows, at the northern tip of Newfoundland. The Ingstads unearthed traces of Norse sod buildings, ironworking and a few Norse artifacts, all at a site that matched the Groenlendinga Saga description. As no archaeological evidence has come to light anywhere south of this site, it seems apparent that Leif Eiriksson's Vinland was the northern tip of Newfoundland, which had been rendered a more habitable place by a warmed climate.

Following a successful overwintering at the settlement they built, known as Leifsbudir, Leif and his crew loaded their vessel with hides and other treasures—including the mysterious *vin*—and sailed for Greenland. Leif's voyage inspired one by his brother Thorvald, who sailed to Leifsbudir and overwintered, then spent the following summer exploring far down the western coast of Newfoundland before returning to overwinter again at Leifsbudir. The following spring they sailed north to Markland, where Thorvald was killed in a skirmish with *skraelings*, the name the Norse gave to the Inuit inhabitants of the land. This incident, on the forested Labrador shore, is the first record in preserved human

Thorvald Eiriksson's battle with the Indians, 1003 C 5539

history of the moment of contact that closed the circle between the two great migratory movements of the human family that left Africa many thousands of years in the past, one to move east, the other to move west. Leaving many of the skraelings dead, Thorvald's crew reached their ship, and in due course returned safely to Eiriksfjord.

There was now a third voyage, a serious settlement attempt led by Thorfinn Karselfni, who guided three ships and over 150 men and women, with livestock and tools, to Vinland. The expedition crossed to Helluland and then coasted south past Markland—all aboard expressing wonderment at the beautiful, endless beaches, which they named Furdurstrandir, or "marvel strands"—before arriving safely at Leifsbudir in Newfoundland. This settlement voyage would not find the land empty, however. The skraelings were present in great numbers, and the sagas relate that in their skin boats, "brandishing their double paddles, and on their second appearance, so plentiful that it looked as if the bay had been sown with coals," they vastly outnumbered the Norse. A pitched battle was fought somewhere on the Newfoundland coast, at an unknown place the Norse called Hop, and although the Norse prevailed with their iron weapons, they ended their sojourn in Vinland after three tense winters, and sailed for Greenland in 1009. With them was the first European child known to have been born in North America, Snorri Thorfinsson, born possibly in 1007.

There was a final, brief attempt at settlement at Leifsbudir the following year, in 1010. Led this time by Leif's daughter Freydis, the expedition disintegrated into murder amongst themselves and another savage encounter with the skraelings. When the knerrir of Freydis's ill-fated attempt sailed home in 1011, leaving the skraelings in possession of Vinland, the decade of Norse settlement attempts in the New World came to an end.

Yet tantalizing clues remain to suggest that the Norse had not given up entirely on North America. The Iceland annals of the year 1121, a full century after Leif, Thorvald, Thorfinn and Freydis, record that Bishop Eric Gnupsson of Greenland made a voyage to Vinland. Later, in 1347, a storm-beaten ship put in to Iceland from Greenland, having been driven off course after a voyage to Markland. The truth with respect to continuing, but unrecorded, voyaging or even settlement of the Norse in what would become Canada is open to speculation. Certainly the navigational knowledge of how to get there was never lost. What is clearly known is that the hardy Norse, in an extraordinary two centuries of expansion out of their home fjords and mountains, had sailed to the waters of Canada, lived on its shores, and then been driven away by the resolute resistance of another people, who have since vanished, even as their Viking invaders have, into the pages of Canada's maritime history.

4

The Europeans Find Canada, 1490–1610

CANADA is psychologically an island, to a degree few Canadians realize, and that mentality began to be shaped in the seafaring that brought Europeans to Canada's shores in the 1400s. It was a period of extraordinary European innovation in navigation, leading to an expansion out of their territorial waters just as the Chinese were retreating ashore. Europe's society at the turn of the first millennium CE was in a period of turbulence, the tumult abetted to a degree by the warmed climate. The Norse had exploded out of the Scandinavian peninsula in all directions, an energy that by the year 1000 had taken them deep into Russia and down its rivers to the unimaginable splendours of Constantinople; down Europe's western coasts to form fiefdoms as far afield as Normandy and Sicily; and westward to Iceland, Greenland and Newfoundland. In Britain and continental Europe, partly as an outgrowth of renewed vigour and fighting organization in response to Norse raids, partly in enthusiasm over the millennium, and partly because of Church interest in focusing all the militant energy of Europe's warriors on a unifying purpose, the crusading movement arose. This militaristic surge sent European armies off to conquer the Holy Land and install "Frankish" west European Christian kingdoms there that lasted for a century or two before collapsing. The Christian knights' holdings in Palestine vanished, leaving only empty hilltop fortresses to mark their passing, but the returning knights and their retainers brought back to gloomy, rainy Europe and its diet of mutton and beer a permanent taste for the spices and luxuries of the sunlit Mediterranean world. Trade arose in these goods, dominated by Venetian and Genoese shippers, to feed this new hunger for Levantine treasures.

A resurgent Islam, having swept away the Christian kingdoms, now made impossible a general trade with the East, allowing only a virtual monopoly on such trade to the canny Venetians and Genoese. Prices soared, availability fell, and the two Italian cities grew rich with the profits. Then, a misguided later "crusade" sacked and looted the Christian city of Constantinople, weakening the major surviving Christian outpost in the eastern Mediterranean and strengthening even further the hand of the Venetian-Genoese monopoly. But another force was at work, and this was the remaining crusader zeal in Spain and Portugal, where the Muslim Moors were being slowly driven from their former holdings in the Iberian peninsula.

The leaders in the seaward aspect of this pressure were the Portuguese, who could not match Spanish strength on land but were excellent mariners. Under the leadership of King João I, the Portuguese were determined to use their newly developed abilities at sea to expand from trading on the Atlantic littoral in prosaic goods such as fish to an eastward thrust via the open sea in pursuit of gold, spices and the luxuries of the East, as well as profits from a developing trade in slaves. The capture of Ceuta, a Moorish port on the North African coast, in 1415 was the first overt sign of this Iberian expansion. Present at the siege was a member of the Portuguese royal family, Prince Henry, who became fired with the idea that Africa might be merely a peninsula—no one knew what lay to the south of the Moorish kingdoms of North Africa—and a way to the East that both obviated the Venetian-Genoese monopoly and outflanked Islam by sea. Retiring from the court, he established a centre for the development of navigation, geographical knowledge and seamanship. Under his tutelage, and under later Portuguese monarchs such as João II, the Portuguese put to sea to attempt this sea route to the East. The capture of Constantinople by the aggressive Ottoman Turks in 1453 added fuel to the search for the sea route to the East, and produced refugee Greek scholars who contributed to the explosion of knowledge and inquiry that would become known as the Renaissance. On this tidal wave of curiosity, commercial avarice, religious fervour and sudden technical improvements, the Portuguese led Europe to sea in a great exploratory emergence even as, halfway around the world, the Chinese were leaving their ships and looking inward.

In the 1400s, European ship technology went through a rapid change that put in European hands ships as able and seaworthy as the junks the Chinese were dismantling. The Arabs had developed the winglike, triangular sail known as the lateen that allowed a ship to tack well to windward. The Portuguese, who were familiar with this rig and used it in their first explorations, soon combined it with the sturdy square sail of the north European ships that evolved from the Norse knorr. With the square sail's better suitability for heavy open-ocean sailing and the lateen's windward ability, the Europeans had in their grasp ships combining both rigs, which were able to voyage the oceans of the world. Within a generation or two, the Iberians would do so.

The single-minded aim of the Portuguese, and that of the Spanish on their heels, was to secure routes to the fabled riches of the Middle and Far East. With a growing European population hungry for a source of protein, the French and English, rebuffed from sharing in the quest for the East by Iberian power and suspicion, contented themselves for the moment with securing a productive North Atlantic fishery. At the beginning of the 1400s the demand for dried cod, known as "stockfish," became so great that northern European port towns began to send fishing fleets to sea in pursuit of cod. At first the English were overwhelmed at sea by the better-equipped fleets of the French and the Basques, but before long they had copied the new seagoing designs of the Portuguese and were searching for fish off the Orkneys, Shetlands and Faeroes. By

1410, English fishing fleets were reducing the cod stocks around Iceland and casting about for fishing grounds farther afield. In that search lay the roots of Canada's discovery—and its enduring relationship with the sea.

To the west of Iceland lay Greenland, its eastern and western Norse settlements now all but obliterated but still within living memory: the last contact with the remaining few inhabitants had been in 1408. The sea route to the west from Iceland was well known, and several authors, including Kirsten Seaver, have proposed that the aggressive English may have established a fishery in Greenland waters in the early 1400s. The English were not yet the equal of the Spanish or Portuguese on long ocean passage making, but they were capable of the line-of-latitude methods of the Norse of four hundred years earlier; and it has been suggested that the English and others, such as the Basques, sailed on farther and reached the coastal fisheries of North America shortly after their arrival in Icelandic and Greenland waters. This would have put European fishermen on the coasts of Labrador and Newfoundland, and onto the Grand Banks themselves, fully seventy years before Columbus set sail on his southerly voyages. However, there is little archaeological evidence to support this thesis other than a few English artifacts found in Greenland. Still, the slowness and difficulty with which knowledge was disseminated in the late medieval world may have concealed the fact that English fishing hulks of the 1400s were sailing in the way of Norse knerrir to Canada's teeming fisheries. The navigational challenges of reaching Greenland and North America were not greater than those of reaching Iceland, and by 1450 English vessels were far more capable craft than they had been in 1415.

Christopher Columbus is said by some biographers to have claimed an Icelandic voyage in the 1470s, which may have put him in earshot of the sagas and knowledge of the sea route to Greenland and the North American coast, where Greenland and Icelandic vessels routinely sailed to obtain supplies of wood. It is conceivable that in Columbus's mind the lost discoveries of the Norse were outlying

lands of the Asian continent, an idea that took him twenty years to
bring to fruition with his voyage of 1492. It is fascinating to consider that had he made his voyage in northern latitudes, he might
have reached Canada only to find a prosaic English fishing fleet riding at anchor there. The likelihood seems to be that Columbus, and
others such as Cabot, who sailed west after him, was quite aware
that land lay to the west; he was simply unsure *what* land it was. That
knowledge came from the inherited and perhaps not-so-forgotten
legacy of the old Norse course to North America. In any event, the
likelihood is very high that dark, weather-beaten little hulls of English, Basque, Breton and other fishing vessels sailed and worked
Canada's coast well before Columbus's masthead lookout cried out
that land had been found; and the communal memory of that long-
ago Norse landfall may have drawn Europeans back to Canada's
dark evergreen shores in an unbroken tradition of voyaging from
the Viking era right through to the Renaissance.

Their innovations in navigation and seamanship saw the Portuguese sailing out from the Iberian peninsula and rounding Africa
by the end of the century, en route to India. The Spanish were not
far behind, but when, in 1492, Columbus demonstrated to a wider
European audience that the Indies—or whatever that new land
was—could be reached by sailing *west*, the claims of both Spain and
Portugal for rights to the riches of the new lands led to a serious rift
between the Iberian kingdoms. This was resolved by a papal inter-
vention resulting in the Treaty of Tordesillas of 1494, in which a
north-south line was drawn round the globe west of the Azores. All
discoveries east of it were declared the realm of the Portuguese,
while all to the west fell to Spain. The English and other north
Europeans, and certainly the inhabitants of the new lands, were not
consulted in this division and were expected not to interfere.

The Portuguese, in their explorations in the South Atlantic,
were delighted to find that Brazil fell within their sphere of monopoly. Portuguese, Basque, French and English fishermen may well
have been voyaging to Atlantic fishing grounds since the early
1400s, but it had been an open ocean in which all was up for claim,

and no nation wanted another to know what its ships were doing. The 1494 treaty changed all that—at least, the Portuguese and Spanish insisted that it did—and in 1500 the Portuguese Gaspar Cortereal made an ostentatious voyage in the direction of Newfoundland to determine what might lie there of interest to his monarch. Clearly, he had not been keeping up with the news. At any rate, Cortereal was seen by fishermen as he grandly sailed past, only to promptly vanish without a trace.

A second formal Portuguese expedition was sent out in 1520 under the command of Alvarez Fagundes, who prudently followed the fishing fleet to the Grand Banks but then turned in to the Gulf of St. Lawrence and explored it to a degree that has yet to be revealed by research. It must not have impressed Fagundes, for he returned and reported to Lisbon that the cold northern lands held little of immediate value to Portugal except the teeming fishery. The Portuguese were happy to turn their energies again to the warm seas of the Indian Ocean. For the Spanish, any interest they may have had in the serious exploration and exploitation of North America was abruptly eclipsed by the discovery and conquest, between 1517 and 1521, of the astounding Aztec Empire of Mexico. Its seizure and, even more, the spectacular plunder from the Inca Empire of Peru a few years later, kept Spanish interest in the south, and soon opened a floodgate of gold and silver into Spain and the wider European community that brought Spain to a pinnacle of power and revolutionized Europe's economy.

To all this fervid exploration and plundering the English, French and Dutch, the latter of whom were locked in a struggle to free themselves from dynastic Spanish rule, were merely envious bystanders, with little ability to challenge the Iberians' growing power either economically or at sea. In the 1400s it was the de facto explorations of fishermen that largely led north European discovery westward, or perhaps helped in the rediscovery of something that was buried in the collective memory. Although it had hardly been a generation since the last recorded Greenland trading voyage had taken place, English merchants who sensed that something special

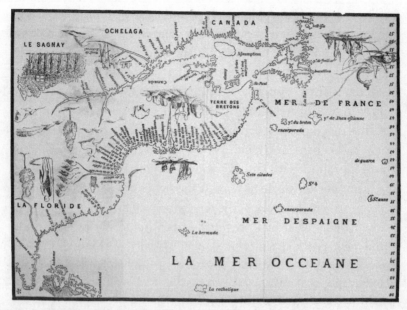

The Dauphine Map of Canada, showing Cartier's discoveries C 99068

lay to the west marvelled at the energy and achievements of the Portuguese and the Spanish, and determined to emulate them without
offending the powerful Iberians. Several courageous investors of
the industrious and disciplined little port city of Bristol determined
that a quest to the west for larger purposes than just the fishery
had to be undertaken. The merchants had been listening to the
grog shop talk about the routes to the fishery, and had an imperfect
but growing idea about fabulous lands underneath the sunset to
which they gave the generic name "the Brazills." Surviving charts of
the mid-1400s show imaginary islands dotted about the ocean west
of Europe, one of which was invariably labelled Brazil. If the cold,
rain-sodden northerners could garner for themselves some of the
wealth the Iberians were pursuing in sunnier climes, it would be
worth the investment to find one of these lands. The first serious
attempt was funded by Bristol merchant John Jay in 1480, who sent
off an eighty-ton ship to the west in search of Brazil. Inauspiciously,
it rolled home empty-handed some months later, but the interest in
the western waters was not about to die.

The news of Columbus's voyage and the continuing success of the Portuguese in their quest for India spurred the Bristol merchants to greater efforts. In 1497, an Italian who had become Spanish, Giovanni Caboto, convinced Bristol merchants and an unenthusiastic Henry VII to support a westward exploration. Sailing in May 1497 with twenty men in a tiny vessel, the *Mathew*, Caboto endured a storm-tossed passage across a grimmer North Atlantic than the Norse had known, and luckily saw what was likely Newfoundland before he ran into it. Turning south, he followed the forbidding shore, finding very little to suggest the riches of Cathay. He and his crew marvelled, however, at the huge stocks of fish they came upon; the knowledge that had previously been held only by fishermen would now reach a wider audience. Historian Heather Pringle quotes Raimondo di Soncino, who wrote from England to the Duke of Milan after Caboto's safe return:

> They declare that the sea there is full of fish that can be taken, not only with nets but with fishing baskets, a stone being placed in the basket to sink it into the water . . . And the said Englishman's partners say that they can bring so many fish that this kingdom will have no more business with Iceland, with which country it has a very large trade in the fish called "stock-fish."

Caboto returned claiming against all evidence that he had found Asia, and if he privately had misgivings about such a statement, it nonetheless earned him support for subsequent voyaging. The dissemination of the news of the wealth of the Atlantic fishery was, however, the more significant result in an era of poor communication. It was as important for North America as the revelation of the Aztec and Inca empires had been for Central and South America. The key lay in the large number of fast days in the Christian calendar, when no meat could be consumed. The Pope had decreed that fish could be eaten on those days, and the market for fish, particularly cod, was large and increasing as Europe's population rebounded after the devastation caused by the Black Death of the 1340s, when a third or more of Europe's population had been carried off.

As in the pioneering mid-1400s, the leaders in the rush to exploit this now wide-open resource were not the English, as aggressive as they had been in penetrating the Icelandic fishery, but the French and Bretons. They had competed with the English for the fish stocks off Iceland through the 1400s, and, astonishingly, they had been on the coast of Africa as early as 1364, well ahead of the Portuguese. As in England there were unsubstantiated rumours in the continental merchant community that French and Breton fishermen were making regular voyages to fishing grounds "beyond Greenland" well before the end of the century, but poor communication meant that few outside the fishing community knew of them. The first actual documentary record of these voyages was finally published in 1504, describing Breton anchorages on the Newfoundland coast. The French and Bretons would continue to fish there until the great wars of the eighteenth century severely limited French fishing rights in Canadian waters they had frequented for three hundred years.

In the nature of the fishery lay the roots of eventual English dominance in this trade with Catholic Europe by the end of the 1500s. The French, Bretons and few Portuguese would transport their catches as "wet bulk." This meant that the fish were caught, heavily salted as they were and stowed below, and the ships sailed for home as quickly as possible. The English lacked large supplies of salt, and so, more out of necessity than choice, they set up stations onshore, where they landed the fish to gut and dry them, then lightly salted them from their meagre supplies before shipping them home. This dried fish was infinitely more portable and storable than "wet bulk," and gradually through the 1500s the European preference for the lightly salted dried cod of the English gave more and more market share to the industrious English over the French, Bretons and Portuguese. Then, in the 1580s, the Spanish and Portuguese crowns were united, and their joint focus turned away even more from the northern fishery to the harvesting of Inca gold and, for the Portuguese, the exploitation of trade with India. By the time of the Spanish Armada, which sailed against England in 1588, not only was England challenging Spanish might where at the beginning of the century she had been fearful of it, but the Spanish imperial court was being fed on fast days predominantly by English-caught dried cod from the Grand Banks that the Iberians, French and Bretons had been the first to exploit.

If English energy slowly overcame the French and Breton initiative as regards the fishery, the French maintained a steady interest in discovering the nature and extent of the vast lands behind those fishing banks. The Gulf of St. Lawrence and the mighty river that empties into it drew their interest almost immediately, and as early as 1506 a Jean Denys of Honfleur created an imperfect but recognizable chart of the Gulf. Two years later, in 1508, Thomas Aubert recorded his ascent of the St. Lawrence a distance of some eight leagues—over 250 miles—and brought back to France seven astonished members of an Iroquoian band he and his crew had happened upon. Aubert was accompanied on that first historic penetration of Canada's inland waters by Giovanni da Verrazano of Florence, who much later, in 1524, would map the east coast of the modern United States and mount the first declared effort to find a Northwest Passage to China around North America. Ten years later, the Baron de Léry is recorded as attempting a settlement on Sable Island. This project soon failed, but left behind were livestock that thrived and provided a boon for later shipwrecked mariners there.

After Aubert, the next serious French effort at exploring Canadian waters came in 1534, when a one-time pirate, rover and adventurer from Saint-Malo with solid seamanship qualifications, Jacques Cartier, sailed on April 20 with two small ships, sixty-one men and a destination of the "new found land." Cartier followed the Breton and French fishing routes to southern Labrador, and then entered the Gulf of St. Lawrence by the Strait of Belle Isle. He continued along Newfoundland's west coast to Cape Ray, then turned southwest and passed along the north shore of Prince Edward Island, marvelling at its beauty. Steering northwest, he entered the Baie des

Chaleurs on a stifling midsummer day—hence its name—and then pressed on past Percé Rock and Bonaventure Island to the harbour of Gaspé. Here he went ashore and erected a tall cross bearing the arms of Francis I of France, and claimed the land for him. Crossing to Anticosti Island's eastern tip, he worked his way westward along its heavily forested north shore, pausing like Aubert to take aboard two Native fishermen, before turning around and steering for home once again through Belle Isle.

In May of the following year, 1535, Cartier sailed again, this time with three ships and 110 men, including the two Native fishermen, who miraculously had survived European food, diseases and sanitation. By late July his flotilla passed through Belle Isle, and he followed the north shore of the Gulf this time, encouraged by the great river's width as it stretched inland. Hopes that it would somehow lead to the Pacific were dashed in September, when Cartier arrived at

Jacques Cartier (1491–1557), engraved by Freeman   *C 7298*

the mouth of the Saguenay River and realized he was sailing on fresh water as much as salt. Nonetheless, he pressed on, and with a favouring east wind he soon arrived at the site of Quebec, where he found a palisaded Iroquoian village named Stadacona. The two captured fishermen were reunited with delighted villagers who knew them, and an amicable visit with the villagers and their chieftain, Donnacona, ensued.

Though the season was growing short, Cartier left his larger ships at Stadacona and set off upriver under oar and sail with fifty men in a forty-ton pinnace and two longboats. After several days he arrived at another village, Hochelaga, on the site of modern Montreal. He scaled the mountain behind the village, erected another cross, and peered off to the west at the great rapids and the river stretching away in the distance. Hopefully naming the rapids and the land beside them La Chine—China—he returned with his little flotilla to Stadacona, where he planned to overwinter. If Cartier was expecting the comparatively mild winter of Saint-Malo, the icy fury of the season when it came was an appalling shock. The crews, huddled in their icebound ships and in the smoky longhouses of the agreeable Natives, suffered miserably from the cold and were decimated by scurvy until the villagers showed Cartier how to prepare a form of evergreen tea that abated the scorbutic symptoms. With the coming of spring in 1536, Cartier abandoned one of his ships, embarked the shaky survivors of his crews and managed a safe return to Saint-Malo. He would make other, unsuccessful colonizing voyages in 1541–43.

As the seventeenth century opened, French interest in voyaging westward beyond the fishing grounds reawakened, and more than one man stepped forward to attempt a Canadian colony. Henry IV granted those rights to a Marquis de la Roche, who found, however, that enthusiasm for colonizing Canada was difficult to generate, and resorted to raiding prisons to secure unwilling participants. The Marquis's dream of colonial grandeur evaporated when he was immediately wrecked on the French coast at departure, and his surviving transports put the hapless convicts ashore on Sable Island, where they began to eat their way through the descendants of the livestock left by de Léry in 1518.

If France's fortunes in the New World were to have any legs at all, champions of greater mettle were clearly needed. Fortunately for France, such men were waiting in the wings. François Gravé, Sieur de Pont *dit* Pontgravé, had been on an early voyage to Canada and saw the possible value of a trade in furs. He approached the king with a request for a monopoly on such trade, in company with Pierre Chauvin of Honfleur and the Sieur de Monts. A wary king granted their request, but on the condition that they agree to plant a successful colony in the new lands. Between 1599 and 1603, Pontgravé and Chauvin established and maintained a successful trading post at Tadoussac, but the effort ended with Chauvin's death. Back in France, the partnership reconstituted itself, with Aymar de Chastes replacing Chauvin, and the men organized another voyage to reopen the little post at Tadoussac. Sailing on that trip was a new associate, a very able seaman and soldier who would have a far-reaching impact on the story of France and Canada: Samuel de Champlain.

Champlain was born in 1567 in Brouage, France, then as now a low-roofed, walled medieval port surrounded by marshes and a shallow inlet of the sea. Champlain had emerged from modest origins into a seafaring career, but then had been caught up in the religious wars and risen by merit to become deputy quartermaster-general of Henry IV's army at the peace of 1598. With his military career at an end, he had reverted to seafaring and accepted a Spanish offer to captain one of the fleet ships of Admiral Francisco Columbo, which was sailing for Mexico. Champlain spent two years in Mexico, recording his experiences with intelligence and perception. On his return to France, he was recruited by Aymar de Chastes for the reorganized Tadoussac venture, and sailed for the St. Lawrence in March 1603.

Here walks onto the stage of Canadian seaborne history one of its most admirable players. Writing in 1902, historian John Fiske said of Samuel de Champlain:

He was a true Viking, who loved the tossing waves and the howling of the wind in the shrouds. His strength and ability seemed inexhaustible, in the moment of danger his calmness was unruffled as he stood with hand on tiller, calling out his orders in cheery tones that were heard above the tempest. He was a stern disciplinarian, but courteous and merciful as well as just and true; and there was a blitheness of mood and quaintness of speech about him that made him a most lovable companion. In the whole course of French history there are few personages so attractive as Samuel de Champlain.

The year's trading at Tadoussac was uneventful, and it ended with the death of de Chastes and the termination of the trading licence. The next year, 1604, the Sieur de Monts assumed the leadership of the group and convinced the king to grant them a trading monopoly in lands stretching from the St. Lawrence to modern Pennsylvania. De Monts adopted a Mi'kmaq word, *Aquoddy* or "place," to refer to his new trading domain, rendered as *Acadie* in French. The 1604 voyage brought the company, joined by the Baron de Poutrincourt and historian Marc Lescarbot, to a disastrous first winter on a small island at the mouth of New Brunswick's St. Croix River. The next spring, Poutrincourt led a transfer of the post to the beautiful Annapolis Basin of Nova Scotia, and a walled and fortified little *habitation* was built there, christened Port-Royal. Friendly and respectful relations were established with the local Mi'kmaq community, and during the years 1605–7 the little post thrived while Champlain took a small vessel and explored the coast of New England. It was an idyll that came to an end in 1607, when de Monts's licence was repealed by the king under pressure from jealous competitors. The little *habitation* was abandoned to the care of the willing Mi'kmaq.

Energetic lobbying led to a one-year renewal of the trading licence, and Pontgravé sailed for Canada in April 1608, with Champlain following a week later. But now their energies shifted again to the St. Lawrence, and the old post at Tadoussac. When Pontgravé arrived, he found that Basque traders had refurbished the post's buildings and were doing a brisk business in furs with the Natives. Only Champlain's arrival prevented a bloody encounter between the French and the Basques. After tempers were soothed and an agreement arrived at, Champlain moved up the river. He found that the village of Stadacona, below the bluffs and on the narrows known as Kebec in Algonquin, had vanished without a trace. There, on the low shore where Quebec's Lower Town now stands, Champlain built a *habitation* in the style of Port-Royal.

The trade was soon everything the company could have hoped for. Pontgravé sailed in the fall for France, his ships laden with rich furs to feed the new European fashion for felted beaver hats, leaving Champlain to overwinter at Quebec with twenty-eight men.

The little post suffered through the grim winter with no helpful villagers to guide them. When Pontgravé returned in the spring, he found only Champlain and eight men alive. A new agreement was arrived at: Pontgravé would manage the post while Champlain would explore the country. It was a decision that began the shaping of the outline of modern Canada.

If the English were latecomers to the exploration of Canada's vast land mass and of its shoreline, the momentum of their interest built slowly and steadily through the 1500s. Intrepid men such as John Davis, Henry Baffin, Martin Frobisher and Humphrey Gilbert were involved in attempts to probe the northern land mass, initially only in an effort to get through it to Asia. There was little if any English interest in exploring the huge new continents, even as English fishermen continued to bring home the lightly salted dried cod that was now in demand all over Europe. Until about 1550, America was seen for the most part as a forbidding barrier to the sea route to Asia's riches. The English could only watch, like children at a candy store window, as galleon fleets groaning under the weight of Potosí silver from Bolivia and treasures transported from the Philippines arrived in an unending stream at Spanish ports. A few tentative southern voyages were attempted, but the English Crown, anxious not to offend Spain and Portugal any more than it already had, showed little interest in sending ships off "on discoverie."

Through the 1500s, English power slowly grew, and the great fear of Spain slowly changed to a determination to make England's own mark on a world the Spanish largely claimed as their own. This new boldness may have brought Sir Francis Drake to the shores of what would become Canada. Over the period 1550–80, as Elizabeth I came to the throne and England moved from a position of fearful avoidance of Spanish wrath to an open animosity toward Spain, the decline of English trade and the threat of Spanish attack galvanized anew English determination to find an independent route to Asia. The writer Richard Hakluyt presented to the queen a "Discourse of

Western Planting," which, far from being an agricultural treatise, argued for an American colony from which to attack the Spanish monopoly on Asian trade.

By 1577, England was in a virtual state of overseas war with Spain, and in that year, on December 13, Francis Drake sailed with three ships for the Pacific in an outright challenge of Spain's authority and monopoly. That voyage may have brought Drake to

the shores of western Canada after he rounded Cape Horn and plundered the Spanish American colonies and shipping in an epic circumnavigation that lasted until September 1580. In 2003, the writer Steven Bawlf published a book that claimed Drake sailed with secret instructions to find a passage from the Pacific into the North Atlantic, and that his actual landfalls on America's west coast were suppressed in the records so as not to alarm the Spanish, who claimed ownership of the west coasts of both North and South America. Drake had repaired his surviving ship, the *Golden Hinde*, at "New Albion," which it has long been assumed meant either San Francisco harbour or one nearby. Bawlf claimed that surviving charts by Drake identify British Columbia landfalls, which would make Drake and his crew the first Europeans to set eyes—and possibly feet—on the soil of western Canada. The change in English thinking about Canada as the century progressed is evident: in 1555, writers claimed Canada was good only for its cod fishery, while by the time of Hakluyt's "Discourse" (1584), Canada, or at least North America, had become a land worthy for colonization, and a post from which to attempt a Northwest Passage rather than merely a heavily forested barrier to it. It was a fundamental shift in thinking.

Martin Frobisher (1535–1594), by Gucht C004727

The end of the 1500s and the opening of the seventeenth century saw a last tragic chapter played out in the early search for the Northwest Passage around Canada, in the story of Henry Hudson. Hudson had spent the years 1607–9 in the pay of Dutch and English merchants, attempting to find a Northeast Passage around Scandinavia. On his last such voyage, in the *Halve Maen*, he had turned back on the Norwegian coast and instead steered westward for North America, where he explored New York harbour—first identified by Verrazano and the French in the previous century—and sailed up the river that came to bear his name. His voyage led the Dutch to claim the Hudson River valley as theirs, but Hudson was censured for having disobeyed his orders.

Undeterred, Hudson found new backers, who chartered him to sail again on a Northwest Passage voyage, providing for him the sturdy fifty-five-ton vessel *Discovery*. He sailed in April 1609 and steered for the mouth of what would become Hudson Strait, which John Davis had remarked was characterized by "furious overfalls" of conflicting tidal currents. He successfully entered Hudson Bay after being trapped by northerly winds in Ungava Bay, the first successful passage of the Strait. In 1602, a Captain George Weymouth had seen the Strait and attempted to enter it, but was stopped when his crew refused to go on. Hudson named Cape Wolstenholme and Cape Dudley Digges, and then, as the vast expanse of the sunlit bay opened to the south, cracked on more sail, certain he was on the coastline of Drake's New Albion. That dream died in the swampy, mosquito-infested shallows of James Bay, where Hudson anchored the *Discovery* over the winter of 1609–10 in Rupert's Bay.

After a harrowing winter, the crew mutinied in June 1610, leaving Hudson, his son and a few others adrift in James Bay in the *Discovery*'s shallop, and sailed off for England deaf to their entreaties and tearful pleas. The mutineers did not escape further disaster, however. Near the mouth of Hudson Strait the ship anchored so fresh water could be found, and Inuit attacked—or defended themselves against—the mutineer crew. Only nine men survived to sail

the *Discovery* home, where their tale was so distorted and unbeliev-
able that no one was prosecuted for the crime. The surviving senior
mutineer, Robert Bylot, eventually had an island named after him
and would sail again to Canada. Of Henry Hudson and his son,
their companions and the shallop, no trace was ever found.

As Hudson morosely contemplated his likely fate, on the far side
of Canada the Spanish and their surrogates were coming to the end
of a relatively brief and strangely half-hearted effort to explore the
Pacific coast north of their Mexican conquests. In 1520, the ruthless and determined Hernan Cortés, with his steel-clad conquista-
dores, had by guile and force seized the Aztec Empire and set about
exploiting it as a source of profit. Fifteen years after his bloody conquest, he was on the Pacific coast at what would become known as
Baja California, unsuccessfully attempting to create a pearl fishery.
But the endless sunburned coastline stretching away to the north
remained unknown. Then, in 1541, an expeditionary voyage of a
single small vessel sailed from Mexico up that long, unknown coast,
commanded by Francisco de Bolaños. Bolaños skirted the new
country, noting the attractive appearance of what would later be the
Los Angeles Basin, and settled on a name for it that was inspired by
a novel he had read. The novel told of an island ruled by Amazons
led by a Queen Califia—and so the land became "California." On
Bolaños's heels came a more determined explorer, João Rodríguez
Cabrillo, who sailed up the coast in 1542 beyond Bolaños's landfall,
only to fall victim to accident and die in the Santa Barbara Channel.
The expedition's command fell to one Bartholeme Ferrelo, who was
made of equally stern stuff. Ferrelo sailed resolutely north along
the stark coast until he encountered a very different kind of landscape from that of California—dark, forested shores and cold seas,
a coastline that could have been anywhere from Oregon to British
Columbia—before turning back.

Ferrelo's brave voyage inspired little interest in the hallways of
Mexico City, however. Of far more importance to the Spanish colonial governors was the beginning of the "Manila Galleon" voyages,

in which each year a Spanish merchantman sailed from the Far East laden with Oriental riches on a long North Pacific track to Mexico. On arrival in Acapulco, the goods were carried overland to the Gulf of Mexico, there to be loaded into the Treasure Fleet sailing via Havana for Spain. The Pacific voyage was an arduous one, following the Japan Current above the North Pacific high-pressure area and then coasting down the Alaskan and Canadian shores for eventual arrival in Mexico. So exhausted and sick were the crews of these galleons that a hospital to receive them was built at the tip of Baja California, and it is possible that these storm-beaten, weed-fouled hulks, with their scurvy-decimated crews, saw and may on occasion have been wrecked on Canadian shores. Not every galleon arrived safely in Mexico.

But knowledge of the dark, cloud-hung northern coasts was not then a priority for the Spanish. There was some continuing interest. Sebastián Vizcaíno sent off several ships on explorations to the north, and one of these, captained by an itinerant Greek named Apostolos Valerianos, may indeed have found the Strait of Juan de Fuca in 1592; it was the name Valerianos went by. His possible voyage into Canadian waters, twenty years before Hudson's lonely death far to the east, marked the limit of possible European exploration of the west coast of Canada for years to come. There was a voyage by Vizcaíno himself in 1602 that may have reached as far north as Oregon, but after that date the Spanish were content to leave the rainy, forested shores of the north to their indigenous inhabitants. The coast of western Canada would lie unseen and untouched by Europeans for the next century or more.

5

Fur Trade
and Forests

The young captain leaned over the alehouse table and stared down at the drawing of a sleek, rakish vessel. He scratched at his beard and swore an appreciative oath. Then he looked up at the man across the table, whose brown eyes were regarding him intently. "Aye, she'll fly right enough, Walter. But why? Why build ships like these?"

His companion smiled. "To command the seas, Richard. Whosoever commands the seas, commands the trade; whosoever commands the trade of the world, commands the riches of the world—and consequently the world itself. Now, ye lay to that!"

A s HENRY HUDSON lay dying of exposure in his long-boat, a resurgent England had moved from fear of the Spanish to a determination that, somehow, England would secure a share in the incredible new riches pouring into Europe. And the words of Sir Walter Raleigh summarized this new thinking. But if the wealth of Central and South America being looted by the Spanish could not be had directly by England, the wealth of Asia and India was another matter, Treaty of Tordesillas or not. The hunt had begun for a northern route by which to reach the wealth of the East more easily than by the lengthy and dangerous voyages round the Cape of Good Hope or the dreaded Cape Horn.

In 1612, with new support from interested merchants, the English returned to the hunt for the Passage. Sir Thomas Button sailed in Hudson's *Discovery*, fifty-five tons, whose very boards must have creaked with grim memories for the man who sailed with Button as his navigator, the unpunished mutineer Robert Bylot. Button crossed the Atlantic without incident, and worked through the extraordinary tidal rips that mark the mouth of the Strait, crossing over the great bay's green, crystalline waters until he made landfall off the flat, low-forested land at the mouth of the Churchill River. From there Button turned south, rounding Cape Churchill and finding a winter anchorage site near the mouth of the Nelson River, named for a crewman who had died on the voyage. Nearby would later be built the fur trading post of York Factory. Prepared by Bylot's experience for the long rigours of the winter, Button brought his crew through it safely, but fled next spring, as soon as the ice would allow, from the ravenous clouds of mosquitoes. Sailing up the west coast of Hudson Bay, Button crossed eastward along the south coast of Southampton Island before re-entering the Strait and steering for home.

In 1615, *Discovery* was once again bound for Canadian waters, this time with the imperturbable Robert Bylot in command and William Baffin as navigator. Entering Hudson Strait, they worked their way along the iron, spectacular south coast of what would become Baffin Island until they reached the end of the Foxe Peninsula at its southwest corner. There they turned north into what would become Foxe Basin, then west, "having a great Swelling Sea out of the west with the Winde which had blowne: which put us in some hope." Instead of a passage opening westward, Bylot found the dead end of Repulse Bay on the Nunavut mainland. Coasting back along the northeast shore of Southampton Island, Bylot steered for England.

Over the winter, Bylot, Baffin and their backers talked over the voyaging results so far. Baffin argued that Hudson Bay offered no westward passage except by "some creeke or inlet" and that the Northwest Passage lay farther north, somewhere above Davis Strait. Accordingly, in 1616, the intrepid pair put to sea again in the hardy *Discovery*. This time they tracked farther to the north, making landfall on Greenland much as Eirik the Red had done five centuries before, rounding its southern tip to sail north along its west coast. With remarkable fortitude Bylot and Baffin pressed on to the edge of pack ice at the latitude of Smith Sound, which for another two hundred years would mark the northern limit of exploration. Turning south, *Discovery* sailed past the mouth of Lancaster Sound—ironically, the true Northwest Passage—which the two explorers felt was only another inlet. Baffin's journal sighed, "Here our hope of a passage began to lessen every day." Steering at last southeast for Greenland, they rounded into the Atlantic and sailed for home. They arrived in England on August 30, 1616, to remain forever unaware of how close they had come to their goal.

Three years later, in 1619, a rare Danish expedition to seek the Passage sailed west across the Atlantic, led by Jens Munk and consisting of the ships *Unicorn* and *Lamprey*. The crossing was uneventful, and the dangers of Hudson Strait were overcome. Munk explored the great bay for a time until the weather closed in, and he attempted to overwinter at the mouth of the Churchill River. Whether from scurvy, a vitamin C deficiency disease, or trichinosis from eating uncooked pork, sixty-one seamen died over the winter, leaving only Munk and two others alive by spring. Incredibly, Munk and his two weakened companions somehow managed to sail the *Lamprey* back to Denmark, an extraordinary feat of seamanship.

A significant effort in the hunt for the China route occurred in 1631, when two separate voyages took place, one by the Londoner Luke Foxe in a little thirty-ton pinnace, the *Charles*, and the other by Welshman Thomas James in a similar pinnace, the *Henrietta Maria* out of Bristol. Both little ships survived the Atlantic crossing and entered Hudson Bay, where they made landfall somewhere on the bay's western coast and then steered south as far as what James called Cape Henrietta Maria. Foxe turned north again at this point, and sailed well up into what would become Foxe Basin until he was stopped by ice. Low on supplies, and aware of the lateness of the season, Foxe turned again for the Strait and safely took his frightened and freezing crew home to England.

Thomas James was determined to overwinter, however, and he brought his little ship with the unwieldy name to Charlton Island, in the southeast corner of the bay that now bears his name. The rigours of the winter proved appalling, but James was resourceful, temporarily sinking the *Henrietta Maria* to put it below the damaging ice level. Hunting and the careful husbandry of their meagre supplies got all but four of the twenty-man crew through the endless months of cold, but James almost brought an unexpected end to the expedition when a fire he set to attract Natives swept across most of the island and narrowly escaped roasting him as he sat up a tree scanning the horizon for signs of the shy inhabitants. With the coming of spring came also the thick swarms of mosquitoes and blackflies, and James and his tormented crew refloated the doughty *Henrietta Maria* and fled north, eventually reaching Bristol in safety.

James wrote a colourful account of his experiences, titled "The Strange and Dangerous Voyage of Captain Thomas James," and in it he expressed the fading hopes of finding a true Northwest Passage, observing gloomily that "even if that merely imaginative passage did exist, it would be narrow, beset by ice, and longer than the route to the East by the Cape." A full century would go by before the next serious attempt by sea to locate and sail through the Northwest Passage.

If the Passage was temporarily set aside as a preoccupation for European minds, something far more accessible and immediately profitable was concerning them, and that was the newly discovered trade in furs with the Native population of North America. Thomas James decried the navigational dead end of James Bay but allowed that it was "the home of the choicest fur-bearing animals of the world." With Europe still in the grip of a Little Ice Age that would not ease for another century or more, the stunning pelts brought back from Canada by the first explorers, particularly that of the beaver, had caused a revolution in European clothing. Among the new fashions that developed in the Elizabethan age were brimmed hats made of felted beaver fur, replacing the earlier soft cloth medieval caps.

As the dream of a quick and easy passage to the riches of the Orient faded, the French and English alike girded themselves for the pursuit of a new Eldorado in North America: the pelt of an industrious, nearsighted little beast whose dams and waterways marked the forested northern landscape. It was a hunt that had profound consequences for Canada, perhaps the most important in its history. As the popular historian Peter C. Newman has written:

> Seldom has an animal exercised such a profound influence on the history of a continent. Men defied oceans and hacked their way across North America; armies and navies clashed under the polar moon; an Indian civilization was debauched—all in quest of the pug-nosed rodent with the lustrous fur. In the conduct of this feverish enterprise, which stretched from the early 1650s to the late 1850s, the cartography of the world trade routes was filled in, and the roots of many a dynastic fortune were planted.

He further observes:

> Just as the stalking of elephants for their ivories lured white hunters into the heart of Africa, so the pelts of the beaver drew the traders from both Hudson Bay and the Saint Lawrence toward the . . . Rocky Mountains and eventually to the shores of the . . . Pacific.

Newman, in an epic two-volume history of the Hudson's Bay Company (HBC), relates how beaver fur, obtained almost as an afterthought by fishermen and explorers, became one of the world's great trading commodities of the colonial era. This was the result of three interlocking realities: the teeming numbers of beaver in "an immense drainage system containing nearly half the world's fresh water"; the insatiable European demand for beaver fur as styles changed; and the willingness of the North American Native population to provide those furs in return for the European trade goods they so deeply coveted. As a result, as Newman neatly summarizes, "the hunt for beaver turned into the quest for a nation."

As attention turned away from the quest for an easy maritime route to riches to a workaday but more promising possibility of wealth through the fur trade, the English achievements in exploration in Canada's cold northern waters, given the limitations of late Elizabethan and early Stuart ships, were extraordinary. As the historian and classicist L.H. Neatby observed:

> In that short period, with little encouragement, next to no material support from the government, and unrewarded by any returns in commerce or plunder, the merchants and seamen of England had defined with considerable exceptions the eastern shores of Canada and Baffin Land, and the coast of Greenland up to 78 degrees of latitude, an achievement which, considering their scanty resources and the exceptional climatic difficulties overcome, will bear comparison with the exploits of the Spanish conquistadors and the voyages of the far-ranging sailors of Portugal.

If the English were concentrating their efforts on probing Hudson Bay and on their first attempts at settlement in Virginia as the 1600s opened, the French were directing their energies to the mouth of the St. Lawrence, the lands surrounding the Gulf and the hinterland upriver. In 1608, three years before the Henry Hudson tragedy was revealed, the trading post of Quebec was founded, with Samuel de Champlain playing a key role. Posts were established as well at Trois-Rivières and then, in 1642, at Montreal. Quite simply, the French were ahead of the English in shifting their attention from attempting to find a way through the mass of North America to exploiting the more immediate resource of the fur trade.

Through an ironic twist of history, French zeal in pursuing the fur trade provided an unexpected push to English efforts in Hudson Bay, through the persons of Pierre Radisson and Médard Chouart, Sieur des Groseilliers. The first half of the 1600s had seen Frenchmen pressing ever westward from their narrow base on the St. Lawrence, in quest of the elusive passage to the Orient; by the 1630s, Jean Nicollet was exploring the Lake Michigan shoreline for

Habitation of Quebec, 1608, by C.W. Jefferys C 73448

a channel leading to the Pacific. Radisson and Des Groseilliers, by contrast, were of the faction who saw greater promise in pursuing the fur trade, and in the immediate gains to be had from exploiting the resources of the huge continent rather than trying endlessly to bypass it.

In the early years of the fur trade, the key French posts at Tadoussac, then Quebec, Trois-Rivières and Montreal, dealt with Huron and Ottawa middlemen, who controlled the trade with the

Shooting the Rapids, by Francis Hopkins C 2774

fur-trapping tribes farther inland. In the middle of the 1600s, however, the powerful Iroquois Confederacy came north from its New York homeland and destroyed the Huron and Ottawa—and very nearly the small St. Lawrence settlements of the French as well. On the coming of peace, the French had a choice: they could either deal with the antipathetic Iroquois or go west themselves for the furs, up the Ottawa River route. Many chose the latter.

In 1659, travelling in the great birchbark canoes that became the galleons of exploration in Canada's early history, Radisson and Des Groseilliers had searched out new beaver lands north and west of Lake Superior. When they returned with their canoes laden with furs, the governor at Quebec punished them for disrupting the existing trade and monopoly system. The two men were refused a licence to trade into the new territory above Superior. Incensed, they determined to find support elsewhere. Radisson and Des Groseilliers travelled to Boston, where they attempted to interest New England merchants in trading for furs in the lands above Superior, which they would reach by sailing into Hudson Bay and entering them from the north. In 1665 a first expedition sailed from New England, Radisson and Des Groseilliers aboard and under the command of Captain Zacariah Gillam. Gillam's little vessel got no farther than Hudson Strait before being forced back by foul weather, but the enthusiasm of the two Frenchmen did not flag, nor did that of the Boston men, who saw promise in what they were proposing.

Two years after the Gillam attempt, Radisson and Des Groseilliers were taken off to London to try to secure more influential backers. Introduced to the court of Charles II by George Cartwright, Radisson and Des Groseilliers must have displayed both considerable charm and marketing skills, as they emerged from St. James's Palace with the protection of the Crown, a weekly pension of forty shillings each, and royal enthusiasm for a plan that would begin sending ships into Hudson Bay in pursuit of Lake Superior furs. In addition, the plan attracted the personal attention of the odd, mercurial Prince Rupert, having, as Newman relates, "ignited his determination to wrest the lucrative fur trade from the French." Very quickly a business association was put together for investors in the project. It would be known as the Company of Adventurers Trading into Hudson's Bay, and it was the direct ancestor of the modern Hudson's Bay Company.

Where Radisson and Des Groseilliers had been met with suspicion and censure in New France, they found enthusiasm, support and investment in England. Within months, a first voyage to Hudson Bay was under preparation. Two ships would be sent. The ketch *Eaglet*, which would carry Radisson and be commanded by Captain William Stannard, would winter on Hudson Bay. The ketch *Nonsuch*, at forty-five tons and under the command of their old Boston friend Captain Zacariah Gillam, would carry Des Groseilliers and be used to bring home the first summer's pelts, returning with provisions.

The two little ships punched bravely westward into the Atlantic on June 5, 1668, only to run into a horrendous storm off the coast of Ireland that forced *Eaglet*, with Radisson, to turn back. *Nonsuch* pressed on and entered Hudson Bay, sailing down to the mouth of the Rupert River, where the hapless Henry Hudson had overwintered. While Radisson fumed and fidgeted in England, Des Groseilliers' experience of the Canadian climate together with Gillam's New England hardiness got the appalled English crew through the rigours of the winter. The trade with the "Indians" was not as extensive as the English wished, the clouds of mosquitoes and blackflies in the spring were an unending torment, and when *Nonsuch* finally fled into the open waters of the great bay, heavy ice in Hudson Strait so blocked the ship's movement that it did not reach England until October. The prince and the other members of the Company of Adventurers were still grappling with the aftermath of the plague, the Great Fire and the humiliation of the Dutch raid on the Medway, but the safe return of the plucky little *Nonsuch* had proven, as Newman points out, that "it was entirely practicable to sail into Hudson's Bay, winter over on its shores, and return with a profitable cargo of fur." The game that would lead to eventual English domination of the continent was afoot.

Charles II, the ghastliness of the recent English calamities and the ongoing conflict with the Dutch weighing heavily on his mind, was still pleased to recognize the success of what Radisson and Des Groseilliers had been instrumental in bringing about. On Friday, May 2, 1670, he signed a comprehensive charter granting the Company of Adventurers Trading into Hudson's Bay a fur trading monopoly in all lands draining into Hudson Bay—a staggeringly huge piece of the earth's surface, encompassing all lands stretching from the Bay to the foothills of the Rocky Mountains. Four weeks later, the charter began to be implemented when the leased frigate *Prince Rupert* and the pink *Wivenhoe* sailed to establish a permanent post on Hudson Bay. The spot they chose was at the mouth of the Nelson River, where Button had anchored in 1612. Radisson and Des Groseilliers had secured their revenge for their humiliation at Quebec.

Seventeenth-century loyalties were a matter of practicality, however, and in 1674 a determined French effort to lure Radisson and Des Groseilliers back into the service of France succeeded. Before long, Radisson would work with a new investor, Charles de la Chesnaye, to form a company for Hudson Bay intended as a rival to the Company of Adventurers; it would be called the Compagnie du Nord. This development joined a number of other threads reeling back to the beginning of the century that had brought French fur trade ambitions in North America to this point.

The French experience in Acadia had been a checkered one. Port-Royal, on its beautiful basin, had been reopened by Poutrincourt in 1610, only to be destroyed by an English raid in 1613, and the lands that would one day be Canada's Maritime provinces now came under English sway for a time. In 1621, Sir William Alexander secured from Charles I a grant of all the lands between Gaspé and the St. Croix River as "Nova Scotia," but he gave up trying to establish a settlement after two years. In 1627, the enterprising and audacious Kirke brothers, who would one day take Quebec, set up an English post in the Annapolis Basin, replacing Port-Royal. Then all this activity in turn came to naught when a treaty in 1632 restored

Acadia to France—and opened a new chapter of French enthusiasm for its distant realms. Acadia would fall to the English yet again in 1654, only to be returned to France after Charles II's restoration in 1660.

If the French had a dizzying, see-saw experience with the contested colonies and fur trade of Acadia, their grip over the St. Lawrence valley and the heartland of New France was far surer, though not unchallenged. After a kind of peace had been established with the Iroquois in the mid-1600s—temporary, as it would turn out, until the Great Peace of 1701—the French confronted the reality that the destruction of the Huron and Ottawa middlemen, and the exhaustion of beaver resources in the immediate St. Lawrence hinterland, made expansion of the fur trade westward and northward a necessity. Soon the French canoes were striking up the Ottawa River route to establish trading posts at Green Bay, Michilimackinac and Sault Ste. Marie, far to the west of Montreal. Behind those questing canoes, a surer administration was falling into place: in 1663 royal government assumed control of the colony, and in 1672, Louis de Buade, Comte de Frontenac, brought his considerable energies and determination to the post of governor.

It was at this time that the French turned away from their single-minded concentration on the Ottawa canoe route west, to include the glittering "silver highway" of the inland seas that were the Great Lakes. If navigation could be established on the Lakes, and the barrier of Niagara overcome, the increase in the volume of fur shipments would be dramatic. The French looked out over the forest-edged, immense surface of Lake Ontario and acted. Within a year of Frontenac's arrival, in 1673, a fortified post was built at Cataraqui—modern-day Kingston, Ontario—and named Fort Frontenac, and the first recorded European ship design to cleave the waters of the Great Lakes was launched the same year. A form of large open boat known as a "bugalet," it was described by a contemporary observer as "a small vessel with two masts, used on the coast of Brittany. The foremast is very short; and on each mast is carried a square-sail, and sometimes a topsail over the mainsail. They have a bowsprit and set one or more jibs."

This little pioneering vessel, possibly named the *Frontenac*, was followed in 1674 by another bugalet, the *Kadaraquay*, and then another, larger, unnamed boat in 1675. In 1679, a much larger vessel, referred to as "the great barque," was built when the French opened the Lakes above Niagara Falls to European hulls and sails with the construction of the *Griffon*, a proper decked ship designed to sail the waters of the Upper Lakes to Michilimackinac and Green Bay and recover their rich holdings of furs. Another ship, similar to the *Griffon*, was built in 1685 below the Falls and christened *Le Général*. With these ships, the true open-water navigation of the Great Lakes began. But the perils soon became evident when the *Griffon* disappeared without a trace downbound from Lake Michigan with one of the new cargoes of furs.

An eyewitness to these momentous first efforts at voyaging in Canadian waters was Father Louis Hennepin, a Récollet friar who had come out from France in 1675, the year René-Robert, Sieur de La Salle, had assumed command at Cataraqui. La Salle had been preoccupied with westward exploration since his arrival in Canada in 1666, and upon Frontenac assuming the governorship he had convinced him of the virtues of a plan to "effect a military occupation of the whole Mississippi Valley . . . by means of military posts which should control the communication and sway the policy of the Indian tribes." Hennepin was dispatched to go along with a detachment under the command of Pierre de St. Paul, Sieur de La Motte, whose assigned task was to voyage west from Cataraqui, get above Niagara Falls, and establish a post on Lake Erie near the mouth of the Niagara River where a ship for use on the Upper Lakes—ultimately, *Griffon*—could be built. The party sailed, possibly in the *Frontenac*, on November 18, 1678:

> That very same year, on the Eighteenth of *November*, I took leave of our Monks at Fort *Frontenac*, and after mutual Embraces and Expressions of Brotherly and Christian Charity, I embark'd

in a Brigantine of about ten Tuns. The Wind and the Cold of the Autumn were then very violent, insomuch that our Crew was afraid to go into so little a Vessel. This oblig'd us and the Sieur *de la Motte* our Commander, to keep our course on the North-side of the Lake, to shelter our selves under the Craft, against the North-west Wind, which otherwise wou'd have forc'd us upon the Southern Coast of the Lake. The Voyage prov'd very difficult and dangerous, because of the unseasonable time of the Year, Winter being near at hand.

On the 26th, we were in great danger about Two large Leagues off the Land, where we were oblig'd to lie at Anchor all that Night at sixty Fathom Water and above; but at length the Wind coming to the North-East, we sail'd on, and arriv'd safely at the further end of the Lake *Ontario*, call'd by the *Iroquese*, *Skannadario*. We came pretty near to one of their Villages call'd *Tajajagon*, lying about Seventy Leagues from Fort *Frontenac*, or *Catarokouy*.

We barter'd some *Indian* Corn with the *Iroquese*, who could not sufficiently admire us, and came frequently to see us on board our Brigantine, which for our greater security, we had brought to an Anchor into a River, though before we could get in, we run a ground three times, which oblig'd us to put Fourteen Men into Canou's, and cast the Balast of our Ship overboard to get her off again. That River falls into the Lake; but for fear of being frozen up therein, we were forc'd to cut the Ice with Axes and other Instruments.

The Wind turning then contrary, we were oblig'd to tarry there until the 15th of *December*, 1678, when we sail'd from the Northern Coast to the Southern, where the River *Niagara* runs into the Lake; but could not reach it that Day, though it is but Fifteen or Sixteen Leagues distant, and therefore cast Anchor within Five Leagues of the Shore, where we had very bad Weather all the Night long.

On the 6th, being St. *Nicholas's* Day, we got into the fine River *Niagara*, into which never any such Ship as ours enter'd before. We sung there *Te Deum*, and other Prayers, to return our Thanks to God Almighty for our prosperous Voyage.

The arrival of the little vessel astonished the local Iroquois—"they were much surprised at our ship, which they call'd the great wooden canoe"—and relations were cordial. The French explored up the river beyond the Falls, encamping likely at the mouth of Chippewa Creek, before returning below the Falls to build a post as high up the Niagara River as the current would allow. The post on Lake Erie would come later; their objective now was to "sail up the River as far as the rapid Current above mention'd, where we had resolved to build some Houses." Hennepin found himself pressed into seamen's work:

The 15th, I was desir'd to fit at the Helm of our Brigantine, while three of our Men hall'd the same from the Shore with a Rope; and at last we brought her up, and moor'd her to the Shore with a Halter, near a Rock of a prodigious height, lying upon the rapid Currents we have already mention'd. The 17th, 18th, and 19th, we were busie in making a Cabin with Palisa-does, to serve for a Magazine; but the Ground was so frozen, that we were forced to throw several times boiling water upon it to facilitate the beating in and driving down the Stakes. The 20th, 21st, 22nd, and 23rd, our Ship was in great danger to be dash'd to pieces, by the vast pieces of Ice that were hurl'd down the River; to prevent which, our Carpenters made a Capstane to haul her ashore; but our great Cable broke in three pieces; whereupon one of our Carpenters surrounded the Vessel with a Cable, and ty'd to it several Ropes, whereby we got her ashore, tho' with much difficulty, and sav'd her from the danger of being broke to pieces, or carried away by the Ice, which came down with an extreme violence from the great Fall of *Niagara* . . .

With the post in the lower gorge built, the party found a reliable path through the great woods up the escarpment, part of which would later bear the name Queenston Heights. Finally the shores of Lake Erie were reached, and construction of the upper post began. Hennepin, inspired by the welcome and the numbers of Iroquois in the area, returned to Cataraqui to recruit more monks for the ministry, and then began a return to the new post a few days before La Salle undertook the same voyage. In this account, Hennepin paused at the "River of the Tsonnontouans," the modern Irondequoit Creek, east of the Genessee River, New York. An important inclusion is the description of the ill-fated *Griffon*, in which La Salle, Hennepin and Henri de Tonty would sail to the end of Lake Michigan but which would be lost on its return.

> After some few Days, the Wind coming fair, Fathers *Gabriel*, *Zenobe*, and I, went on board the Brigantine, and in a short time arriv'd in the River of the *Tsonnontouans*, which runs into the Lake *Ontario*, where we continu'd several Days, our Men being very busie in bartering their Commodities with the Natives, who flock'd in great numbers about us to see our Brigantine, which they admir'd, and to exchange their Skins for Knives, Guns, Powder and Shot, but especially for Brandy, which they love above all things. In the mean time, we had built a small Cabin of Barks of Trees about half a League in the Woods, to perform Divine Service therein without interruption, and waited till all our Men had done their Business. M. *la Salle* arriv'd in a Canou about eight Days after; he had taken his course by the Southern Coast of the Lake, to go to the Village of the *Tsonnontouans*, to whom he made several Presents to engage them in our Interest, and remove the Jealousie they had conceiv'd of our Undertaking, through the Suggestions of our Enemies. All these Impediments retarded us so long, that we could not reach the River *Niagara* before the 30th of *July* . . . [W]e . . . went up the Streight to look for our Ship, which we found riding within a league of the pleasant Lake *Erie*. We were very kindly receiv'd, and likewise very glad to find our Ship well rigg'd, and ready fitted out with all the Necessaries for sailing.

She carry'd five small Guns, two whereof were Brass, and three Harquebuze *a-crock*. The Beak-head was adorn'd with a flying Griffin, and an Eagle above it; and the rest of the Ship had the same Ornaments as Men of War use to have.

On August 7, 1679, the *Griffon* sailed with Hennepin, La Salle and others aboard on a voyage that would take them to the limits of Lake Michigan, and send Hennepin on a wandering journey of capture and adventure with western Indians until he finally returned to Cataraqui in 1681. Hennepin would eventually end his days in a monastery in Rome, while La Salle would go in 1682 to explore the Mississippi and claim what would become Louisiana for France, only to die there by a murderer's hand five years later. Of the *Griffon*, no trace was ever found after she left Lake Michigan for her return voyage to the post on Lake Erie.

The third great theatre of France's pursuit of the fur trade was, along with the English, Hudson Bay. As we saw earlier, the Company of Adventurers had lost Radisson and Des Groseilliers in 1674. By 1682 the two men had secured an influential French backer, Charles de La Chesnaye. Together, Radisson and La Chesnaye inked an agreement that created the Compagnie du Nord, which ironically had the express purpose of competing with the Company of Adventurers. In that same year Radisson and Des Groseilliers sailed for Hudson Bay with two small ships and twenty-seven men, intent on erecting a fur trade post at the mouth of the Hayes River. On their arrival, they were accosted by two vessels of the Company of Adventurers, but poor navigation on the part of the larger vessel, the *Prince Rupert*, caused it abruptly to sink, leaving Radisson and Des Groseilliers to rescue a clutch of sodden and shivering prisoners. The French sent them off toward English safety in the remaining ship's boats, then loaded the surviving English vessel, the *Batchelor's Delight*, with a prime cargo of furs at the end of the season, sailing triumphantly off to Quebec to sell the furs. Once again the bureaucracy of the colony punished them, leading Des

Groseilliers to retire in disgust into obscurity, and Radisson to become once more an employee of the Company of Adventurers. He would make one further voyage to Hudson Bay in the *Happy Adventure*, but his luck and fortunes failed him, and he died in poverty in 1710.

If the strange shifting allegiances of Radisson and Des Groseilliers make for a confusing story of the fur trade and shipping on Hudson Bay, there now began a period that would bring the savagery of real warfare to the Bay, and it would last until the century's end. Central to these years of open conflict was the most effective soldier, fighting seaman and brigand Canada has ever produced: Pierre Le Moyne, Sieur d'Iberville.

In 1686, two years before the Glorious Revolution of 1688 that brought an end to the Stuart dynasty in England—thereby beginning the long period of implacable war and competition with France that would not end until 1815—the French launched an expedition by canoe from the Ottawa River against the English posts on James Bay. This hardy force was led by the Chevalier de Troyes, and included d'Iberville. In one of the most daring and well-executed raids ever carried out in North America, de Troyes's column fought its way north to the shores of James Bay and in quick succession took the Hudson's Bay Company posts at Moose Factory and Rupert House. In a captured HBC ship, the *Craven*, d'Iberville then sailed to take the small HBC post at the mouth of the Albany River. In one sweeping stroke, France had made itself master of much of the great bay, and much of its fur trade.

D'Iberville returned to Quebec with the triumphant de Troyes force, then sailed back around Ungava into James Bay in the French vessel *Soleil d'Afrique* to recover the stacks of captured furs in the English posts. While rowing in from the anchorage to the mouth of the Albany River, he came upon two HBC ships, the *Churchill* and the *Yonge*. D'Iberville so impressed the masters of both ships with the overwhelming power of his distantly anchored *Soleil d'Afrique* that both surrendered immediately. The *Soleil d'Afrique* rolled home to Quebec trailing two prizes and bearing a fortune in English furs. It was an extraordinary coup—but more was to follow.

In 1690, with war well under way, d'Iberville returned to Hudson Bay with three small ships, determined to capture the remaining major English post, at York Factory. As he approached the offshore anchorage, known as Five Fathom Hole—the waters of the west shore of the Bay were dangerously shallow—d'Iberville made out the topmasts of an English frigate outlined against the dark evergreen line of the shore. Realizing at once that he was heavily outgunned, d'Iberville immediately steered for the lesser remaining post at Fort Severn, and took it. Four years later, in 1694, d'Iberville returned again to attempt York Factory, and this time was successful. The English, however, would regain it a year later.

Finally, in 1697, as the century was drawing to a close, the seesaw struggle for control of the fur trade of the Bay was encapsulated in a final confrontation that brought d'Iberville back to the cold Bay waters. The previous year, the French had decided to launch a strike against English commercial interests in the western Atlantic, notably the fishery, by conducting a destructive raid on English fishing settlements in Newfoundland. France maintained a small post at Placentia, named Fort St. Louis. A plan was developed to gather a French force there, then sail round to capture the port of St. John's and destroy as many of the small coastal settlements as possible. Ordered from Quebec to take part, d'Iberville arrived at Placentia in September 1696 only to find that the irascible governor there, the Sieur de Brouillon, had already sailed with a recently arrived squadron of seven French ships. When de Brouillon sailed dejectedly back after failing to take St. John's, d'Iberville helped plan a second effort, a combined land and sea attack, which not only succeeded in taking St. John's but led to the destruction of most of the little fishing posts and settlements of the Avalon Peninsula.

On d'Iberville's return to Placentia, he found waiting for him a small fleet of ships newly arrived from France, bearing orders for him to enter Hudson Bay and attack York Factory, also known as Fort Nelson, again. D'Iberville, a born fighting man if ever there was one, had despised the work of burning out poor fisherfolk on the Newfoundland coast. Now his orders were for nobler pursuits, and he accepted them gladly. In July 1697 he sailed for Hudson Bay, in command of the squadron's lead vessel, the 44-gun *Pélican*. Supporting him would be the *Palmier*, 40 guns, and three smaller vessels: the *Profond*, the *Wasp* and the *Violent*, a supply ship.

The voyage into the Bay was long and tedious, with contrary winds and, once into the Bay, moving fields of pack ice that threatened to entrap the squadron. By dint of good seamanship d'Iberville managed to keep *Pélican* free of ice, sailing on until he anchored on September 4, 1697, at the mouth of the Hayes River, not far from the Nelson River and York Factory/Fort Nelson. He had become separated from the other ships of the squadron, however, and the ice had trapped them near Digges Island. There they were found by a powerful HBC squadron entering the Bay, led by the large frigate *Hampshire*, 56 guns, and accompanied by the *Hudson Bay*, 32 guns, and the *Derring*, 36 guns. The ice prevented the English from closing with the French, so they sailed on, content to leave the French locked in the ice where they could cause no trouble, after exchanging some fruitless cannonading at long range. *Pélican* would have to face the English alone if they found her. The French lead vessel was now anchored some ten miles from York Factory/Fort Nelson. To scout out the state of the fort—which the French called Fort Bourbon—d'Iberville landed twenty-two of his already scurvy-weakened crew. This left barely enough men to sail and "fight" the ship—man its guns—if the enemy appeared. And it did.

The next morning, September 5, 1697, d'Iberville's lookouts squinted eastward in the cold dawn light and made out the shapes of *Hampshire* and its consorts beating purposefully up toward *Pélican's* anchorage. The odds were stacked against d'Iberville: with his landing party sent away, he had at most 150 men to face an estimated English force of 600. In addition, the three ships now closing into gunnery range mounted a total of 124 long guns against *Pélican*'s battery of 44 guns.

D'Iberville had a quick council with his officers, if only to determine that they agreed with him that surrender was out of the question. Knowing that to stay trapped in the anchorage to await recovery of the landing party would be tactical suicide if the wind changed, d'Iberville broke out his anchors and raised sail, running out before the westerly wind toward his attackers. So unexpected was *Pélican*'s rush down on *Hampshire* that the English captain turned away, fearing a boarding attempt. *Hampshire*'s failure of nerve put it out of the picture for a moment, as it attempted to tack or wear around to get back into the action. *Pélican* swept down unchallenged toward the remaining English vessels, the *Derring* and the *Hudson Bay*. Before *Hampshire* could close the gap, d'Iberville put two thunderous broadsides into *Derring* and *Hudson Bay* before rounding up to work into range for a second pass. But now *Hampshire* had worked back into range, and the other English vessels, shaken by the ferocity of d'Iberville's attack, had regained some self-discipline and opened fire.

All three were soon directing a storm of round shot at the lone French ship. By skilfully manoeuvring *Pélican*—French ships were as a rule swifter and more manoeuvrable than those of the English, which one wag said were built by the mile and cut off as required—d'Iberville managed to keep *Pélican* at extreme gunnery range, where his weakened and outnumbered crew were not at risk of boarding from the far more numerous English. D'Iberville had his gunners bang away at *Hampshire* and the other ships in a waiting game that could only benefit the French, particularly if the French squadron trapped in ice at Digges Island had got free.

After three hours of tacking and wearing, *Hampshire*'s captain succeeded in crossing *Pélican*'s stern at close range, and her raking fire cut bloody swaths along the French decks. D'Iberville rallied his shaken gun crews, and as *Hampshire* wore around to bring her other broadside to bear, d'Iberville managed to turn *Pélican* and fire a full broadside before *Hampshire* had completed her turn. The flying cloud of round shot struck *Hampshire* at the waterline as it was heeling over in the turn, shattering the hull. *Hampshire* suddenly wallowed low in the icy seas, her canvas rumpling and collapsing, and then in a moment the big frigate was gone, the masthead pennant and ensigns vanishing last as she sank away in a huge rumbling circle of foam and debris.

Pélican had suffered heavily from *Hampshire*'s close firing, but d'Iberville still had to contend with the remaining ships of the English squadron. With his gun crews almost incapable of reloading after the supreme effort of the broadside that had sunk *Hampshire*, and with barely enough hands to brace around the yards, d'Iberville turned *Pélican* toward *Hudson Bay*. Stunned by the fate of *Hampshire* and unaware of *Pélican*'s desperate condition, *Hudson Bay* struck its colours without a fight. The remaining English vessel, *Derring*, on seeing the surrender, fled off to leeward and away from the fight. With *Pélican* leaking and damaged, her crew barely able to manoeuvre the ship, d'Iberville managed to let go the anchors.

But now the ferocious weather of Hudson Bay took the upper hand, and as night fell a howling northern gale came up, smashing the prize *Hudson Bay* ashore. Her captain and fourteen of her crew managed to survive the breakup in the icy surf and stumble, frozen and near death, to Fort Nelson. In *Pélican*, d'Iberville tried to get his ship to sea after his best anchor gave way. Slipping the remaining anchor cable, he attempted to tack the ship out to sea and deep water, only to have the rudder tackle give way. Despite a frenzied effort to repair it, the ship drifted off to leeward and ran hard aground on a shoal six miles from shore, out in the shallow bay. Knowing *Pélican* was doomed, d'Iberville launched a boat in the stormy darkness, and then used it to lead a collection of crude rafts bearing his surviving men and wounded ashore. In the freezing conditions, many of the wounded died during the ordeal, and d'Iberville gathered the survivors around fires on the shore in an attempt to get them through the night alive. In the morning he formed up his

D'Iberville's ship *Pélican* wrecked off the Nelson River   *C 12005*

freezing, exhausted survivors and marched them along the shore to the mouth of the Hayes River, to see to his enormous relief the remainder of the French squadron, freed from the ice, riding there safely at anchor. Within hours, *Pélican*'s men were aboard, and the final phase of the grim struggle could be planned.

The English, characteristically, were not about to make it an easy contest. The governor of Fort Nelson, Bailey, was supported by the surviving captain of *Hudson Bay* in a determination to resist the now more numerous French. D'Iberville sent in a demand that the fort surrender, which Bailey rejected. D'Iberville countered calmly with an observation that, with the English ships scattered or sunk and the French weight of numbers, resistance was futile. Twice more Bailey refused, and then d'Iberville sent in a stern warning: he would negotiate no further, the fort would be assaulted and the defenders would be at the mercy of the French. With his small garrison lacking enthusiasm for a fight, Bailey surrendered. As Henry Kelsey, who was second-in-command of the fort, would later write, the garrison marched out to an uncertain fate and "ye French took possession of ye fort, this being ye end of a tedious winter and tragical journal by me, Henry Kelsey."

The Treaty of Ryswick, signed during d'Iberville's foray into the Bay, ended for a time the ongoing hostilities between the English and the French. France ended the seventeenth century in possession of the frigid waters of Hudson Bay, but the grim little victory won by d'Iberville marked the end of an era. The courageous engagement fought by *Pélican* would be d'Iberville's last service in the cold waters of the north. In continuing duty to his king, he fought in the West Indies, and both explored and served in Louisiana, only to die of fever at Havana, Cuba, in 1706 at the age of forty-seven. With his death ended the phase of the great struggle for Canada, its waters and its riches, that had been fought between France and England on a more or less equal footing.

Now, in the century just opening, the rising naval power of Britain would slowly tip the scales in her favour, and in mid-century bring an end to the struggle for control of the riches of the fur trade and the limitless potential of the forested land itself. Throughout this bloody and eventful history, the sea and the sea-like waters of the Great Lakes had been the principal highway and theatre for the actions of the men—and women—who were laying the historical foundations of the future nation. Neither they nor many who came after would realize how much the sea was already shaping a special character in the people who fought to possess the land on which that sea broke, and who would make that land their home. Canada and its people were, and have remained, shaped by the sea more than has ever been adequately expressed.

6

The Great Struggle for Empire, 1700–1763

With a steep heel the French frigate swept round, the bowsprit swinging in long, dipping curves around the horizon. The frenzied hauling of the men on the braces eased the tremendous thundering aloft from the luffing canvas, and within a few minutes the frigate had begun its beat up to windward, punching now into the full force of wind and swell, sails arched and taut, clouds of spray bursting over the plunging bow to rattle on the decks and drench the hands belaying the braces or crouched, wide-eyed and expectant, at the upper-deck guns.

The frigate's commander jammed his tricorne more firmly on his head against the wind and squinted at the approaching British frigate, trying to make his mind work. The Englishman was frighteningly close, a towering dark shape against the silver dappling of the sun on the sea. What was the weakest part of that beautiful thing rushing down on them? The hull? The rigging?

"Ready your larboard guns, there!" he barked over the roar of wind and sea. "We'll fire on the uproll!"

WITH THESE GRAPPLINGS of eighteenth-century warships came the climactic era in which the vast struggle between Britain and France for worldwide empire, and in particular for North America, would find its bloody resolution. With few interruptions, it took its deadly course over the first half of the century, in three great spasms of fighting: the war that began in the 1680s and lasted until 1713; the war of 1739–48; and the final demise of the French Empire in North America, 1754–63. In all instances the waters of Canada were scenes for military and naval catastrophe or success, culminating with the great amphibious assault of 1759 that put James Wolfe's redcoats ashore at Quebec and ended France's dominion forever.

In essence, the conflict between France and England in North America was the struggle for survival between the larger British colonies along the Eastern Seaboard and the far smaller French colonies of New France and Acadia. Each side had its warrior allies, but the pattern of the struggle was one in which the French attempted to maintain a vast fur trading empire in a great arc from the St. Lawrence to the Mississippi, while the much more numerous British sought to settle and develop that same land in an inexorable march westward that had little interest in respecting the French trading empire or the warrior allies who dealt with it. It was a clash of two incompatible concepts: the one a trade-based business that saw the warrior and his tribe as a needed ally, and had little interest in re-creating the ordered parkland of Europe; and the other a deliberate process of pushing back or destroying the wilderness and its neolithic inhabitants to build an agricultural society, with no regard for preserving the wild places and the way of life they had sustained since the last ice age.

The conflict, when it came, most often took the form of savage raiding from the small settlements of Canada and Acadia, with warrior allies, who fell on the outlying villages, farms and settlements of the British colonies and left smoking ruins and scalped bodies—and produced ponderous retaliatory moves from the British colonial assemblies, which returned often to the preoccupation of the colonies since the seventeenth century: the defeat and removal of French influence in North America. In the great war that was launched at the end of the 1680s in Europe and North America between Louis XIV's France and Britain and her allies, and which would not end until France teetered on the edge of disaster and ruin in 1713, the first serious naval efforts to seize or destroy the French presence in New France and Acadia were mounted.

The French lay in their lair at Quebec, approachable only by the almost endless stretch of the great St. Lawrence, along the long and storied Lake Champlain corridor, or via the Great Lakes, at this time still difficult to reach and impenetrably forested on their shores. In 1690 the northern British colonies convened a conference at New York to plan an attack on the French in Canada. With resources from Britain itself unlikely to be available, the colonists determined that they would put an end to the galling presence of the French by themselves. After much tumultuous argument, a plan was devised that provided for an advance by a small body of four hundred men by canoe and longboat up Lake Champlain, to attack Montreal. This force would support a simultaneous expedition by a fleet of armed colony vessels that would embark 350 musketeers and sail up the St. Lawrence to attack Quebec itself. The colonies of New York and Connecticut would provide the militia soldiery, while New England, principally Massachusetts, would provide the vessels and crews.

Enthusiasm for this plan ran high in Boston, particularly if, en route to Quebec, the colonial force could attack Port-Royal on the Annapolis Basin. This had been a base for French privateers, privately owned warships licensed by the Crown to make war on the enemy, and to profit from the sale of any prize vessels they might take. The privateers had bedevilled Boston shipping, so Port-Royal was, if anything, a more important plum to pick than Quebec to many a New Englander. To command the seaborne expedition, the General Court of Massachusetts appointed Sir William Phips as "Major General" of the force, with a commission dated March 12, 1690. Phips was a rough, burly and unlettered man who had earned his place in Massachusetts society with a mixture of shrewd wits and the application of hard fists. He had been awarded a knighthood by the Crown for sailing to the Bahamas and successfully salvaging more than a quarter of a million pounds' worth of bullion from a wrecked Spanish vessel. Now he threw his characteristic energy and bullish leadership into assembling a force of eight small ships and seven hundred eager if untrained men to assault the first prize in the campaign against the French, Port-Royal.

The force sailed from Boston on April 28, 1690, and by May 11 Phips had his squadron riding to anchor in Annapolis Basin off Port-Royal, and was demanding the surrender of the small fort. The governor of Acadia at Port-Royal, Meneval, knew a losing fight when he saw one, and Phips's little fleet sailed triumphantly back into Boston by May 30, bearing on board not only Meneval but a substantial hoard of loot from the fort and the little settlement. Flushed with success, and with the congratulations of the General Court and of relieved merchants ringing in his ears, Phips prepared for the next, and more daunting, task: the assault on Quebec itself.

The "armament" that was ready to sail under his command on the morning of August 9, 1690, was considerably larger than the little force that had overawed Meneval at Port-Royal. Phips now had a total of thirty-two ships, merchantmen under charter for the most part, which would be escorted by New England provincial vessels including Phips's own frigate, the *Six Friends* of 44 guns, as well as the *John and Thomas*, 26 guns. The colony of New York provided armed vessels, including a 24-gun frigate and two smaller sloops of 4 and 8 guns. In due course the entire fleet bore away, carrying a total of 2,200 men, of whom 1,300 were musketeers and the remainder seamen. It was a prodigious undertaking for the English colonies, and it presaged a growing power that would lead, eighty years later, to their successful struggle for independence.

But for now, all thought was on advancing British interests by defeating the threat posed by the French in the north. As correspondence from the General Court expressed it to London, "There is no expectation of putting an Issue to the Indian Warr, nor will Their Majesty's subjects here ever live in peace, but by the dislodging and removal of these ill neighbours." There was little experience in the colonies of mounting such enterprises. Phips had succeeded at Port-Royal by luck and audacity, and he stormed off to assault Quebec with more energy than preparation. The Reverend

Cotton Mather, a colonial clergyman, would observe later that "there was more haste than good speed in the attempt . . . [The leaders] were not enough concerned for the Counsel and presence of God in the undertaking; they mainly propounded the plunder to be got among a people whose trade was that where wild beasts enriched them; so the business miscarried."

The "business" soon lost its accompanying attack up the Lake Champlain valley when the encamped militia were riven in their sodden camps on the shores of the lake by smallpox and the defection of the canoe brigades that were meant to carry them north. A few remaining men trudged north and mounted a brutal little raid on the harmless village of Laprairie, south of Montreal, before wandering home. The "undertaking" would have to be Phips's alone.

Phips had always believed in, and relied upon, his own good luck as a given in his life. Astonishingly, that luck held as the thirty-two ships rounded Cape Breton and turned into the Gulf of St. Lawrence for the uncharted passage up to Quebec. Phips knew that others had made the passage before him, and he hoped audacity and luck would see them through. At first it did: a steady east wind drove the fleet westward up the river, and by dint of solid seamanship and Phips's continuing good fortune the myriad shoals, ledges and rocks that mark the river were avoided. But then Phips's luck broke. Some sixty miles below Quebec—a good day's sail with fair winds—the fleet was forced to come to anchor as strong west winds swept down the river. For three maddening weeks the fleet lay at anchor as word spread along the shore of the English presence, finally reaching Governor Frontenac at Quebec, who ordered a feverish improvement of the town's defences. Finally the wind swung to the east, and Phips completed his epic and remarkable ascent of the river, bringing his fleet safely to anchor in the basin below the heights of Quebec—where the fleet bearing James Wolfe and his army would anchor sixty-nine years later—on October 16, 1690. It was ominously late in the season.

Phips repeated the tactics that had worked so spectacularly at Port-Royal: an officer was sent ashore to offer surrender terms to

Frontenac. But Frontenac was no Meneval, and the bluffs and walls of Quebec were a tougher nut to crack than little Port-Royal. Frontenac scorned Phips's terms and dared him to do his worst. Phips sent in his militiamen by boats to the Beauport shore, successfully landing where, a half-century later, British infantry would be bloodily repulsed by French defenders. The New Englanders then marched through the cold October drizzle to cross the Rivière St-Charles. When they had crossed it and were about to assault the town, Phips was to bring his ships closer to the Lower Town and begin a supporting bombardment.

The plan went quickly awry. Phips did not wait for the signal that his men had reached Quebec's walls—they had not—before beginning his bombardment. Now the haste and lack of planning for such an "undertaking" became evident, as Phips's gunners reported that they had too little gunpowder and round shot to carry out the bombardment. Furious, Phips ordered them to reduce their charges by a half. The French watched in amusement as Phips's rounds lofted slowly up toward the town, only to bounce harmlessly off walls and roofs. The French batteries found their own range and began to deliver a hail of shot down on the anchored colonial ships, which were soon bracketed by leaping geysers of spray. As round shot splashed into the river, the *Six Friends* was struck several times and seriously damaged. With his cursing gunners carefully doling out their remaining powder and the carpenters working feverishly to repair the shot damage, Phips received word from the men ashore: their assault had failed. Even as Phips digested this news, surrounded by the smoke of the gunnery and with the river leaping from shot splashes, a worried ship's officer drew Phips's attention to the black, looming wall of a squall line that was bearing down on the anchorage.

The storm struck in lashing clouds of white spray just as the boats bearing the exhausted and muddied landing force came alongside the ships, dodging through the hail of French shot. Half blinded by the stinging rain, Phips's crews hauled the cursing men aboard, tied off the boats astern, and then, as the ships heeled to the force of the gale, broke out their anchors and fled off before the squall downriver, to anchor again in the lee of the Île d'Orléans. The storm continued unabated into the next day, keeping the ships huddled at anchor behind the island, with Phips gloomily assessing his prospects, which were few. Abruptly, a French boat under a flag of truce arrived through the rain: Frontenac had several of the landing party and other English as prisoners, and Phips had taken some French during his progress upriver. Could an exchange take place? Phips agreed.

With his captured men recovered, the stormy weather shaking the ships at their anchors, Phips conferred with his captains and decided to sail for Boston. Still battered by the unending gale, the fleet straggled off downriver. Again Phips's luck was not in evidence, as they missed two French vessels crammed with stores and an accompanying frigate, which had hidden themselves in the mouth of the Saguenay River when the approaching New England fleet was spotted.

Now, as the vessels reached the wider river and the open waters of the Gulf of St. Lawrence, and the storms continued unabated, the cohesion of the fleet began to break down. Vessels started to vanish. Some foundered outright from damages sustained at Quebec, while others ran aground on the shoals missed so effortlessly on the ascent. More than a few, blown out to sea through Cabot Strait, were carried to an unknown fate, several fetching up with starving and scurvy-ridden crews in the West Indies. As recounted by historian Joseph Rutledge, the story of one ship was typical:

The brig *Mary*, with Captain John Rainsford in command, went ashore on Anticosti Island in a bleak night. The captain and the sixty on board made the shore and developed a Robinson Crusoe talent for adapting the vessel to their needs. Its timbers provided rude shelter against the winter, and salvaged supplies gave a distant hope of survival. The supplies did not amount to much, but it was agreed to divide them. They ran to a weekly ration of two biscuits, a half pound of pork and as much flour, a pint and a quarter of peas, and two small fish. Hunger and cold quickly began to take their toll, but the record points out that they were all convinced of the necessity of keeping their allowance, "unless they would at last eat each other." Early in December the surgeon died, and in a matter of a few weeks forty of the sixty followed him. At the end of March, Captain Rainsford and four of the company remaining set out in a small skiff they had lengthened to provide a cabin for two or three men. With a sail salvaged from the brig the five began their impossible voyage to Boston. It was the 25th of March. On the ninth of May the skiff, with its tattered, starving crew miraculously arrived and was sighted. Soon a vessel was dispatched to Anticosti to rescue the other survivors.

Phips's own luck had returned, but only to a degree. His *Six Friends* had come to anchor in Boston harbour the previous November 19, and he was soon petitioning the General Court for more funds and a renewed mandate for attack. The General Court, aghast at the expense for no gain of the Quebec expedition, cautiously pondered his request. The French, pleased with their successful defence of Quebec, plotted to recover Acadia, which they achieved a year later when the Port-Royal garrison surrendered to a French warship with the familiar and alluring name of *Soleil d'Afrique*. But the English assault on Port-Royal, on Acadia and on New France itself would be relentlessly renewed.

With the return of Port-Royal to the French in 1691, its role as a home port for audacious privateers that preyed on New England shipping was once more in play. The war on the inland frontier continued to ebb and flow in its litany of slaughter and burning, and the waste left by the tomahawk and the torch along the edge of the English colonies. But then, in 1704, a particularly savage raid on the village of Deerfield, Massachusetts, spurred New England to renew plans for the retaking of Port-Royal as a preliminary step to taking the final prize of Quebec itself.

The unending naval war on the Acadian and New England coasts had made Port-Royal rich. But now another determined New Englander, Benjamin Church, harnessed fury over the Deerfield raid, together with the prospect of financial gain, to form a plan for attacking the privateer haven again. Obtaining permission from the General Court of Massachusetts, Church displayed volatile energy in assembling a force of seven hundred militiamen, and convinced the Court to requisition several merchant vessels as well as Massachusetts's own *Province Galley* and two Royal Navy frigates to transport the force. Stopping at the island of Matinicus for final preparations, the force sailed on to a French outpost at the present site of Castine, Maine, where they killed or captured everyone they could find before sailing on into the Bay of Fundy. Arriving off Grand Pré, the New Englanders rowed ashore to find the village deserted. Having to content themselves with burning what homes they could and damaging the dike system, the Massachusetts men trudged back to their boats through the red mud with little sense of satisfaction. Church was now facing a dilemma: Governor Dudley of Massachusetts, fearful of French reprisal or secretly reluctant to damage a profitable trade with the privateer haven, had given Church last-minute instructions *not* to attack Port-Royal. Church ignored the instructions, and within a day the squadron rode at anchor in the beauty of the Annapolis Basin.

Benjamin Church was quick to send a note ashore demanding that the French garrison surrender. When the French refused, Church was dismayed to find the officers of the two British frigates opposed to launching a bloody assault and bombardment. Fuming, Church satisfied himself with burning a few outlying farms before the ships withdrew, sailing somewhat ignominiously back to Boston. The revenge for Deerfield had not been at the level Church had hoped, and Port-Royal remained in French hands. As the nineteenth-century historian Francis Parkman would write:

If Port Royal in French hands was a source of illicit gain to some persons in Boston, it was also an occasion of loss by the privateers and corsairs it sent out to prey on trading and fishing vessels, while at the same time it was a standing menace as the possible naval base for one of those armaments against the New England capital which were often threatened, though never carried into effect.

If in 1704 Governor Dudley had wanted Port-Royal left alone, by 1707 his attitude had changed. That year he proposed to the General Court that an unhesitating attack be launched against Port-Royal. The General Court duly considered the concept, and once again approved a substantial "armament" of its own.

On May 13, 1707, the garrison of Port-Royal was sobered to see, advancing up the Annapolis Basin on the incoming tide, another flotilla of New England vessels, escorted by the *Province Galley* and the frigate HMS *Deptford*. These vessels soon disgorged into their boats a landing force of some one thousand Massachusetts, New Hampshire and Rhode Island troops, who landed on the north and south sides of the Basin, quickly driving in French pickets sent out to oppose them. The French commander, however, refused to consider surrender demands, and the garrison troops cleverly displayed themselves in a manner that convinced the New Englanders they were there in great numbers. Bickering and disagreement among the independent-minded attackers soon turned into a chaos of missed opportunities, and the glum troops were re-embarked, the flotilla sailing home from the Basin to a fall dominated by recriminations, accusations of cowardice and discontent at all levels of Massachusetts society—not least in the General Court, which had amassed a staggering debt in paying for all these abortive naval adventures.

Two years later, however, in 1709, the gentlemen of the General Court heaved a collective sigh and agreed yet again to consider the Port-Royal question. They were presented with a plan to attack not only Port-Royal but the heartland of New France itself. The initiative came from a bullish and determined merchant, Samuel Vetch, who convinced the General Court that substantial help from London had to be sought if an assault on the northern tormentors was to succeed. Accordingly, Vetch sailed off to Britain with the Court's plans and returned as quickly as the transatlantic passage under sail would allow, with a heartwarming package of offered support. The Crown heartily approved of the Court's plan; Vetch was to become "Governor of Canada" upon a successful outcome; a naval squadron and transports bearing five full regiments of British infantry were assured, all to be sent off for arrival in the early summer, provided the colonies did their part.

With Vetch hounding and hectoring everywhere, the colonies sprang into action. A force of eight hundred New York militia was joined by several hundred men from New Jersey, Pennsylvania and Connecticut, and together they marched through the forests of the New Hampshire grants under Colonel Francis Nicholson to the shores of Lake Champlain. There they were to strike north into Canada when word came of the arrival of the British force at Boston. This latter force would strike at Port-Royal then ascend the St. Lawrence for nothing less than a Phips-like assault on Quebec itself: the time-honoured plan.

All summer long the colonists drilled and readied themselves in a fever of expectation, which gradually faded as no ships appeared. Nicholson's force, sweltering in its bark huts and tents on the shores of Lake Champlain, was swept by disease, until finally Nicholson buried his dead and sent his survivors marching off through the wilderness for home. At Boston, the exasperated General Court finally informed Vetch in October that a letter had been received simply stating that the Crown's larger interests had caused the fleet to be sent to Portugal.

As the winter of 1709–10 closed over Boston, the Court held its collective temper in check and determined that the following summer, 1710, they would try again for the "enterprize" to the north. This time it was the turn of the long-suffering Colonel Nicholson, rather than the choleric Vetch, to travel to London and beg for support. He returned in some triumph, having had assurances that naval support would be sent. Further, Nicholson was named as commander, with Vetch, not forgotten, appointed adjutant-general.

To almost everyone's astonishment, a Royal Navy squadron of five frigates, bearing on board four hundred men of the "sea regiment"—later to be formally known as marines—arrived in Boston harbour in midsummer 1710, ready to do Nicholson's bidding. Ecstatic, Nicholson and Vetch called up every militiaman and coastal vessel available, and on September 18 they sailed off for Port-Royal with the five frigates grandly escorting more than twenty-four colonial vessels, including the redoubtable *Province Galley*, a bomb ketch, and over 1,500 colony troops crammed in seasick expectancy into every available space in the ships. The fleet had an easy passage, sailing through Digby Gut to the Annapolis Basin on September 24, and soon anchored off Port-Royal to begin ferrying the marines and militia ashore.

This time the serious preparations of the New Englanders for a ruinous bombardment and assault led the governor of Port-Royal, Subercase, wisely to surrender. Between the ranks of the drawn-up marines and colony troops, Subercase and his garrison marched out of the little fort with drums beating and all the honours of war. It was a bittersweet moment of success for the New Englanders, and the end of an era. As Parkman would later observe:

> Port Royal had twice before been taken by New England men, once under Major Sedgewick in 1654, and again under Sir William Phips in the last war; and in each case it had been restored to France by treaty. This time England kept what she had got; and as there was no other place of strength in the province, the capture of Port Royal meant the conquest of Acadia.

The year closed with no further effort against the French by sea, but the industrious Nicholson was off to Britain again to press the need to resolve, once and for all, the question of the French in Canada.

The Crown agreed, and early in 1711 Nicholson returned to Boston with news that Britain would mount a major seaborne operation up the St. Lawrence against Quebec. Nicholson was to repeat his assembly of a force on the shores of Lake Champlain, ready to strike north at the heart of French Canada.

Again, true to the Crown's word, a fleet arrived after a seven-week passage on June 24, but this time it was of a size and scale that astonished the colonists. No fewer than nine warships, two bomb ketches and almost sixty transports came in, the last bearing over five thousand men of seven infantry regiments and artillery detachments, as well as the six hundred marines of the ships. In command of this formidable force was Admiral Sir Hovenden Walker in his flagship HMS *Edgar*, a flag officer not noted for sharp efficiency. The army was under the command of Brigadier John Hill, a brother of a favourite of the queen. Of "Jack" Hill, the illustrious Duke of Marlborough had been heard to mutter that he was "good for nothing." Any misgivings the colonists may have had over the leadership, however, were buried in the scale and excitement of the preparations, and 1,500 colonial militia were easily found to clamber aboard the transports in wide-eyed anticipation. On July 13, 1711, with a fair wind out of the southeast, the fleet sailed for the Gulf of St. Lawrence and Quebec.

The captains of the vessels, and Walker himself, were woefully unprepared for the navigation of the great river and its perils. No charts of any reliability existed for the river—Phips was considered simply to have been lucky that he got through at all—and a French pilot taken from a fishing vessel found in the Gulf and bribed to guide the fleet talked ominously of treacherous channels and an oncoming early winter. Walker had sought out every man in Boston with any knowledge of the river, even some who had sailed with Phips, and Samuel Vetch was along for the expedition, urging prudence but no competent navigator either. Walker would have to feel his way to Quebec; but the luck of Phips would not be with him.

At first the voyage was uneventful, and fair winds carried the fleet along the Nova Scotia shore, around Cape Breton and in toward the mouth of the river. The first hint of trouble came on August 18, when fierce winds out of the west forced the fleet to shelter in Gaspé Bay for two days. But then the fair winds returned from the southeast and the fleet "rounded the corner" of the Gaspé Peninsula and began to ascend the river. By August 22 the fleet believed itself to be well to the west of Anticosti Island, at about a point where the river was some eighty-five miles wide. There had been no sight of land since the previous day, and the ships were now in fog, footing ahead before a steady east wind. Walker believed his position to be close to the south shore, but his reckoning was tragically wrong. The fleet was in fact sixty miles north of its estimated position, dangerously close to the north shore.

At eight o'clock in the evening of August 22, with the wind now building out of the southeast, Walker ordered the fleet to "lie to," or adjust sails to make minimum progress for the night, but to steer southward. At ten, Captain Paddon of HMS *Eagle* reported to Walker that his lookouts had seen white water ahead. What the sighting actually was is unknown, but Walker assumed it was the south shore and ordered the fleet to steer north. The winds increased, and in a short time Walker was awakened with news that breakers were visible dead ahead. It was the north shore, and after at first angrily refusing to believe the information, Walker allowed *Edgar* to come about in a frantic lather of work and claw away from the breakers. Other ships of the fleet, in *Edgar*'s wake, were not as fortunate, and the night was punctuated with the flare of rockets and the firing of alarm guns as, one by one, the fleet blundered in toward the rocks. By luck and seamanship the Royal Navy's warships managed narrowly to pull clear, but ten other vessels, including eight of the transports carrying the army, were wrecked and destroyed in the wild night on the rocks of what was later revealed to be the Île aux Oeufs. Just under one thousand men died in the wild tumult of that night, their screams and cries, the crash of collapsing rigging and the grinding of the hulls as they splintered on the rocks audible to the ships desperately tacking past the wrecks to get clear. Through the night the fleet tacked back and forth off the fatal shore, sending in boats as daylight came and the wind abated to try to bring off survivors.

Walker and Hill called a council of war in *Edgar*, at which the officers of the British warships argued for turning back, notwithstanding what Phips had achieved. Though sufficient troops had survived the disaster to make an assault on Quebec still possible, Walker and Hill had had enough. To the anger and disappointment of the Massachusetts men, they ordered an end to the attempt. Samuel Vetch, whose vessel had survived the wreckings through prudent seamanship and a distrust of Walker's navigation, wrote in protest to the Admiral:

> The late disaster cannot, in my humble opinion, be anyways imputed to the difficulty of the navigation, but to the wrong course we steered, which most unavoidably carried us upon the north shore. Who directed that course you best know; and as our return without any further attempt would be a vast reflection upon the conduct of this affair, so it would be of very fatal consequence to the interest of the Crown and all the British colonies upon this continent.

Walker ignored both the accusation and the plea. He steered for the harbour of what is now Sydney, Cape Breton, where he held another council of war. The council recommended no further attempt be made, and Hill and Walker were quick to agree.

A frigate was sent off to Boston with the news—the faithful Nicholson having to bitterly burn his huts and once again disband his waiting army on Lake Champlain—and the New England vessels were sent off home in a black mood of failure. The Royal Navy vessels, including HMS *Edgar*, sailed for Britain, where *Edgar* blew up spectacularly in the Thames shortly after Walker went ashore, a final endnote to a failed campaign. Hill went on to greater glories, secure in courtly "interest," but Walker was removed from command, to die in obscurity in the West Indies. Behind him, on the rocky shores of the Île aux Oeufs, the French picked for months over the wreckage of the ships he had led to disaster.

In two years' time, in 1713, the first of the three great Anglo-French struggles for North America would come to an end by treaty. Acadia, with the exception of Cape Breton Island, had been lost by the French, although the New England joy at taking the privateer haunt of Port-Royal was soon to fade as the French built a new and more powerful base at Louisbourg on Cape Breton Island. The seas of eastern Canada had witnessed the passage of great "armaments" and the thunder of guns, and received their share of wrecked ships and dying men. But more was to come.

By the Treaty of Utrecht in 1713, an old and defeated Louis XIV surrendered significant portions of his empire in North America. The Five Nations of the Iroquois were henceforth to be seen as subjects of the British Crown. Territorially, France surrendered its claim to the posts and shores of Hudson Bay, most of Newfoundland, and the indistinctly defined territory of Acadia. On the Atlantic, only Île St-Jean (Prince Edward Island) and Île Royale (Cape Breton Island) remained in French hands. Inland, France still controlled the St. Lawrence, the Great Lakes, and—theoretically—the curving sweep of tiny settlements that stretched south and west to Louisiana.

Withdrawing from Placentia in Newfoundland and the mainland of Acadia, the French looked to Île Royale as a place to establish a naval, military and trading foothold. On the southeast shore of the rugged island a kidney-shaped harbour, with a narrow entrance guarded by rocky islets, was selected. An ice-free fishing vessel refuge known as Havre à l'Anglais, it was selected over two other ports, Port Dauphin and Port Toulouse. On the south side of the harbour, on a low arm of land that reached out from low land marked by tundra-like bogs and shallow ponds, the French began the construction of a major walled town. Over the next thirty years, heavy bastioned fortifications were built facing the land approaches, while the anchorage in the harbour was protected by gun batteries in the fortress itself and on the island guarding the harbour entrance, as well as by a separate "grand" battery sited on the inner shore of the harbour, facing seaward. Soon, Louisbourg became a transshipment point for cargoes inbound from India, Asia and the Caribbean to France, pausing before the last long run across the Atlantic. It became a hub of the thriving fishery, with its proximity to the teeming Atlantic banks; an ice-free guardian naval base to the approaches of the St. Lawrence; and, to the bedevilment of Boston merchants and shipowners to the south, a home port for daring privateers who waged an unceasing and untiring war of plunder and seizure on New England shipping. Louisbourg captains such as Morpain, who commanded the privateer *Caribou*, became feared and detested names on the Massachusetts coastline, clauses of faraway treaties notwithstanding. After 1713, this war between New Englanders and the French, and warriors allied to the French, went on unabated without regard to the treaty, as the following appeal to Governor Dudley and the General Court, recorded by historian J.S. McLennan, illustrates in part:

Mem'l of Capt. Cyprian Southack to
Gov'r Joseph Dudley and the Council at Boston,
September 15, 1715

On 30 Apr. 1715 he sailed with 2 sloops & one two mast vessel for a fishing voyage to Nova Scotia. 14th May arrived at Port Rossway & landed 17th, vessels sailed on to their fishing 18th. Welcomed by Mons. Tarranquer & Joseph Muess. 23rd. welcomed by the chief Captain of Cape Sables & 8 Indian officers. 25th. M. Tarranquer came and threatened to lead 100 Indians to capture all the fishing vessels on the coast. 28th June received news of capture of an English vessel and men. 3rd July. Informed of the capture of another fishing sloop by the Indians, who threatened him with capture and death; saying Costabelle had given to the Indians a great present. 11th July. 2 vessels came in and told him of a capture of 7 sail at Port Seigneur, that the Indians were on their way to capture him & his, & would kill him. They refused to carry him, his people & effects away, unless he first gave them a bill of 500 current money of Boston & 125 pounds to be p'd in Boston. Agreed to . . . Loss sustained at Port Rossway—450 pounds & the fishing season.

This virtual state of sea war off the coasts of Massachusetts, Nova Scotia and Newfoundland continued unabated until 1739, and as Louisbourg's walls grew and its harbour filled with more shipping and with the prizes gleefully brought in by the privateer fleet, it became as much of an obsession to the men of Massachusetts as Port-Royal had been. They saw it as the hotbed that inspired bloody raids on English frontier settlements, and as the home harbour for such large numbers of marauding privateers that it was called the "Dunquerque [Dunkirk] of North America" after the famous French privateering port.

In 1739, on the pretext of defending the honour of a British captain named Jenkins whose ear had allegedly been sliced off by a Spanish coast guardsman in the Americas, Britain declared war on Spain. The War of Jenkins' Ear was more about gaining the profits of the African slave trade than the severed ear, and France was officially neutral, but the privateer sea war along the Atlantic coast continued as before. Then, in 1744, European arguments as to who should be the successful claimant to the Austrian throne led by a convoluted process into an official declaration of war between Britain and France. The unofficial privateer war now had the full authority of the French Crown and purse behind it, and the Louisbourg men were soon off to sea with an expanded list of English targets. For the Bastonnais, the grim-visaged men of Boston to whom Morpain and his ilk were a pestilential scourge, Louisbourg itself had to be taken or destroyed. As historian Joseph Rutledge wrote:

If Louisbourg might stand for the nadir of the French spirit in the New World, there were few knowing or willing enough to admit the fact. To the French, Louisbourg was a great gesture, a new guardian of the gates of Canada. To the English it was a challenge in part to their vanity but, more importantly, to their trade with the American continent. To the American colonies it was a never-ending threat to their lives, to their seagoing commerce, and to the fisheries that were the backbone of that trade.

With formal war declared, the governor at Louisbourg was quick to send off vessels bearing part of the Louisbourg garrison to attack the English posts at Canceau, on the Nova Scotia mainland (successfully), and Annapolis Royal (unsuccessfully). The privateering war soon became the preoccupation of the mariners of Louisbourg. The New England fleet was large, with eighty or more vessels trading to the ports of Île Royale despite the state of war, so oddly did business and conflict intersect in the eighteenth century. Soon, captured New England vessels choked the fortress's harbour, awaiting sale in Quebec or France.

The New Englanders were quick to retaliate, and as English privateers themselves flooded the seas off Nova Scotia, Île Royale and the Gulf of St. Lawrence, shipping to Louisbourg began to dry up. In the deliberations of the General Court a grand conviction was growing, that of the necessity of marshalling the colonial forces and seizing Louisbourg itself. The idea was floated to the British government in a letter from Massachusetts governor William Shirley, sent in November 1744. That winter, Shirley argued that the French attacks on Canceau and Annapolis Royal, the threat to the fishery, and the inroads Louisbourg privateers were making in New England shipping rendered the capture and destruction of Louisbourg an absolute necessity rather than a luxury. In his proposal Shirley was supported by an influential merchant, William Pepperrell, and the General Court agreed to the plan. It was an ambitious undertaking for the colonists to consider.

The colonies applied to the Royal Navy for support in mounting the effort against Louisbourg, and the commodore of the North American station, Peter Warren, readily agreed. By April 1745 the

Capture of Louisbourg, April 30, 1745 *C 40575*

colony troops and their transports—over sixty ships—had been assembled, and they sailed for Canceau, or Canso as it was increasingly called, to prepare for the awesome task of assaulting the fortress. Warren's squadron of over a dozen warships arrived to escort the fleet, and with additional transports bearing more colony troops and supplies coming in daily from Boston, it was a fleet of just under one hundred vessels that sailed north from Canso on April 29, 1745, bound for Gabarus Bay and the sole beach where troops could be landed within striking distance of Louisbourg. Coming to anchor there on April 30, the fleet presented an astonishing spectacle to the watching French on Louisbourg's ramparts, who soon saw longboats pulling for various points along the shore.

The energy of the New Englanders was breathtaking, and by nightfall over two thousand troops had landed and set up an encampment on the shores of Gabarus Bay, busily wrestling guns ashore and sending parties of men out to encircle the harbour and skirmish with the French. With more enthusiasm than skill, and by dint of an extraordinary effort, the New Englanders hauled siege guns overland from the beach on sledges, captured the grand battery on the harbourfront after the French had abandoned it, and soon forced the French governor, Du Chambon, to sue for surrender terms. By

June 17, 1745, it was all over, and Warren's squadron was able to anchor in safety in Louisbourg harbour.

One French vessel might have briefly helped the hapless Du Chambon resist the New England onslaught—the 64-gun *Vigilant*, outbound from Brest to assist Louisbourg. *Vigilant* could not have fought off Warren's squadron, but its stores, guns and personnel might have prolonged the siege. On approaching Louisbourg, however, *Vigilant* found and pursued a smaller English vessel, the 44-gun *Mermaid*. The English ship wisely led *Vigilant* into the trap of Warren's waiting squadron, as the log of *Mermaid* relates:

Mermaid 20th May

Hazey wear [sic], Gave Chace to the S.W. at 1 wore Ship to the No. Wd. The Chace hoisted. A French ensign & pendt. We fired our Stern Chace on her wch. She returned from her Bow we made ye Sigl. Of Discovering a Strange Ship to ye Fleet who were all in shore at 2 the Chace perceivg. Our Fleet wore to ye So. Wd. & gave us his Broadside we wore after him and returned it he made all the Sail Possible we kept Close under his Starboard Quarter he kept plying his stern Chace as we did our Bow we Portd. Our Helm twice and gave him two broadside at 6 came up Capn. Rouse in a privateer Snow who Ply'd his Bow Chace very well at 8 the Commodr. In the Superbe and Eltham Joyn'd us the Chace Engaged us Large the Superbe on the Starbd. & we on the Larboard quarter at 9 the Chace, struck sent on bd. Our boats and brot. From thence the 1st and 2nd Caps. & part of the Officers it being a Thick Fogg could see no other Ship but the Prize wch. Was a French Man of War of 64 guns & 500 Men called the Vigilant Capn. Maisonfort Am Imployed shifting Prisoners & Securing our Riggin Recd. On board 130 Prisoners at 8 A.M. the Commodr. Joynd us . . . , 21st May.—Modt. & Foggy sent on board the 1st Mate 1 Midshipman 20 Men Laying too in Compy. The Eltham and Commodr. At 4 A.M. the Commodr. Stood in for the Land sent on bd. The Prize 1 Midshipman and 15 Men to Assist she being much shattered . . .

The siege took the lives of over two thousand New England men, by either wounds or disease, and the cost of the expedition was a heavy burden on the New England economy for years. Louisbourg itself attracted few merchants or settlers willing to relocate to its grim, fogbound world. In 1749 the treaty that concluded the war returned Louisbourg to the French, to the bewilderment and anger of the New England colonists. But it would not remain in French hands for long.

Between 1749 and 1754, the undeclared but continuing war between the English and the French in North America became muted for a time. Inland, the French had begun to establish at Cataraqui—now Kingston—a sizable Lake Ontario squadron that could guarantee the vital route up the lake to Fort Niagara and the lakes above the great Falls. The French had built several general-purpose cargo vessels at Cataraqui, beginning with the *Frontenac* in 1673, but now their shipbuilding took on new purpose.

In 1749, the year the French returned to Louisbourg, the first addition to the Lake Ontario squadron was launched. It was the 40-ton schooner, later a sloop, *Saint-Victor*, pierced for 6 four-pounder guns, and named after the little settlement that clustered around the walls of Fort Rouillé, on the site of present-day Toronto. In the next year, 1750, the little yard at Cataraqui launched *La Louise*, a 50-ton schooner of 8 guns. By 1755, when warfare had become an open fact once again, they were joined by the 90-ton *La Hurault*, a square topsail schooner, and the Lake Ontario flagship *La Marquise de Vaudreuil*, a 120-ton square topsail schooner carrying 14 long guns and 8 swivel guns. With this force the French dominated the lake and cowed the fewer and smaller British vessels that were based at Oswego, on the lake's southeastern shore. This squadron would figure large in the successful attack and capture of Oswego in 1756 by French troops and warriors. It would only be scattered and destroyed when, in 1758, a great three-pronged pincer movement against Canada brought a sizable British force to Lake Ontario that captured Cataraqui and burned or took over the remaining French squadron. The simple white ensign of France had flown briefly, but bravely, in control of the most important of the Great Lakes.

In 1754, the seemingly quiet frontier between the holdings of France and the English colonies walled off behind the Appalachian Mountains burst into open warfare. English traders and land speculators were probing into the Ohio valley, and one party, under the command of a young Virginian named George Washington, came out on the losing end of a bloody confrontation with the French, precipitating an eventual worldwide war that lasted until 1763, known as the Seven Years War, or the French and Indian War. It would end with the conquest of France's empire in North America, a conquest effected largely through the growth and exercise of British sea power.

The British government and its American colonies were very much uncertain of victory as the war began in earnest. French frontier war strategy, with strong Indian alliances, gave them victory after victory to begin with, including the capture of Oswego by the French military commander in Canada, Louis-Joseph, Marquis de Montcalm-Gozon. But the situation began to unravel for the French after 1757, when worldwide British sea power, growing in ability and reach, slowly crushed France's navy and made contact with Canada and Île Royale steadily more difficult. Along with the rise of British sea power came the leadership of William Pitt in Parliament, who determined on a relentless and overwhelming strategy of conquest in North America; a strategy that would rely on British naval expertise and its ability to place the king's troops anywhere that ships could go.

Pitt's plan for the conquest of Canada was not very different from the plans of fifty years earlier. It called for a column to move west from the English colonies to seize Fort Niagara at the head of Lake Ontario and retake Oswego before moving on to take

Cataraqui; another column to voyage by bateaux and longboats north along Lake Champlain toward Montreal; and a third to sail to Louisbourg for its recapture before ascending the St. Lawrence to assault Quebec itself. The heartland of Canada would then be taken by British forces moving west from Quebec toward Montreal, there to rendezvous with the columns coming from Lake Champlain and Lake Ontario. Over the period 1758 to 1760, the British accomplished everything they set out to do in this plan.

In 1758, a huge force of some 140 ships was gathered at Halifax, Nova Scotia, where a permanent Royal Navy dockyard would be established the following year. Carrying a large army of British regular troops, the fleet sailed northeast and repeated the form of the 1745 New England capture of the fortress of Louisbourg. The great fleet anchored in Gabarus Bay, landing its thousands of troops on the sands of what became known as Kennington Cove, and then besieged the fortress until its surrender six weeks later. The climactic and decisive moment came when British seamen in longboats rowed in to attack two French warships that were protectively anchored in the fortress harbour, the *Prudent* and the *Bienfaisant*. With the burning of one of these ships and the capture of the other, French resistance ceased.

The following year, 1759, Louisbourg was used as a staging base for the second of the two great amphibious operations of the war, the assault on Quebec itself. A huge force of 8,000 soldiers and 13,000 sailors in a fleet of 141 vessels, ranging from the 90-gun *Neptune*, flagship of Vice Admiral Charles Saunders, down to tiny cutters and bomb ketches, sailed for the St. Lawrence. Guided by charts assembled by two men of later historical impact, James Cook and Samuel Holland, the fleet slowly made its way up the great river, succeeding where Walker had failed. Carefully negotiating its dangers with a fortuitous east wind driving them, the great fleet arrived in the basin below Quebec by June 27, 1759, and the army commander, James Wolfe, began probing the French defences. French naval defences were non-existent, with the exception of several attempts to launch fireships and rafts at the anchored fleet, as

A view of the Landing Place above the Town of Quebec, by Hervey Smith *C 788*

well as the gallant resistance of a small French flotilla upriver under Jean Vauquelin. It would take until September 13, for Wolfe to find his chink in the French armour. On the previous night, landing barges from the anchored British warships and transports had carried troops to a small cove called the Anse au Foulon, where they climbed in the darkness to the Plains of Abraham above. A set-piece battle with the French gave Quebec to the British, and in the following year the great pincer movement seized Montreal and ended the French Empire in North America.

The war would drag on until ended by treaty in 1763, the last spasm of fighting coming in 1762 when the French made a brief and unsuccessful attempt to seize a foothold again in Newfoundland. In a rising wave that culminated in 1759, the Royal Navy of Britain had crushed *la marine royale* of France in several battles that ensured Britain emerged from the global war with a worldwide empire based on her sea power.

There is no event so indicative of the gallant futility of French naval efforts to defend their North American empire in the face of this overwhelming power than the engagement that has come to be known as the Battle of the Restigouche. In spring 1760, the British conquerors of Quebec were hanging grimly on in their battered walled town, besieged by French troops under the determined and capable command of the Chevalier de Lévis. Both sides watched anxiously to see which nation's ships would be first to arrive at Quebec after the ice had cleared, for that would signal whether the British conquest would succeed or fail. In the event, the arrival first of the frigate HMS *Lowestoffe* sent the British defenders into delirium and Lévis's army into retreat westward.

France had tried to help; it just came too late. On April 10, 1760, a French convoy of eight supply ships with stores and four hundred troops, escorted by six smaller French warships and the frigate *Machault*, all under the command of Lieutenant François Chénard de la Giraudais, sailed from Bordeaux for Quebec. Within a day of sailing, the convoy had been seen by two patrolling British frigates, which characteristically closed under all sail to engage the French. La Giraudais ordered the convoy to disperse and managed to drive the British vessels off, but not before the supply ships had turned tail and fled back toward the French coast, while another sank. La Giraudais managed to reassemble the convoy and stood on manfully for the entrance to the Gulf of St. Lawrence. Arriving in the middle of May, the French intercepted and captured a small British vessel only to learn from it that a British squadron—of which *Lowestoffe* was the harbinger—had already passed up the river to Quebec.

Hove to in mid-Gulf, La Giraudais called a conference of captains in the great cabin of *Machault*. La Giraudais had orders to sail to the Caribbean or Louisiana if a Canadian resupply was impossible. Before resorting to that, the officers agreed that the convoy would sail into the Baie des Chaleurs and the mouth of the Restigouche River. There, an effort would be made to send the supplies overland to Quebec, if that seemed feasible.

La Giraudais brought the convoy to anchor off the small refugee Acadian settlement that had sprung up at the mouth of the Restigouche. Mooring his ships defensively, he managed to get heavy guns on shore to set up a defending battery, and encamped the four hundred troops ashore, away from the fetid atmosphere of the ships' lower decks. A volunteer messenger was sent off through the woods for the trek to Quebec, to reach Vaudreuil and obtain his orders. The reply, when it came after the superhuman exertions of the messengers, told La Giraudais to stay where he was and await additional orders. With an eye to his defensive preparations and his limited stores, La Giraudais settled down to wait.

The news of La Giraudais' convoy had put two separate British squadrons at sea in pursuit. From Louisbourg, five ships under the command of Captain John Byron—known as Foul Weather Jack for the bad weather that seemed to follow him everywhere—sailed for the Baie des Chaleurs, with Byron flying his commodore's pendant in HMS *Fame*, 74 guns. Arriving in blustery weather in the offing of the mouth of the river, Byron spent from June 22 to 25 sounding and charting the channels leading in to La Giraudais' anchorage with his squadron's longboats. During this work an additional six ships under Captain Samuel Wallis arrived from Quebec.

Entering the inner approaches on June 25, *Fame* went hard aground, chart work and soundings notwithstanding, and lay vulnerable to French attack for the full day it took to work her off the ledge. But La Giraudais did not risk a foray from his lair to attack *Fame*. The next day, June 26, Wallis and the remaining ten ships came in, only to have two more ships run temporarily aground. Relentlessly, however, the British closed the distance to the *Machault* and the other moored French ships, until on June 27 La Giraudais' shore battery found the British within range and began firing at them. The British paused, edging their vessels just out of range of the French guns, but La Giraudais could see that he was hopelessly outgunned. Trying to buy time, La Giraudais had his ships lift their anchors and work by sweeps and sails farther up into the river, only to have Byron's smaller craft inch their way toward him in turn. This advance was temporarily slowed by La Giraudais' sinking of several of his smaller ships in the channel, but the inevitable loomed now in the French commander's mind, with his ships effectively trapped. Nonetheless, he made preparations to fight as best he could. He moored his ships on "spring" lines, which allowed them to be pivoted at the mooring for more effective use of their guns, and then supported them by a new shore battery that was hastily erected.

Within a few days the leading three British vessels were within gun range of the French, and HMS *Repulse* moved in first to engage *Machault*. *Repulse*'s fire was met by a furious cannonading from *Machault* that soon rendered the British vessel damaged and unmanageable. It drifted off and ran aground, out of the fight. But now La Giraudais faced another difficulty: his powder magazine was almost empty, expended in the battle with *Repulse*. The crews of the remaining French ships were beginning to flee ashore, and *Machault* faced certain capture. La Giraudais assessed the situation, determined he had done all that honour demanded, and gave the fateful order to abandon ship, with fuses lit in the remaining powder supplies in the magazine. The blasts were tremendous, but with the smoke of the explosions still lying over the river, longboats from the British squadron packed with marines rowed in to the remaining French vessels, and as their crews watched from shore, the torch was put to the convoy in a towering pillar of smoke and flame. Over thirty French vessels, ranging from warships to colonial sloops, were either burned, sunk or captured. It was July 8, 1760.

La Giraudais' gallant naval effort encapsulated all that had marked the French adventure in America: courage, audacity, skill and gallantry, but too little of everything to face the growing power of an implacable enemy. That it occurred in a bay and waters first named by another audacious Frenchman, Jacques Cartier, 226 years earlier, poignantly revealed that more than just wood, tar, rope and canvas was vanishing in the flames that rose above the dark waters of the Restigouche.

7

A
Kingdom
Won and
Lost

I N 1713, the Hudson's Bay Company found itself in control of all of Hudson Bay and its limitless, ill-defined hinterland. But the very success of the Bay's operations in its little posts on the edge of that cold sea had generated little interest in probing the great interior that had now become unassailably the domain of the British Crown. The Company had, at the midpoint of the eighteenth century, barely two hundred men on station on Hudson Bay, content, as one writer put it, to be "asleep by the frozen sea." So uninterested was the general British mind in even the location of this distant wasteland that John Oldmixon, writing tardily of the Hudson Bay holdings in his 1708 work *The British Empire in America*, observed that "there being no towns nor plantations in this country, but two or three poor Forts to defend the Factories, we thought we were at liberty to place it where we pleas'd, and were loath to let our History open with the description of so miserable a wilderness."

That the Hudson's Bay Company put little value on an inland pursuit of furs was borne out in 1754, when the Company sent Anthony Henday inland from York Factory to "draw down many of the [inland] natives to trade." Henday gamely trudged west as far as the foothills of the Rockies, and reported on his return in 1755 that he was astonished to find vigorous and ambitious French fur traders from Montreal at the current location of Edmonton and elsewhere, actively pursuing a lively trade with the Plains Indians. This alarming report produced no shock of effort in the Company, and the cloud of war soon settled over the continent.

In 1764, the French elite having been sent home from Canada and the Union flag of Great Britain now flying from Florida to Ungava, the Hudson's Bay Company directors in Britain expectantly contemplated a full continent's worth of fur trade that they assumed would be theirs to exploit. But they had not reckoned with a new and unexpected source of competition. The French fur trade had been strictly controlled by the French colonial administration, but even though the elite that had governed the trade had been sent home to France, the able and experienced *voyageurs*, the canoemen, remained. British merchants and entrepreneurs were quick to see the potential for profit in the newly conquered lands, but none so quick as the Scots, who arrived in numbers at Quebec and Montreal, and soon put in place partnerships with the willing voyageurs that had the canoe brigades paddling west again in search of furs. Liberally interpreting the Hudson's Bay Company's charter to mean that any new fur trade initiatives had free rein in former French territory that had not been covered by the Company's charter, the Scots and their cheerful *Canadien* employees burst into the western lands with an energy that caught the Hudson's Bay Company by surprise.

The great waterways of Canada were the highway of the trade, as before. The furs were assembled at remote posts and gatherings in the west and carried to the head of the Great Lakes in smaller north birchbark canoes, which rarely exceeded twenty-five feet in length. At the head of the Great Lakes and the waters of the Ottawa and St. Lawrence rivers, the packed furs and the canoemen's supplies were transferred to the huge "five fathom" or "Montreal" canoes, forty feet in length, which made the final descent to Montreal. The goods on which the trade relied were ferried out to the west in the spring, in a reverse process. The canoemen were extraordinarily hardy and tough, paddling for up to ten hours a day and sleeping under their overturned canoes, living on pemmican and dried peas, and dogtrotting over the portages often with two ninety-pound packs. Joined to the canny business sagacity and energy of the Scottish managers, the Montreal-based "pedlars"—as the Company disdainfully referred to them—had by 1774 secured a stranglehold on the inland fur trade and were a serious threat to the Hudson's Bay Company's north-based trade.

The coming of the American Revolution and the brief occupation of Canada by rebel troops over the winter of 1775–76 slowed the trade for a time, but on the retreat of the rebels in 1776 it rebounded, and by 1779 the "pedlars" had decided to form a company, the North West Company, that would focus their challenge to the Hudson's Bay Company. Peter Newman described them this way:

> Unlike the more sedentary Bay men, the Nor'westers were constantly in motion. Their canoes were propelled by voyageurs, free spirits and galley slaves both, their only reward a defiant pride in their own courage and endurance. Their subculture was based on custom, dress and circumstance, but the French language was their unifying ethos. As the beaver lodges in relatively accessible corners were trapped out, the canoe brigades aimed always further afield—and the longer the network, the greater the hardships.

The Treaty of Paris of 1783, which ended access of the fur traders to the Ohio and Mississippi valleys, only redoubled their efforts to seek new fur sources to the north and west. In 1793, the Nor'wester Alexander Mackenzie's exploratory voyage reached the Pacific at Bella Coola inlet; in 1808, Simon Fraser descended the turbulent river that bears his name to the sea; and in 1811, David Thompson capped his extraordinary mapping and exploration of the Alberta–British Columbia lands by reaching the Pacific. A temporary rival to the Nor'westers, the XY Company, had mounted a strong challenge for control of the trade, ending with a merger with the Nor'westers in 1804. The final chapter of the fur trade, before its decline after 1821 with the shift in hat styles to silk from felted beaver, would be the merger of the Nor'westers with the Hudson's Bay Company in the early nineteenth century, even as the heyday of the fur trade was coming to a close. The nature of the trade itself had changed over the years 1750 to 1820 as well, with the gradual introduction of the sturdy, single-sailed York boat, a kind of cargo-carrying large dory or bateau that was rowed rather than paddled, and was infinitely more durable and capacious than the fleet but delicate birchbark canoes. The first York boat, based on an Orkney Islands design that in turn drew from Norse traditions, had been hammered together by Scots boat wrights at Albany Fort in the 1740s, and it would stay in use on the western and northern rivers, and the uncounted lakes, until the great prairie settlement days of the 1870s. Its career spanned the heyday and the decline of the single most important commercial and transportation activity in the early history and shaping of Canada.

By the terms of the Treaty of 1763 that ended the Seven Years War, France's empire in North America had been reduced to two small islands off the south coast of Newfoundland, St. Pierre and Miquelon, where the French were allowed to base their fishing fleets. In contemplating the vastness of their conquests, stretching from tropic swamp to Arctic tundra, the British were faced with the daunting realization that, other than the practised and familiar routes of the fur trade, there were few if any reliable maps of the interior, and equally few useful charts of Canadian waters. New England and European fishermen and trading schooners that had plied up to Louisbourg or the Newfoundland fishery—even in time of war—had built up a body of practical knowledge of how to navigate the Canadian coasts, but the British soon realized that an empire of this scope required more than word-of-mouth navigation. Both the land and the sea needed to be laid down on paper. There was a burst of charting and land surveying activity in eastern Canada after the British conquest, and it revolved principally around three men: J.F.W. DesBarres, Samuel Holland and James Cook.

James Cook was an extraordinary British naval officer and explorer whose name is forever linked with several navigational and cartographic accomplishments: three monumental Pacific voyages in the eighteenth century; success in dealing with sickness at sea; and the delineation of the coastlines of Australia and New Zealand. He was a somewhat mysterious man of simple Yorkshire origins who came to be a towering figure in eighteenth-century history, but it is understood by few that Canada and its waters were the crucible that shaped Cook from a simple warrant officer into arguably the world's greatest navigator and maritime explorer.

Portrait of Captain James Cook *C 034667*

When Cook arrived at Halifax in the spring of 1758 as part of the force gathering to attack Louisbourg, he was a capable but undistinguished master, a senior but non-commissioned rank in the Royal Navy, serving in HMS *Pembroke*, 64 guns. Over the next nine years, as his active professional life developed in the waters of coastal Canada and Newfoundland, he was transformed into a competent navigator, an innovative chart-maker and a surveyor whose superior skills led him to be commissioned as an officer and selected to command the first of three epic voyages of oceanic exploration, a role in the forefront of European scientific and philosophical investigation of the Pacific. Cook's experiences on the coasts of Nova Scotia, in the Gulf of St. Lawrence and the river itself, and on the coast of Newfoundland, as well as his exposure to the work, instruments and methods of Samuel Holland, J.F.W. DesBarres and others, were, it can be argued, the basis on which he and others developed the first reliable chart-making methodology in Western experience. Cook's achievements in North American cartography not only led to his selection for the Pacific voyages but provided, together with works such as DesBarres's *Atlantic Neptune*, a secure navigational basis for the post-1763 settlement of British North America and for the inshore fishery.

Cook's transformation began with his chance encounter with the Dutch-born military surveyor Samuel Holland at Louisbourg in the summer of 1758. Cook learned from Holland the techniques of land surveying, and then combined those techniques with existing chart-making usages to produce chart work of a wholly new level of accuracy. His participation in the ascent to Quebec in 1759 of the Royal Navy fleet carrying James Wolfe's troops, his key role in the success of that venture and his preparation of subsequent charts led to his selection to undertake a survey of the west and south coasts of Newfoundland. The excellence of this work led him to be chosen to command the first Pacific voyage of HM Bark *Endeavour* to Tahiti in 1768.

Cook had remained in Canada after the capture of Quebec, transferring into HMS *Northumberland*, which joined a new squadron that overwintered at Halifax in 1759–60, during which time the Royal Navy dockyard there was established. Cook continued to develop his chart-making ability, completing a masterful chart of the Gulf of St. Lawrence and the river that could be used for reliable navigation well into the modern era.

In 1762, Cook visited Newfoundland when *Northumberland* was sent there to repel a last, futile French attempt at an attack on British settlements there. Cook produced charts of Placentia, Harbour Grace and Carbonear, and then, from 1763 to 1767, was involved in charting both St. Pierre and Miquelon as well as carrying out his principal work on the coasts of Newfoundland. In 1768 he left for the Pacific.

If one individual may have had an even greater impact on navigation in colonial eastern Canada than Cook, it was Joseph Frederick Wallet DesBarres. DesBarres was a Huguenot Swiss who had attended the Royal Military Academy in Britain and entered the British army as an engineer with a particular talent for surveying and map-making. When the Seven Years War broke out, he was sent to North America and took part in most of the major campaigns, including Lake George in 1757, Louisbourg's siege in 1758 and Quebec in 1759.

In 1761, DesBarres was stationed at Halifax, where Cook in *Northumberland* was working with his engineer friend Samuel Holland to develop his chart-making skill. It seems evident that DesBarres worked with both men and that Cook learned a great deal from DesBarres. During the 1762 expedition to Newfoundland, DesBarres worked with Cook in the surveying and charting that was done. On the squadron's return to Halifax, DesBarres found himself now commissioned by the Admiralty to prepare "accurate Surveys and Charts of the Coast and Harbours of Nova Scotia." He applied the new inclusive chart-making and surveying techniques pioneered collectively by Cook, Holland and himself in that key period of 1761–63. The result of DesBarres's work would be the exhaustive survey of the complex Nova Scotia coastline known as *The Atlantic Neptune*.

After spending the period of the American Revolution in England, DesBarres returned to serve for two years as governor of the then-separate colony of Cape Breton Island, during which time he established its capital at Sydney, and then from 1802 to 1812 he was governor of St. John's Isle, later Prince Edward Island. He died in retirement at Halifax in 1824, having been instrumental in improving navigation along Canada's east coast to the enormous benefit of the fishery, trade, the immigration of Loyalists and the work of the navy.

The departure of the French threat from the north allowed the differences and arguments that had threatened to divide the so-called Thirteen Colonies from Britain to burst into full flower, and by 1775 these grievances had broken into open warfare. For reasons ranging from a religious revival to the proximity and power of the military and the Royal Navy, Nova Scotia did not join the rebellion, although it flirted with it; nor did Canada, in spite of a winter-long occupation by American troops, who were greeted by the French-speaking population with disinterest. The Royal Navy secured the eastern waters and the St. Lawrence River, and to take the place of the small French squadron on Lake Ontario the Quartermaster

The American schooner *Franklin*, in company with the *Lynch*   C 40571

Corps of the British army established a small squadron of warships known as the Provincial Marine. Based on Carleton Island in the St. Lawrence River just below its opening into Lake Ontario, the Provincial Marine voyaged from the Long Sault rapids all the way up to the head of the lake at Fort Niagara, serving a general-purpose role of cargo carrier, passenger line, fur trade consignment forwarders, troop transport and—almost as an afterthought—naval force. Other vessels were operated in the Upper Lakes, above Niagara Falls. Manned largely by Canadians, the Provincial Marine operated ships such as the little full-rigged *Limnade* throughout the Revolution, and was never challenged in its control of Lake Ontario and the river. That challenge would not come until the War of 1812, when in 1813 the Provincial Marine surrendered its mandate and ships to the Royal Navy. The base at Carleton Island was abandoned in 1794–96, when the British government at last gave up posts it nominally should have surrendered to the Americans, but which it held on to after 1783 in a vain hope of pressing the American government to honour Loyalist reparation claims.

If the Great Lakes were relatively quiet during the American Revolution due to the presence of the Provincial Marine, the coast of Atlantic Canada was the scene of active privateering, which we will look at in the next chapter. And Canadian waters were not free of rebel privateers, who sailed north from Massachusetts and other colonies to attack British shipping, and on occasion raided ashore. Serious incursions were made at several Nova Scotia communities, and a less bloody one on Prince Edward Island, in 1775. In November of that year two Massachusetts privateer vessels, the *Lynch* and the *Franklin*, appeared off the colonial capital of "Charlotte Town" and sent a party ashore that plundered some possessions, including the Great Seal of the colony, and took members of the governor's staff hostage. The hostages were later released by an apologetic George Washington, but the Seal was never returned.

The rebel privateer threat to Nova Scotia was far more serious. Washington had ordered that Nova Scotian shipping and communities should not be interfered with unless they were evidently supporting the British military suppression of the Revolution. Massachusetts privateers largely ignored this directive, and the Nova Scotia coastline was plagued with attacks from small sloops and schooners bent primarily on looting, from the Halifax approaches to Annapolis Royal. Fishing craft were taken or destroyed, coastal schooners intercepted, and communities attacked and looted, until the hardships of the privateer war led to the revival of an old term for the colony: Nova Scarcity.

The peak of the rebel privateering campaign against Nova Scotia came between 1781, when French assistance to the rebel cause began to show real effect, and 1783, when the peace treaty was signed that ended the war. Typical of the rebel privateer raids was one mounted on Lunenburg on July 1, 1782. Four American vessels had anchored at some distance from the town and put an armed party ashore. This group was seen by a local woman who was about to milk her cow, and she sent her husband on the run into the village to give the alarm. As the privateers approached, the townsfolk hurriedly buried possessions, some throwing them down wells. A handful of militiamen got to one of the town's two blockhouses, but they soon surrendered after a brief fight when it became evident that resistance was futile. General plunder and looting followed, and a

A Southeast View of Cataraqui, 1783, by James Peachey C1511

threat to burn the town down unless a thousand-pound promissory note was paid, a demand backed by the seizure of three hostages. The coming of peace in 1783 restored a more usual relationship with New England, one of neighbourly goodwill and trade.

The end of the Revolution produced a massive northward flow of Loyalists. Those who crossed at the Niagara frontier, or gathered at Sorel, Quebec, to be allotted lands on the upper St. Lawrence and Lake Ontario, eventually established English-speaking Upper Canada, later Ontario. The thousands who flooded into Nova Scotia gave a brief flowering to Shelburne before moving on or embedding themselves in Nova Scotian society, and their settlements along the St. John River led to the creation of an entirely new colony, New Brunswick. When, in 1792, John Graves Simcoe, newly appointed lieutenant-governor of the new province of Upper Canada and son of the Captain John Simcoe with whom James Cook had sailed to Canada, stepped ashore at Newark—later Niagara-on-the-Lake—it marked the beginning of a new age in British North America. That the one just ending had been shaped by events on the sea was borne out by the fact that Simcoe and his family encamped at Newark in tents that had previously been carried around the world on Captain Cook's third world voyage. The sea and the glittering lakes were now to be the setting for new chapters of gripping drama in the era that lay a few years ahead.

There was a last sputter of warfare at the end of the Revolution that also served as a kind of exclamation point to the 150 years of activity of the Hudson's Bay Company. In 1782, the French warships *Sceptre*, 75 guns, *Astrée*, 36 guns, and *Engagéante*, 36 guns, fresh from serving in the losing battle off Les Saintes in the Caribbean, arrived in Hudson Bay. They were under the command of Jean-François de Galaup, Comte de La Pérouse, who would later vanish mysteriously in Pacific waters during an exploratory circumnavigation. Carrying aboard a force of three hundred marines equipped with artillery, La Pérouse arrived off the huge stoneworks of Fort Prince of Wales at the mouth of the Churchill River, a stone fortification that had taken the Hudson's Bay Company forty years to build, and which was commanded by western explorer Samuel Hearne. Hearne, faced with the overpowering strength of the French, struck his flag before a shot was fired, to spare lives. La Pérouse ordered the guns of the great fort to be spiked, and its casemates blown up; it would never again be used by the Company.

With his prisoners on board, La Pérouse sailed down to the mouth of the Hayes River and anchored off York Factory at Five Fathom Hole. The night before the French landed, the Company staff managed to escape to sea in the Company vessel *Prince Rupert* with as much trade goods and furs as they could cram into the ship. Undeterred, La Pérouse burned York Factory, and then used a captured HBC vessel, the *Severn*, to send his prisoners safely off to England. Of La Pérouse one of the prisoners, Edward Umfreville, is quoted by Peter C. Newman as saying the French leader's "politeness, humanity and goodness secured him the affection of all the company's officers." It was the polite and mannered end of an era.

8

Black Flags in Northern Seas

They entered the Harbour of Trepassi, with their black Colours flying, Drums beating, and Trumpets sounding. There were two and twenty Vessels in the Harbour, which the men all quitted upon Sight of the Pyrate, and fled ashore. It is impossible particularly to recount the Destruction and Havock they made here, burning and sinking all the Shipping, except a Bristol Galley, and destroying the Fisheries, and Stages of the poor Planters, without Remorse or Compunction; for nothing is so deplorable as Power in mean and ignorant Hands, it makes Men wanton and giddy, unconcerned at the Misfortunes they are imposing on their Fellow Creatures, and keeps them smiling at the Mischiefs, that bring them no Advantage. They are like mad Men, that cast Fire-Brands, Arrows, and Death, and say, are not we in Sport?

OF THE MANY ICONS of Western culture captured by these words of Daniel Defoe, few have become as instantly recognizable as the pirate—the pig-tailed, eye-patched rogue of adventure under billowing canvas, in pursuit of buried treasure and at once a fearsomely fun figure of childish delight and an ever-intriguing subject for inaccurate films and books. That few pirates ever took on the elaborate persona so beloved of Hollywood, and that most were murderous thugs with little to love about them, is rarely considered. Nor is it well known that Canada was as much a haunt to pirates as some waters of the Caribbean.

In recent years, perhaps as a reaction to the faceless homogeneity of so much of modern Western culture, the pirate as a figure of adventure and freedom has made a comeback of sorts in public entertainment, but also as the subject of serious study by respected scholars such as David Cordingly and Marcus Rediker. Writing in 2004, Rediker explained that the pirates of Western culture enjoyed a "golden age" from about 1650 to 1730, divided into three distinct eras. The first phase took place between 1650 and 1680, and consisted mostly of British, Dutch and French outlaws who survived by their wits and the hunting of wild game and escaped cattle in remoter parts of the Caribbean. From hidden coves they used dugout canoes and small boats to pounce on the shipping of the Spanish. Over time these men made larger and greater conquests, until by the 1690s, unhindered by British and French fleets preoccupied with fighting one another, the pirates became true ocean-going predators, moving into the warmer waters of the Indian Ocean and entering the second phase, which largely related to the establishment of a pirate stronghold on the island of Madagascar and the creation of the "Pirate Round" between the Indian Ocean and the Caribbean Sea. The final, most successful era of piracy in the West was the decade 1716 to 1726, when legions of unemployed privateers, paid-off navy and merchant seamen, and other products of the end of the exhausting wars with Louis XIV took to the sea for their livelihood.

As mentioned in a previous chapter, privateers were privately owned armed vessels manned by volunteers that were given authorization by governments to pursue the shipping of enemy nations. Captured ships and cargoes were disposed of by admiralty courts, and the volunteer crew and the owners shared in the profits. Pirates, on the other hand, were men who recognized no law or limitations with respect to their depredations at sea. Frequently ex-privateers, they declared their loyalties to be only to themselves, banding together in an oddly democratic society with elected captains and agreed-upon "Articles" that governed pirate life. All vessels or coastal communities that caught their eye were fair game, and having rejected duty to their former sovereigns or countries, they sailed under a variety of flags, usually black, with terrifying designs of skulls, weaponry or dripping blood. Many were content merely to loot captured ships, harming no one who did not resist, while as many others were sadistic criminals who visited death, torture, rape and mutilation on those unfortunate enough to cross their path at sea. As Rediker points out, the number of pirates in that key decade of 1716–26 did not exceed four thousand. But those four thousand men brought intolerable disruption and destruction to the Atlantic system of trade before they were hunted down by the navy, and they died kicking in droves at the end of hangmen's ropes before audiences torn between admiration and loathing.

Pirates were essentially men who had given up hope that a lawful life could bring them a degree of happiness or fulfillment. It was a bitterly unfair age of privilege for a few and grinding drudgery for the majority, and piracy offered a brief, incandescent escape from the cheerless hardship that was the lot of most Europeans in the seventeenth and eighteenth centuries. As Rediker observes, "Piracy may have held out hope for a good life, but it was not to be a long one. The typical man sailed under the black flag for a year or two, and many if not most pirates lost their lives for it. Unusual was the man who served—or lived—longer."

Most pirates were males, between the ages of eighteen and thirty, and they placed their hopes on selling their plunder to the black markets that flourished on the coasts of southern France, Ireland and Cornwall, or in a number of American colonial ports where bribed governors were willing to look the other way, and frequently were business partners of successful pirates. The chance for success was appealing, if one lived.

> The glittering reward, the great hope that lured men into piracy
> and banditry, was wealth, and its attendant power and ease.
> In the 17th Century . . . the annual wage for a working man

ranged from five to ten pounds sterling. But the payoff at the end of a pirate voyage was often a thousand pounds or more—enough to buy an estate or, prudently invested, to support one's family in comfort for life.

Marcus Rediker's succinct summary of the pirates' goal—if they had any goal at all—paraphrases the words of one of the most successful pirates of the "Golden Age," the Welshman Bartholomew Roberts:

> There is [in law-abiding sailor work] thin Commons, low wages, and Hard Labour; in this, Plenty and Satiety, Pleasure and Ease, Liberty and Power; and when all the Hazard that is run for it, at worst, is only a sower look or two, at choaking [being hanged]. No, a merry Life and a Short one, shall be my motto.

Another great myth about pirates' exploits is that they carried out their foul deeds only under waving palms, and off gleaming sand beaches or the coral lagoons of the tropics. It was an easier process to stay alive in the warmer climes of the south—providing mosquito-borne fevers did not carry off most of a crew in a few days, as it could—but there was booty and swag to be had in the cold waters of the north as well, and the lure of that sort of wealth brought its share of pirates to the waters of Canada, as revealed by scholars such as the Canadian Roger Marsters.

Writing in 2004, Marsters revealed that a principal lure for northern pirates was the huge industry surrounding the Grand Banks fishery, which had been in place since the 1470s and was now led by the British, French and Portuguese, the Spanish being busy plundering South America of its seemingly inexhaustible treasure. The North American fishery required some ten thousand men and over four hundred well-equipped ships, as well as shore stations to support the visiting fleets, particularly the English, who dried their catch onshore rather than carrying it home whole, as the Portuguese and others did. The fleets that congregated each year on the Newfoundland, Nova Scotian and Labrador coasts were governed by no authority other than that of the first captain to arrive each year, who was given the title of Fishing Admiral. With hordes of seamen to prey upon as potential additions to a pirate crew, and with ships and shore stations brimming with equipment, supplies, gear, and the services of shipwrights and men skilled in all the seagoing trades, the fishery became a rich prize that the pirate brethren could not resist, particularly off Newfoundland. And if the pickings in the fishery were lean, the great convoys of the Plate Fleets sailing their ponderous way home to Spain from Havana passed a mere three hundred miles to the south. This flame soon attracted the black-flagged pirate moths. And a rum lot they were.

Remarkably few true pirates put to sea from the ports of Acadia or New France to prey on shipping in what would become Canadian waters. A more bureaucratic control over who went to sea to do what, and the reality that piracy committed in home waters is a risky business at best, meant that most French armed vessels in Canadian waters that were not part of *la marine royale* were licensed privateers. European French pirates, and more than a few from New France, preferred the pickings of the Caribbean, the Indian Ocean, and the wealthy, ill-defended towns and shipping of colonial Spanish America. A number of New France or Acadian seamen did enter the notoriety of open Atlantic piracy, among them Chevalier, Maissonate and a rather unlucky individual known as Pierre Le Picard. Le Picard's origins are not recorded, but it is likely that he was an *acadien*. Le Picard first heaves into view in 1688, when he is listed as a crewman in a pirate vessel commanded by the Frenchman François L'Ollonais, cruising in the Caribbean. L'Ollonais, who had a reputation for sadistic cruelty, was intending to raid the coast of Nicaragua but was blown off course to Honduras. Undeterred, he sacked the town of San Pedro de Puerto Caballos, then waited three months to attack a reputed treasure galleon, only to find that it carried no bullion. Le Picard left L'Ollonais at this point with a few followers, determined to march overland to the town of Panama and attack it. The Spanish repelled his little band with ease, and afterward Le Picard appears here and there around the Caribbean in varying and mostly unsuccessful raids on small towns and ports. Having earned little but adventure from his wanderings, he appears to have returned to Acadia to settle around 1690, going to sea once more at the time of William Phips's attacks, during which he apparently took part in a privateering raid on the coast of Rhode Island.

Newfoundland waters continued to be the great northern magnet for piracy, or for privateering attacks that bordered on piracy. The first true pirate worthy of the name to inflict himself on Newfoundland waters was the handsome and aristocratic Peter Easton, who arrived in St. John's harbour in 1611 with no fewer than ten ships, bristling with armament, including his own flagship, the 350-ton *Happy Adventure*. Easton demanded that the local Fishing Admiral, Richard Whitbourne, provide him with five hundred fishermen and supplies with which to attack Spanish shipping, particularly the treasure fleets crossing from the West Indies to Spain by the northern Atlantic route. That Spain and England were officially at peace was not lost on Whitbourne, who nonetheless yielded to Easton's superior manner and air of entitlement: Easton got 1,500 men and supplies enough to establish a fortified base for himself at Harbour Grace.

Easton was not without nerve. Secretly bankrolled by the Killigrew family of Pendennis Castle, Cornwall, Easton had built a lucrative trade in bold piracy in the English Channel and coastal Europe until, by 1610, he commanded a formidable squadron of forty ships. King James, the din of protesting merchants ringing in his ears, finally appointed an aristocratic lawyer and opportunist, Henry Mainwarring, to assemble a fleet and put an end to Easton's depredations. Hearing of this, Easton took his best ships and fled south to the coast of West Africa for a year's profitable, if unhealthy, cruising before deciding to make Newfoundland his base.

Having earlier secured Whitbourne's grudging acquiescence, Easton put up at Harbour Grace a well-provided shore station, featuring a solid small fort and the stockpiled lootings from twenty-five French, twelve Portuguese and one unlucky Flemish vessel, in addition to a hundred ship's guns purloined from English vessels. Once his fleet had been readied, and with a watchful garrison left behind in the bristling fort, Easton sailed off to Puerto Rico, where he captured not only El Morro Castle, the guardian of San Juan harbour, but the treasure galleon *San Sebastien*, which was about to depart for Spain. Easton's loot-packed ships wallowed back to Harbour Grace only to find a fleet of Basque ships, fresh from capturing his fort and station, sailing out to do battle. Easton was in no mood for half measures, and in the ferocious battle that ensued every single Basque ship was either sunk, captured or run aground.

Now in undisputed mastery of the coast, Easton built a personal "retreat" at Ferryland while still maintaining his operational base at Harbour Grace. This period, 1612–14, was the high point of his piratical career, and he capped it by sailing with his fleet to the vicinity of the Azores Islands, where he captured the Spain-bound treasure fleet and sailed home to Harbour Grace with his ships almost awash with the weight of the spectacular plunder.

A fight between a pirate vessel like those of Easton's fleet and a Spanish plate galleon or Basque fisherman was a fearsome process, made deliberately so by the pirate fighting methods. The preferred pirate vessel was a single-masted sloop, a light, handy and swift craft that could easily sail away from trouble if the prey proved too stubborn to capture or danger approached in the form of a pursuing warship. Easton, however, commanded a heterogeneous fleet that included multi-masted, heavily armed larger ships that were the equal of government warships. As in those naval warships, Easton's crews were notoriously overcrowded into their vessels, with many men being carried to simultaneously sail and "fight" the ship, and to overwhelm their opponents in the savage work of hand-to-hand fighting after boarding.

A pirate vessel approaching for the attack was a formidable and frightening sight indeed. The pirate usually tried for the "windward gauge," the position upwind of the prey that allowed the pirate to run down at will for the attack or sheer off if the defence seemed too stalwart. The decks of the vessel would be crammed with noisy pirates who delighted in adding outlandish additions to their normally drab seaman's clothing: broad sashes, earrings, brocaded coats and other oddities. Frequently they blackened their faces to effect a more threatening air. They equally delighted in weapons, and often fought overladen with dirks, cutlasses, boarding axes, pikes and braces of long flintlock pistols, sometimes hung about them on ribbon lanyards for easy use.

As the pirate vessel rushed in for the attack, aloft it would be flying huge, oversized banners and flags emblazoned with threatening designs and in either the traditional black or the dreaded red of the flag of no quarter—the *jolie rouge* or Jolly Roger that meant slaughter to all who resisted. The pirates on deck not handling lines would be baying out dreadful threats and curses to overawe their victims, and, in an incongruous touch, any musicians on board would be gathered somewhere on deck, blaring out drum-heavy anthems and fanfares that added to the general nightmarishness of the spectacle. All this was calculated: surrender without a fight was what most pirates wanted—damaged ships and goods were of little value—and those who did not resist were usually plundered but not harmed. It was a different matter for those crews who fought back, for the pirates were merciless if opposed, and there were psychotics and sadists among them who killed or tortured even the meekest of victims.

Boarding was the preferred method of taking a prize, as it avoided damage and brought the numbers and infighting skills of the pirates into play. Surging in from windward, the pirate vessel's whipstaff would be put "hard over" and the hulls would crash together, grapnels flying across the leaping foam between the ships, and the boarders would launch themselves over the rail of the victim with a collective roar in their throats and the gleam of gold in their eyes. Rare was the opponent vessel that successfully resisted such an attack.

As Easton's Newfoundland fort rang with the roar and clink of rum-soaked celebration, the somewhat tardy arm of the Crown in the form of Henry Mainwarring was closing in, albeit slowly, on the pirates. Learning of Mainwarring's approach, Easton sped off a note to James I, supported by appropriate gifts, requesting a pardon. In timely fashion it arrived before Mainwarring's fleet did, and Easton paid off his crews in handsome fashion before sailing off alone to the Mediterranean, a pardoned and extremely wealthy man. There he concluded a deal with the Duke of Savoy that allowed Easton to buy a beautiful estate by the sea, title himself Marquis of Savoy and Master of Ordnance for the Duke of Savoy, and live a lengthy life in supreme luxury, perhaps the most fortunate pirate of them all.

The man sent in pursuit of Easton was cut from much the same cloth of aristocratic entitlement and scant regard for the law. Henry Mainwarring was but twenty-seven when in 1610 he received the commission to hunt down Easton, or at least put a stop to his flagrant piracy in the English Channel. Easton, as we've seen, hustled off to Newfoundland on the news, but Mainwarring was not one to miss a main chance. Convincing the king to grant him a privateering commission to attack Spanish ships outside European waters— one had to do *something* while looking for Easton—Mainwarring spent two years enriching himself and his crews by attacking Spanish shipping off Africa before finally sailing off to Newfoundland in pursuit of Easton, if "pursuit" is the right word. Arriving at St. John's, Mainwarring cornered the hapless Whitbourne, by ill luck once again the Fishing Admiral, and used the privateering licence to demand stores and men from the fishing fleet. Mainwarring occupied Easton's fort and buildings at Harbour Grace, plundered any Spanish or Portuguese vessels within reach, then sailed off to the African coast to prey on more Iberian shipping. When King James received complaints from the Spanish ambassador about Mainwarring's attacks, they were politely ignored. Incensed, the Spanish determined to bring an end to Mainwarring's career on their own. A powerful Spanish squadron was assembled, which fell on Mainwarring's ships off Portugal as they were returning to England. When the pitched battle drew to a close, Mainwarring emerged victorious, to the enormous chagrin of the Spanish.

Pressed again by the humiliated Spanish and now the Portuguese, the king cleverly resolved the dilemma by issuing Mainwarring a pardon and immediately commissioning him in the Royal Navy. Mainwarring countered with a hefty cash gift to his accommodating monarch, and was made the commander of Dover Castle, a highly prestigious appointment. The honours did not stop there, as Mainwarring was knighted and rose to become Vice Admiral Sir Henry Mainwarring. Ironically, he would later lose all during the time of Cromwell due to his understandable royalism.

The dashing Easton and Mainwarring loom as large, fictional-seeming characters in the history of eastern Canadian waters. But there were many minor figures who were carried along on the same wave of adventure and plunder, and the careers of a few are worth notice. One whose story is yet to be fully told is beautiful Sheila Na Gara, so-called Pirate Queen of the Newfoundland coast. The girl's real name was Sheila O'Connor, and she had been taken prisoner by a Dutch privateer, where her beauty both made her a great prize and put her at great risk. In a savage mid-Atlantic battle, one of Peter Easton's ships had defeated the Dutch privateer and O'Connor had found herself with Easton's band. Sharing in their freebooting adventures, she finally fell in love with one of Easton's lieutenants, Gilbert Pike. Together with Pike, she left Easton's service when the latter sailed off to Savoy, and with their share of the payout they set up a fishing station and seamen's tavern at Mosquito, which is now Bristol's Hope. For years afterward it was rumoured that unmarked longboats rowed out of hidden coves with pirate crews led by a beautiful woman, and plundered vessels of the anchored fishing fleets. Her story has never been fully revealed.

Pirates and brigands were as often murderous psychotics as romantic adventurers, and one particular villain, with an air of madness caused by sorrow, was the pirate Edward Low. Low had arrived at Boston from England in 1714, and soon met a New England girl with whom he fell deeply in love, Eliza Marble. Proposing marriage, Low was accepted, and soon he and Eliza had a baby. Low was gainfully employed as a shipwright at a Boston shipyard. This promising start was cut short when both Eliza and the baby died, leaving Low a grieving and darkly moody man. He became unreliable as a ship-yard worker and was released.

This tragic death of his wife and child, and dismissal from the shipyard, sent Low off on a long spiral into sadistic mayhem. Sign-ing on a sloop bound for log cutting in Honduras, Low murdered the ship's captain once in the Caribbean and sailed off with the ship's longboat and twelve other men, intent on turning pirate. Soon they seized a small trading vessel and, having "disposed" of its crew, sailed it to a known pirate rendezvous on Grand Cayman Island. There, Low and his companions signed on with the experienced pirate commander George Lowther, and Low soon became the first mate of Lowther's *Happy Delivery*. After months of indifferent suc-cess in Caribbean waters, Low split with Lowther and sailed north in his own ship. Attacking New England shipping, he was pursued by a Massachusetts provincial warship sent out from Boston to find him. Low eluded the Massachusetts vessel by abandoning his ship after capturing another, and sailed off with the latter into Nova Scotian waters.

Rounding into Roseway Harbour, near Shelburne, Low cap-tured no fewer than thirteen fishing vessels, taking one for his new flagship, which he named the *Fancy*. Uncharacteristically releasing the fishermen to sail home in his former ship, Low sailed northeast along the Nova Scotia coast, then crossed to the south coast of New-foundland. Working round to St. John's, he peered in through the rocky gates of the harbour and spotted what appeared to be a sub-stantial merchant ship. When Low sailed in to attack the anchored vessel, it opened up a thunderous broadside—the ship was a naval frigate—that sent Low hustling out to sea. Furious at this rebuff, Low looted a settlement near Carbonear with almost gleeful bru-tality and then took eight Grand Banks vessels in quick succession before fleeing south to warmer climes for the winter.

Somehow surviving a hurricane, the *Fancy* cruised the Spanish and west African coasts, with Low's cruel treatment of his captives building an even greater demonic reputation for him. With the

Fancy laden with bullion and other plunder, Low returned to North American waters in the fall of 1723, sailing quietly up into the Bay of Fundy A number of sources claim that Low and his crew dragged chests of treasure ashore on the high, cliff-faced Isle Haute and buried them there, confident that Fundy's dangerous tides and the remoteness of the island would keep the stash safe. Sailing away from the Bay of Fundy, Low began to act with such maniacal cruelty and sadism toward the crews and passengers of captured ships that his sickened crew finally put him over the side in a small boat with three other men and sailed away. A short time later Low was found by a French warship and taken to Martinique, where the French lost no time in stringing him up to a gibbet. The vast hoard he allegedly left on Isle Haute, far to the north, has never been found.

A figure who claims right of recognition for sheer audacity on a level with Peter Easton and Henry Mainwarring is the Welsh pirate Bartholomew Roberts, known as Black Bart for his swarthy good looks. Roberts went to sea in 1719 on a slaving voyage to West Africa, during which his ship was captured by another Welshman, the pirate Howel Davis. Davis forced his countryman into service in the pirate vessel, and Roberts's skills and natural leadership were such that, upon Davis being killed in a sea battle, the crew elected Roberts captain. Roberts's style became legendary: he wore scarlet velvet clothing, particularly in battle, and cut an elegant and imposing figure at all times. He insisted on a strict code of behaviour in his ships, a code that distributed the proceeds of piracy fairly to all, forbade the mistreatment of women and even prohibited an overindulgence in swearing. Roberts was that rare thing, a civilized and even at times honourable pirate, who nonetheless led a spectacular if brief career that saw him net over four hundred ships captured and looted.

In 1720, he sailed north from the West Indies to prey on the Atlantic fishing fleets. Pausing at Canceau to attack the fishermen gathered there, he sailed on in his 32-gun vessel to Trepassey Harbour, Newfoundland, there finding twenty-two ships at anchor while their crews were working ashore. Roberts sailed in amongst the anchored ships with a band playing on his afterdeck and flying the usual oversized flags, including his own ingenious version of the Jolly Roger, from his mastheads. As the crews watched in helpless astonishment from the shore, Roberts went methodically from ship to ship, pillaging, burning and sinking all twenty-two ships except for one. This he kept as his new flagship, renaming it the *Royal Fortune*. As a footnote to the destruction of the ships, Roberts then went ashore with a large armed force and plundered the small village that tended to the fishermen's needs before sailing off from the smoking scene of destruction, his band still tootling away. Roberts steered for Cape Breton Island, where he capped his Canadian raid by attacking and taking six merchant and fishing vessels inbound to Louisbourg.

Roberts's career ended two years later. Captain Chaloner Ogle of the Royal Navy frigate HMS *Swallow* caught Roberts's flagship, the *Royal Fortune*, alone off West Africa. Seeing battle as inevitable, Roberts dressed in his usual elegant style as he observed *Swallow* beating determinedly up toward him amidst lightning and prophetic blasts of thunder overhead. Ogle's log records Roberts's last moments:

> About eleven a clock she being within pistol shot abreast of us, and a black flag, or pendant hoisted at their main topmast head, we struck the French ensign that had continued hoisted at our staff till now, and displayed the King's Colours, giving her at the same time our broadside which was immediately returned by them again but without equal damage, their mizzen top-mast falling and some of their rigging being disabled.
>
> The pirate sailing better than us, shot ahead above while we continued firing without intermission such guns as we could bring to bear . . . till by favour of the wind we came alongside again, and after exchanging a few more shot, about half past one, his main-mast came down, being shot away a little below the parrel.

At two she struck, and called for quarters, proving to be the
Royal Fortune of 40 guns . . .

Bartholomew Roberts was dead, struck in the throat by a blast of
grapeshot at the height of the battle. In accordance with his wishes,
his scarlet-clad body was thrust out of a gun port over the side, to
sink away in the sea he had mastered and not to rot on a gibbet.
For Chaloner Ogle, a knighthood would reward his victory, and
he would eventually rise to become Admiral of the Fleet. Roberts's
death marked the end of the Golden Age of piracy, and it is fitting to
note that the most telling exploit of this most notorious but oddly
gentlemanly of pirates took place in the cold northern waters of
Canada, and not in the emerald seas of the tropics.

In contrast to pirates who used Canadian waters as cruising
grounds but preferred to base themselves in warmer climes, there
were a few who rivalled Easton's and Mainwarring's use of Canadian
shore bases. The names of Charles Bellamy, George Lowther and
Samuel Hall are among them. But the careers of these or even the
spectacular exploits of Easton and Mainwarring could not match
the twenty-year commitment to ruthless killing and looting of a
rare piratical man-and-wife team, Eric Cobham and Maria Lindsey. Cobham had stolen money at an inn in Oxford, England, early
in the eighteenth century—for which the innocent innkeeper was
hanged—and used it to buy a small armed vessel at Plymouth.
Enlisting a particularly murderous crew, he put to sea and fell upon
a returning East Indiaman in the Irish Sea. After emptying the
merchantman of a priceless cargo, Cobham sank the ship with all
its crew sealed below before sailing off to sell his loot in the unques-
tioning marketplace of the French Mediterranean coast. Returning
to Plymouth, he fell in with a woman who equalled him in ruthless-
ness, Maria Lindsey. Together, the two embarked on a marital career
of piracy, their first joint victim being an American vessel taken off
Nantucket shortly after the Cobhams had arrived in those waters.
They continued with the policy that "dead men tell no tales," and
were it not for their own recollections their depredations would

never have come to light, due to their expedient of killing everyone on board any vessel they took and sinking it—presumed "lost at sea"—after unloading what they wished of the cargo.

The Cobhams found that Cabot Strait, between Newfoundland and Cape Breton Island, was a highway for French ships laden with goods and money steering for Quebec, and others laden with furs outbound for France. Scouting the innumerable coves of the Newfoundland coast, the Cobhams set up a fortified base at Sandy Point, on Bay St. George. From there, they swept out in all seasons but the deepest cold of winter to prowl their hunting grounds of the Strait and the shores of Prince Edward Island. In their extraordinary twenty-year career their activities were never suspected, their base at Sandy Point never attacked, all as a result of their unhesitating murder of all and any they came upon.

Finally, tiring of this harsh life, they paid off their murderous minions and sailed eastward to Europe with their twenty years' worth of plunder. Unwilling to risk England, they settled instead on a comfortable estate near Le Havre, where the wealthy pair became respected citizens, with Cobham even serving as a magistrate in local county courts. Periodically the blood lust would arise in both—or a need to top up their coffers—and they would take a ship to sea, plunder a hapless merchant vessel, butcher the crew and sell the goods in southern France. Neither was ever caught in any of this, or even tainted with suspicion. Cobham died in his bed, mourned and respected by the unsuspecting French, while Maria, the weight of those years of murder possibly bearing on her, sank into madness and committed suicide. The truth of their bloody careers only came to light after their deaths.

Large-scale piracy in North American waters was for the most part eradicated by determined naval authorities not long after 1720. But from time to time a piratical act reminiscent of the former era would take place, and such was the story of Edward Jordan. In July 1809 the schooner *Three Sisters* sailed out of Halifax harbour and turned northward for Canso and the port of Gaspé. Captain John Stairs had aboard as crewmen Thomas Heath, Benjamin Matthews and John Kelly, the last as mate. One of two passengers was Edward Jordan, Irish in origin. The voyage to Gaspé was uneventful, and at that port Stairs took on board a cargo for Halifax, as well as Jordan's wife and three children.

Between Canso and Whitehead Island, on September 13, 1809, Edward Jordan and his wife, Margaret, joined by the mate John Kelly, suddenly and inexplicably made a move to take the ship. Heath and Matthews were knifed where they stood and thrown over the side. Captain Stairs, seeing the killers turn for him, seized a hatch cover and leapt over the side into the sea. The *Three Sisters* swung northward along Cape Breton, leaving Stairs to his fate. By luck, an American fishing schooner en route to Massachusetts spotted Stairs and rescued him. Within hours of the schooner's arrival in Boston, Stairs was in the office of the British consul, and the hunt for the pirates was on.

Meanwhile, Jordan and Kelly had manhandled the schooner across Cabot Strait to Fortune Bay, Newfoundland, where they found an inshore fisherman, John Pigot, and forced him to join the crew. With Pigot's unwilling help, the *Three Sisters* sailed east to the Avalon Peninsula at St. Mary's, where Jordan attempted to find more crew and a competent navigator for a voyage to Ireland. A row developed with the mate, Kelly, who stormed off the ship. Undaunted, the Jordans set sail for Ireland, only to be intercepted at sea by HM Schooner *Cuttle*. The sword of justice fell swiftly, and on November 23, 1809, Edward Jordan was hanged in public at Halifax, and his tarred corpse was hung in chains on a gibbet at the end of Maugher's Beach as a warning to would-be pirates. No such fate awaited Margaret: she pleaded the needs of her children and the court released her to care for them.

There are many more odd, sometimes grisly but always fascinating tales of piracy off Canada's coasts awaiting discovery.

As for Canada's freshwater lakes and rivers, they had their share of lawless miscreants prowling their coves and channels, but none quite so bold as the man known as "Pirate" Bill Johnston. Johnston was a native of Quebec, born in 1782 at Trois-Rivières to a Loyalist family. In 1784 the family took up a land grant at Bath, west of Kingston, Ontario, where Johnston grew up as a farmer and small merchant. When the War of 1812 exploded between Britain and the United States, Johnston faced divided loyalties: his young wife was American, and he had many trading contacts with New Yorkers at Cape Vincent and elsewhere. Accused by suspicious British agents of smuggling, Johnston had all his property confiscated and was thrown in jail. He and six other inmates managed to escape and made off perilously in a stolen canoe for the American shore, where an American steamer picked them up and landed them at Sackets Harbor, New York. From there, Johnston wrote to the British authorities, pleading his innocence and requesting the return of his property. Incensed by the curt refusal he received, Johnston determined to seek revenge, and began conducting his own private war against Upper Canada, as Ontario was then known. Recruiting a gang of tough characters, Johnston secured a six-oared longboat and used it in various "acts of war" against British shipping on the St. Lawrence, picking off bateaux and other small craft as they threaded their way through the Thousand Islands. It was a technique of attack he would remember for the future.

At the end of the War of 1812, Johnston settled with his family at French Creek (now Clayton), New York. There he resumed a profitable cross-river trade with a twelve-oared rowing launch that soon became an even more lucrative smuggling platform. By the 1830s, Johnston maintained a substantial force of loyal and unprincipled rivermen, governed as much by Johnston's leadership as by admiration for his beautiful daughter Kate, who hefted an oar like a man and was talked of as the Queen of the Thousand Islands, but who so far had spurned her many suitors.

The Rebellions of 1837 and the upheavals of 1838 were an opportunity too good to pass up. Offering his services to the rebels, he was named by the "patriot" leader Van Rensselaer as Commodore of the Navy in the East. Johnston aimed to live up to his grand title, and his first plan was to attack and take Fort Henry, the massive limestone citadel at Kingston. The attack was planned for February 1838, but it came to nothing when a courageous American schoolteacher, Elizabeth Barnett, carried word to Kingston of the impending attack. Undaunted by this setback, Johnston and twenty-five of his men raced on board the British steamer *Sir Robert Peel* on May 29, 1838, when it stopped at Wells Island for firewood en route from Brockville to Kingston. Driving the terrified passengers ashore and locking them in a shed, Johnston and his men made off with the ship, plundering it of general loot and the British army payroll before burning it on the river. The passengers and crew were rescued from Wells Island by a passing American steamer. Later that year, in November, Johnston took part in the abortive Battle of the Windmill near Prescott, Ontario, slipping away on the river when the rebel force that had landed and occupied a windmill were evidently about to be defeated by British troops and Canadian militia.

Johnston's role in the battle, in the steamer *United States*, led the British government to accuse Washington of aiding piracy. Stung, the American administration mounted a serious effort to take Johnston. He was finally cornered near Ogdensburg, New York, and sentenced to a nominal one-year term in an American federal penitentiary. Even this was too much for the old pirate, who escaped, hid in the Thousand Islands and wrote letters to President Van Buren that finally earned him a presidential pardon. Unrepentant, Johnston returned to Clayton once more in some triumph, and eventually died there in 1870.

Johnston was lucky, living, like Peter Easton and a few other pirates who plied their "sweet trade" in Canadian waters, to enjoy a full life and die in his bed. Most pirates, as we have seen, suffered harsher fates, eventually being tracked down by the navy or other authorities, and ending their days hanged, jailed or killed at sea. Their lives, to borrow a phrase from another context, were nasty, brutish and usually short, but if they were fortunate, there was a certain drama to their inevitable end, beyond the merely sordid extermination of seagoing vermin—a drama that intrigues us still.

9

Dividing the North: The Great Struggle of 1812–1814

A s THE 1800s began, North America was divided into the Canadian colonies to the north of the Great Lakes, the colonies of what would become the Maritime provinces, and a newly emerging republic to the south, anxious to get on with its perceived destiny of mastering the continent. The custodian of the North, Great Britain, was enmeshed in an interminable war with revolutionary and then Napoleonic France that would not end until 1815, and had little inclination to concern itself with the problems of its distant North American colonies. The Royal Navy had its dockyard at Halifax, a slim garrison of overworked regular soldiery manned the thin defences of Upper and Lower Canada, and the Great Lakes were sailed on by a largely cargo fleet of indifferently manned small vessels of the Provincial Marine, an agency of the quartermaster branch of the British army. In the context of the great struggle with France, the fortunes of backwater Canada were low on the British list of priorities, but they were anything but to certain ambitious minds in the American Congress.

The young republic of the United States, still clustered essentially along the Eastern Seaboard but expanded recently by Thomas Jefferson's purchase of Louisiana, was attempting to maintain a strict neutrality in the Anglo-French struggle, insisting that its trade with

Britain and the Continent, which was vital to the American economy, should be unmolested by the two warring nations. The Americans also chafed at what they saw as a British refusal to take their nationhood seriously and afford it due respect. As France sank into the clutches of the Napoleonic dictatorship, Americans were no more supportive of the Corsican dictator than Englishmen were, but a series of ill-considered acts by the British played into the hands of those in Congress who had little love of Britain and who eyed the Canadas as more stars to be added to the American constellation. Rightly or wrongly, the Americans believed the British supported Indian tribes who were resisting American westward settlement, and men from the frontier states such as Kentucky were loudest in arguing for expulsion of Britain from North America.

The Royal Navy, since the American Revolution, had refused to recognize the legitimacy of the American flag and citizenship, and routinely claimed the right to stop American ships and take off men whom they considered to be British subjects or deserters, regardless of the papers they carried. In 1807 a British warship, HMS *Leopard*, fired without warning on an American warship and took off several men who claimed to be American, unleashing a storm of resentment in the United States. Far more seriously for American trade, Britain imposed a blockade on Napoleon's Continental empire that closed the door on American shipping. When Napoleon countered with similar acts of his own, the seaborne trade of the United States began to die. New Englanders, at peace with their Maritime neighbours and willing to take their chances in risky trade with Britain, opposed talk of war. But the insult to the flag, the issue of "free trade and sailors' rights," and the frontiersmen's desire to expunge British support for the Indian population were enough to push a slim majority in Congress to vote for war with Britain in 1812. President James Madison had little in the way of a navy with which to fight Britain, so the key would be an overland assault on Canada, the conquest of which Thomas Jefferson said would be a "mere matter of marching," since aside from the French of Quebec, most inhabitants of what would become Canada were American in origin by 1812.

New England opposition to the war and the perceived loyalty to Britain of the Maritimes made problematic the simplest and most obvious strategy Madison could have used: the seizure of Montreal or Quebec, and the strangling thereby of the vital artery of the river and Gulf of St. Lawrence. Instead, the war would be fought by attempting major invasions across the Niagara and Detroit frontiers to begin with, followed by a Lake Champlain effort. On paper such a plan seemed feasible: the majority of the inhabitants of Upper Canada were recent American arrivals, and the militia of the frontier state of Kentucky alone overmatched the total number of men-at-arms in all of the Canadas. The first attempt at conquest by marching would be across the Detroit frontier, where an army of three thousand men led by General William Hull would, it was hoped, "neutralize" Indian resistance and, in his words, "probably induce the enemy to abandon the Province of Canada without opposition. The naval force on the Lakes would in that event fall into our possession & we should obtain command of the waters without the expense of building such a force." Not all in Congress were as sanguine about so easy a victory. The statesman Henry Adams quietly observed: "This hazardous plan required energy in the American armies, timely cooperation from Niagara if not from Lake Champlain, and, most of all, assumed both treason and incompetence in the enemy."

The war began on June 18, 1812, and six months later, far from abandoning Upper Canada, the British had by dint of aggressive use of their small forces—and thanks to the vital Indian warriors, of whom the Americans were terrified—defeated two American invasion attempts and forced the Americans to look to their own frontier defences. With an easy land campaign out of the question, a competition for naval control of the Great Lakes now loomed as the key to the war's successful prosecution. For British North America, the great weakness was the thousand-mile supply route that stretched from Quebec up the St. Lawrence to the Great Lakes, along which all the supplies of war and life would have to pass, often within gunshot of American territory. Maintaining that route at all costs would be vital to Canada's survival, and that survival was most seriously threatened when part of the supply corridor fell to American naval power.

When the war began in 1812, the army's Provincial Marine was the only naval force on the Lakes, and it performed a multitude of tasks in supply, transportation and constabulary. With the exception of the 17-gun brig *Oneida* on Lake Ontario, the Americans had no naval forces on the Great Lakes that could challenge the Provincial Marine. But that would soon change.

The Provincial Marine had been established by the army in 1760 as essentially an armed transportation service, and its initial base, through the years of the American Revolution, was Carleton Island in the St. Lawrence River. When, in the 1790s, the British finally relinquished their frontier posts as the 1783 peace treaty had stipulated, the Provincial Marine relocated to Kingston, Ontario, barely 38 miles from the little American Lake Ontario base at Sackets Harbor, New York, where the *Oneida* was based. The Provincial Marine was by no means a crack fighting force: its commodore in 1812, Alexander Grant, was eighty-five years old, and the commander on Lake Ontario, Captain John Steel, was seventy-five. Its fleet, as war began, provided on Lake Ontario for two ship-rigged vessels, one of which was the 20-gun "corvette," or small frigate, the *Royal George*, which had been launched in 1809, and three schooners. On Lake Erie, based at Amherstburg, where Fort Malden stood on the Detroit River, the flotilla was formed of one ship, the *Queen Charlotte*, and two schooners. The St. Lawrence River, above the great rapids that began below Prescott, was patrolled by a single 8-gun schooner. The men of the Provincial Marine had no illusion that the Americans would not soon challenge them, and the commander at Amherstburg, George Hall, observed matter-of-factly that "as the enemy has undoubtedly got a number of seamen on the Frontier of the Lakes, there can be little doubt of their risking everything to try and obtain command of them."

The Americans were all too aware of their naval weakness on the Great Lakes. Ironically, the naval blockade of the American Atlantic

British attack on Sackets Harbor   C 40598

coast instituted by the Royal Navy had rendered idle many able seamen, who were now free to be sent to the Lakes. Madison was quick
to use this resource, remarking to the overall American commander
on the Canadian frontier, General Dearborn, that "the command
of the Lakes by a superior force ought to have been a fundamental
point in the national policy from the moment the peace [of 1783]
took place."

Beginning in the summer of 1812, with only the *Oneida* to rely
on, the Americans began a rapid expansion of their naval power on
Lake Ontario at the Sackets Harbor base, which under the command of Master Commandant Isaac Chauncey had by November
of that year added the 20-gun *Madison* and no fewer than seven
lightly armed civilian schooners to the fleet. The Provincial Marine
had sailed over to Sackets Harbor for a half-hearted attack and had
been driven off by enthusiastic if inaccurate American gunnery, and
before the snow flew Chauncey replied by chasing the *Royal George*
right into Kingston harbour as a demonstration of his new mastery
of the lake.

The winter of 1812–13 saw a feverish shipbuilding race under
way at Kingston and Sackets Harbor. The Americans also began to
build flotillas on Lake Erie and Lake Champlain, two schooners on

the latter that they promptly lost to the British on the Richelieu River. It was clear that 1813 might prove the decisive year for the lake war. The Provincial Marine stood to be the loser, as its largely civilian crews, untrained for war, manned ships carrying close-range "carronades" as guns, while the Americans, their ships full of prime seamen from the Atlantic coast, were arming with long-range guns that would pound the British vessels to pieces unless the British could close the distance.

Captain George Hall at Amherstburg learned early in 1813 that a competent American regular navy officer, Oliver Hazard Perry, had arrived on Lake Erie and begun the construction of a credible flotilla at Presque Isle, on the lake's south shore. The omens for the aged gentlemen of the Provincial Marine were not promising, and the general ascendancy and initiative of the Americans were all too evident as, in April 1813, Chauncey's Lake Ontario flotilla sailed to York (now Toronto) and landed an assault force that took the town after a sharp fight and burned public buildings. A short time later, Chauncey put American troops ashore at what is now Niagara-on-the-Lake, where they took possession of the Niagara frontier.

In May, however, a seasoned British naval officer and veteran of Trafalgar, Captain Sir James Lucas Yeo, arrived at Kingston with a draft of 450 Royal Navy seamen and placed the naval assets on the lake under Royal Navy control. Yeo sent forward another Trafalgar veteran, Robert Heriot Barclay, and a few officers and men, to do what he could at Amherstburg. Yeo's arrival brought a just-in-time energy to the British naval defences, and only two weeks after his arrival Yeo packed soldiery into his ships and mounted a serious assault on Sackets Harbor on May 29, 1813. The assault had almost won the day, and eliminated the major USN base on the Lakes, when the overall British commander, Sir George Prevost, lost his nerve and called off the attack at the key moment. Deprived of his chance to cripple Chauncey while the latter was away up the lake, Yeo would have to settle for a shipbuilding war, and the manoeu-vrings of fleets that could win or lose the war in an hour's ill-considered fighting.

On Lake Erie, Robert Barclay found when he arrived there in June 1813 that he had the *Queen Charlotte*, two smaller gun vessels and two light schooners. Manning these were Provincial Marine crews and volunteers, about whom Barclay wrote to Yeo: "I am sure, Sir James, if you saw my Canadians you would condemn every one, with perhaps one or two exceptions, as a poor devil not worth his salt." Sir James could only offer sympathy, and Barclay would have little help in the way of men or materials. Nonetheless he set about the building of a 20-gun small frigate, the *Detroit*, aware that across the lake in Ohio an invasion force under General William Henry Harrison was awaiting only a seizure of control of Lake Erie and the Detroit River by Oliver Perry's squadron to cross the border and invade Upper Canada. Opposing Harrison would be an over-matched and overworked small garrison at Fort Malden under General Henry Procter, and a desperate band of warriors and their families led by the great Shawnee chief, Tecumseh. Tecumseh was the implacable enemy of Harrison and the Americans, for he and his warrior alliance stood in the way of American expansion into the "Old Northwest," the rich lands south and west of Lake Erie. Harrison's army, if it could get across the Detroit River, would attempt the destruction of Fort Malden, the defeat of its garrison, and the extermination of Tecumseh and his warriors.

Through the summer of 1813, Perry prepared his fleet at Presque Isle, while Barclay attempted to watch him and build his flagship, *Detroit*. Finally, when Perry by dint of superb seamanship had got his fleet to sea, and Barclay's dwindling supplies forced him into risking a fight, Barclay sailed to engage Perry with what was still an ill-armed and ill-managed fleet. Of 440 men manning the British ships, only 50 were trained seamen; the rest were unskilled volunteers. In September, Barclay and Perry met in almost windless conditions off what is now Put-in-Bay, Ohio. The luck of the bloody and hard-fought engagement went to Perry, and Barclay's defeat led to Procter's precipitate evacuation of Fort Malden, an invasion of western Upper Canada, and the death of Tecumseh at a losing rearguard battle near London, Ontario. The loss of the lake led to

Naval Action on Lake Ontario, by
C.W. Jefferys C 70259

invasion, but only briefly, as the overextended Americans could not hold the territory and retired back across the frontier. They were aware that its control was theirs any time they wished to use it, and Perry's naval victory had bought that control for them.

On Lake Ontario, the fate of Canada now rested with Yeo's fleet. The feverish shipbuilding had given Yeo a sturdy, well-constructed squadron of seaworthy ships that could weather any conditions the lake had to offer. Chauncey, relying on many civilian schooners made top-heavy with the addition of guns, could "keep the sea" less well. Yeo's short-range carronades, however, made him far more vulnerable to long-range gunnery from Chauncey's weapons. Thus handicapped, both commanders gingerly manoeuvred through a series of inconclusive engagements in 1813—August 7 to 10, September 11, September 28 and October 2—each burdened by the knowledge that one mistake could cost the war. Chauncey knew that if he had commanded more weatherly ships, the gun advantage might have given him victory; the lack of long-range guns almost spelled disaster for the British, but a repetition of the Lake Erie defeat was avoided by Yeo's caution and the superior seakeeping abilities of his squadron. This avoidance of defeat, rather than the gaining of victory, led, as the respected Canadian naval historian W.A.B. Douglas has noted, to the losing campaign of fall 1813, in which American armies descending the St. Lawrence toward Montreal, and another marching north from Plattsburg, New York, were each defeated in turn, ending the greatest threat of capture Canada would face in the war.

The seamen of Chauncey's squadron knew what they had lost by not having ships of the quality of Yeo's squadron. Commandant Sinclair of Chauncey's force mourned the British ownership of "six regular-built vessels of war, all sailing alike and able to support each other in any weather—capable of keeping the sea and acting efficiently when our gunboats dare not cast loose their guns."

As the snows swept over the cold waters of Lake Ontario, they obscured the last, best chance for a comprehensive American naval victory on the Great Lakes. British shipbuilding efforts at Kingston were now turning out ever more powerful warships—one, HMS *Saint Lawrence*, would be a monster larger than Nelson's *Victory*—and the Sackets Harbor shipwrights had to struggle to keep up. The war had become a shipbuilding race. And, as Douglas has observed, time was now on Britain's side. The long struggle against the French was coming to a successful conclusion. The overwhelming power of the Royal Navy had strangled American seaborne trade, and the American Treasury was approaching bankruptcy. New England was threatening secession. And aside from the lightning strike of Harrison's one-sided victory over Procter and Tecumseh, American military efforts against Canada had proven embarrassingly inept.

With the sailing season of 1814, the two sides confronted one another with fleets that dwarfed the little flotillas of 1812. On Lake Ontario the United States Navy now operated twelve vessels, seven of which carried 17 guns or more, against a British fleet of ten vessels, seven of which carried 16 guns or more. In addition, both sides maintained shoals of cutters, sloops, bateaux, wherries, yard boats and tenders of varying size, rig and capacity. On Lake Champlain the Americans maintained four vessels, of which three had 17 guns or more, facing a British fleet of four, in which two carried at least 16 guns. Here, both sides were again supported by lesser craft, including a number of barge-like "gunboats" powered by sweeps and Arab-looking lateen sails. But caution still governed both Yeo and Chauncey. When Chauncey was at sea with his new *Mohawk*, 32 guns, and *Superior*, 58 guns, Yeo remained under the protection of his shore batteries. When Yeo countered with the *Burlington*, 44 guns, the *Kingston*, 60 guns, and the behemoth *Saint Lawrence*, which loomed up over the horizon with no fewer than 112 guns, Chauncey remained prudently at anchor at Sackets Harbor. The year 1814 saw no major confrontation between these astonishing "fleets in the wilderness," and *Saint Lawrence*'s principal role became that of troop transport and supply vessel. Meanwhile, British operations on the remote Upper Lakes were largely successful in retaining British control there.

Lake Champlain was another matter. The battle-shy governor at Quebec, Prevost, had received in 1814 almost twelve thousand British veteran troops of the war against Napoleon, and was ordered to attack American posts with them. Rather than seize the obvious target, Sackets Harbor, Prevost inexplicably elected to march south toward Plattsburg, New York, from Montreal. Faced with the first serious American resistance at Plattsburg, Prevost ordered the unfinished and hastily manned British naval squadron from the Richelieu River, which had accompanied him, to attack the American Lake Champlain squadron, anchored defensively before Plattsburg. When the American ships under Thomas McDonough shattered the British squadron, Prevost called off the assault and marched his twelve thousand untested—and disgusted—veterans back to Canada. Plattsburg Bay joined Put-in-Bay as the two decisive naval engagements of the 1812–14 war on the inland lakes, both of them creditable American victories.

In the larger view, however, the British and Canadian naval effort had succeeded in what it was intended to do: prevent American success against Canada. Barclay's loss on Lake Erie left western Upper Canada open to American predations, but the heartland of the Lake Ontario–Quebec core had been kept secure. Seamanship, prudence and an extraordinary logistical achievement lay behind the success, for the Royal Navy had manned and supplied itself along a transportation route that began at British dockyards, crossed the Atlantic and then stretched two thousand miles up the river, through rapids and flanked by enemy territory, to the Great Lakes. The solutions were often ingenious, or simply demonstrations of bloody-minded determination. The frigate *Psyche*, 56 guns, had been built in England then dismantled and sent out as a "kit" to be hauled by bateaux to Kingston, where it was reassembled in 1814. Forty-six heavy guns were hauled from Montreal to Kingston, astonishingly by two hundred teams of American oxen hired in Vermont and New Hampshire to do the job. And to get 216 needed sailors up from the Maritimes to Kingston, Yeo had them march the 1,000-mile distance on snowshoes in mid-winter. They made the incredible trek in fifty-three days, but lost twenty-six men in the process.

At sea in the Atlantic, the story was all about the Royal Navy's crushing blockade of the American coast, and isolated single-ship actions in which the small but able American frigate force inflicted humiliating defeats on British frigates until the blockade forced them too into port. Halifax witnessed a bright exception to that series of single-ship defeats when HMS *Shannon* brought into harbour the captured American frigate *Chesapeake*, which it had taken in a brief but bloody gunnery battle off Boston. But what Atlantic Canada experienced most in the War of 1812 was not the business of great ships of war but rather the war of the privateer, as the next chapter will reveal. And that war, like the sea war on the Great Lakes, not only saved but deeply shaped the Canada that was to be—and the men and women who would be its citizens.

10

Booty and Adventure: The Canadian Privateers

CANADA DERIVED much of its early wealth from the sea. And nowhere was that more evident than in the quasi-piratical world of the armed Canadian privateer. The privateer vessel was a remnant of former times in European history, when city-states or kingdoms maintained no standing fleets of warships, but merely chartered merchant vessels for warlike purposes when the need arose. During the Middle Ages, prosaic sailing vessels such as North Sea "cogs" would have temporary fighting platforms—the "forecastle" and "aftercastle"—affixed to their hulls, and would carry men-at-arms into battle for a substantial fee. By the time of the European discovery and colonization of the Americas, standing "national" navies maintained by monarchs or parliaments were coming into existence. However, the great colonial struggles between the French and British—and, later, between the British and their rebellious colonies—created demands for armed ships that far exceeded the numbers of naval vessels available for the task. The colonial administrations offered "privateering" commissions to the owners of merchant vessels, authorizing them to arm their ships, hire fighting crews and sail after profit that came from selling the captured prizes or their cargoes. As Atlantic historian Roger Marsters succinctly summarized, "Through the long wars of the eighteenth century, privateering was a legally prescribed way for European nations to increase their military strength in an economical fashion, at the same time offering their merchants opportunities for profits to replace those lost to wartime interruptions in trade."

There were other merchant vessels that did not sail with the direct purpose of preying on enemy shipping, but which sailed either with cargoes to sell or in search of them. These ships, if armed and willing, were offered "letters of marque and reprisal," which allowed them to pursue their trading opportunities but also to pounce on an enemy prize if success looked possible. In many respects the world of the letter-of-marque vessel in wartime was very similar to the life of plunder, trade and opportunism of the Viking raider eight hundred years earlier. For the dedicated true privateer, the pursuit of glory and gain was a far more regulated process, or was meant to be. Privateer historian Faye Kert observed:

> Privateers were . . . obliged to follow strict rules for disposing of their captures: they had to be taken to a port that had a Vice-Admiralty Court [such as Halifax] and the legality of the capture had to be proven before a judge. Once the judge ruled that the prize was "good and lawful," the ship and/or cargo would be sold at auction and the proceeds shared among owners, officers and crew according to their pre-cruise agreement. Since [naval] vessels were also entitled to prize money and naval officers counted on prizes to supplement their salaries, public and private armed vessels frequently found themselves competing for captures.

During the French regime in Canada of the seventeenth and eighteenth centuries, the colonial administration relied heavily on the armed private ship for defence and for prosecution of the endless war against the English and their colonies. The French were far more legalistic in their allowance for privateers and, some would observe, far more practical. There were several categories of privateers, vaguely resembling categories of legitimized pirates. *Armateurs* were consortiums of private investors who secured the use of royal warships for privateering expeditions at their own expense, while *corsairs* were licensed private warships more similar to the English concept of privateers. The French had another category, that of *filibustiers*, vessels whose purpose seemed to combine the elements of both a licensed privateer and an uncontrolled pirate: the status was unimportant so long as investors and officialdom received a sufficient share of the voyage profits. Manning these varied vessels in the waters of New France and Acadia during times of war were enlisted civilians of various "sea militias," men called out in similar fashion to the farmer militias that defended the settlements ashore. The French *marine royale* never operated in Canadian waters in sufficient strength to challenge the English by itself; it was left to the various types of irregular vessels to defend the colonies of King Louis.

The career and achievements of Canadian soldier-privateer Pierre Le Moyne, Sieur d'Iberville, were outlined in an earlier chapter. A man cut from similar cloth was Pierre Maisonnat, later known simply as "Baptiste." Baptiste was a Huguenot, a French Protestant from the town of Bergerac, not far from Bordeaux. He had arrived in Acadia in 1690 to seek his fortune, only to land in the middle of Phips's attack on Port-Royal. Baptiste—still known as Maisonnat at this point—fought well if uncomprehendingly in the defence of Port-Royal, but was carried off to Boston as a prisoner. As a Huguenot he was accorded a degree of welcome, and for a time he accommodated himself to New England, joining the Huguenot church and swearing allegiance to the British Crown. By 1692, however, he had a change of heart, possibly for romantic reasons, and escaped from Boston, embraced the Catholic Church and assumed the name Baptiste. Arriving on the Saint John River at the Acadian capital of Nashwaak, near present-day Fredericton, Baptiste petitioned the governor, Joseph Robineau de Villebon, for a privateering commission. With some misgivings Villebon granted one to the unproven petitioner, who in rapid sequence found himself a vessel, arms and a willing crew, with which he sailed off to Boston and promptly captured eight New England ships.

Clearly, Baptiste was a man to be reckoned with and, to the court of Louis XIV, beset by a losing and financially disastrous war, a valuable one who might help preserve France's holdings in Acadia. Baptiste was summoned to France and found himself given command of the corvette—a small frigate, or sloop of war—*Bonne*, with which to attack New England shipping. Baptiste sailed back to North America in April 1694 and cut a bloody swath through the New England fishing fleet on the Grand Banks, taking five prizes and driving off many more, followed by several captures that he made in sight of Boston itself. The English were not slow to react, and when Baptiste appeared in New England waters again in 1695, he was confronted by the sloop of war HMS *Sorlings*. During a bloody battle *Bonne* was pounded into an almost unmanageable mass, and Baptiste drove her up onto the shore in order to escape before she sank. Fleeing into the woods, he and his crew managed to return overland to Acadia.

Undeterred by the experience, Baptiste was back in New England waters in 1696 to take part in an attack on the English post at Pemaquid, Maine, and managed to return home in time to help repel a New England raid on Nashwaak. In 1697, still without a replacement for *Bonne*, Baptiste took a hardy band of volunteers along the Atlantic coast in canoes to Casco Bay, where in a whirlwind of flashing cutlasses and barking pistols they took six fishing schooners and repelled a fierce English counterattack before sailing off to the Minas Basin with their prizes. Within a few weeks, now once again commanding a ship, he was back off Boston. But this time the *bastonnais* were ready for him, and he and his crew were captured and imprisoned, only to be released and allowed to sail home as part of larger negotiations. He was back at his raiding in 1702, was captured again and thrown in jail as a pirate, only to be released and return in 1709 to harass Boston shipping once more while commanding a small armed vessel out of Port-Royal. The loss of Port-Royal in 1710 ended his mercurial privateering career, but he is heard of in 1713, helping to select the site of the greatest French privateer haven of all: Louisbourg.

A fascinating contemporary of Baptiste was Pierre Morpain, known to the merchants of Boston as "Morpang ye pirate." Morpain was born in Blaye, France, on the Gironde, in 1686. He went to sea as a youth, drifting from merchant ships into more lucrative privateering when war broke out. By 1706 he had risen to command a heavily armed sloop, the *Intrépide*, based at St-Domingue. In 1707 he sailed north with *Intrépide* from his usual Caribbean hunting grounds to the busy waters off Boston, surprised himself by taking two ships almost immediately, and brought them into Port-Royal. Pleased with his welcome and reception there, he sailed back to St-Domingue in pursuit of a ship large enough to make serious inroads into New England shipping. Within a year he had captured and traded his way up to a substantial full-rigged ship of 20 guns, which he grandly renamed the *Marquis de Choiseul-Beaupré*.

In 1709 he took the *Marquis* northward to Port-Royal, and his contribution to that banner year was considerable: on one ten-day cruise alone off Boston, Morpain took nine prizes and sank four others, which exploit earned him the "Morpang ye pirate" title from the infuriated Boston merchants. When Port-Royal fell in 1710, Morpain was at sea. Undaunted, he relocated the home port of the *Marquis* to Plaisance, on the southeast coast of Newfoundland. When he sailed from there to join an attempt to retake Port-Royal, he was intercepted at sea by a powerful English warship based at St. John's, which took the *Marquis* after a long and bitter gunnery battle. Morpain became an English prisoner, and was treated with great courtesy as a recognition of his valour and personal character until his release at the war's end. But his career had only begun.

By 1713, the war with the English had come to an end, and France had nominally lost all of Acadia except for Cape Breton Island, or Île Royale. Like Baptiste, Morpain was involved in the selection of the ironically named English Harbour on Cape Breton Island as the site of the new fortified port of Louisbourg, and for his services he was named Port Captain of the new post. Until the coming of war again in 1744, Morpain led a long and productive life at Louisbourg, losing his wife in 1726 but himself seeming to be indestructible. With the reopening of hostilities, the old captain put to sea in command of the privateer *Succès*, with a crew of over one hundred, and after raiding the English post at Canceau he took two large New England vessels in quick succession. "Morpang ye pirate" had not lost his touch.

The impressed French Ministry of the Marine, anxious to employ good fighting officers, gave Morpain the command of the impressive warship *Caribou*, 52 guns. With this formidable vessel Morpain cruised the New England and Acadian coasts, but he cut short his privateering depredations when news came of the New England "enterprise" against Louisbourg in the summer of 1745. Morpain left the command of *Caribou* and returned to Louisbourg, prepared to fight in its defence. When New England troops successfully got ashore on beaches west of the town, the old privateer was one of a few officers who carried out a counterattack against the beachhead. His small force was quickly cut to pieces, and Morpain escaped capture only when a slave hid him in the swampy marshland and got him back to the fortress. On Louisbourg's surrender, Morpain said farewell to the town that had been his home for thirty years and accepted a commission in France's *marine royale*. In 1748 he sailed to Louisiana in command of a French warship, finally dying aboard his ship at Rochefort the next year.

If the outgunned and outnumbered French in Acadia and New France were able to muster swashbuckling figures such as Baptiste and Morpain, the more numerous English were no less able to do so. Some, like the New Englander John Rous, used their privateer backgrounds to pursue formal careers as naval officers. But there were others who never took off the vaguely piratical guise of the privateer throughout their bloody and violent careers. One such character was Sylvanus Cobb, whose life came to symbolize the brutal and pitiless warfare that was waged along the Atlantic seaboard between Acadia and New England. Cobb was born in Plymouth, Massachusetts, in 1710, and led an obscure career ashore and at sea until he was caught up in the huge New England effort of the 1745 siege of Louisbourg. After the successful capture, Cobb became involved in the raising of wrecked and sunken ships from Louisbourg harbour, so adroitly that he was sent off to do the same work at Annapolis Royal. By 1747 Cobb had amassed enough money to secure command of a small armed vessel, the *York*, which he manned with hardy volunteers, and sailed off to join the floating "sea militias" raised by John Rous to raid and plunder French ships and settlements in the Saint John River valley. So efficient was Cobb at this sort of thing—some would say ruthless—he attracted the attention of the colonial administration as someone who could get things done. From 1749 to 1754 he remained in the Crown's service during the brief peace, transporting troops and even ferrying supplies to the newly established town of Lunenburg, on Nova Scotia's Atlantic shore.

When George Washington's ill-fated clash with the French in the Ohio Valley in 1754 propelled France and England into open warfare, Cobb was quickly off to sea again in *York*, with a privateer's commission in his pocket and a keen eye for prizes. In 1755, he made his most lucrative haul when he intercepted the large, heavily laden French vessel *Marguerite* off Port La Tour on the Nova Scotia coast, on its passage from Louisbourg to the Saint John River packed with military supplies. Unable to take the pugnacious *Marguerite* on his own, Cobb cleverly manoeuvred to prevent the French vessel from escaping until a nearby Royal Navy vessel could intervene. For his efforts Cobb received a hefty share of the prize money when *Marguerite* was sold at the Port-Royal Vice-Admiralty Prize Court. With his new wealth Cobb paused in his privateering to begin a substantial family home on the Chignecto Peninsula. Conveniently, the British laid siege to nearby Fort Beauséjour, between modern New Brunswick and Nova Scotia, and Cobb was everywhere, using *York* to ferry men and supplies up the Missaguash River in support of the siege, and then throwing himself and his crew with enthusiasm into the brutal business of looting and burning Acadian farmsteads, finally participating in the expulsion of the wretched settlers in accordance with the British edict of 1755.

In 1758, Cobb brought *York* around to Halifax, and sailed north with Admiral Richard Boscawen's huge fleet that was carrying the British force intended to capture Louisbourg. With his knowledge of the place from thirteen years before, he was relied on for pilotage information, and carried a very seasick but determined James Wolfe into within musket shot of the beach at Kennington Cove where Wolfe would later win a landing—and doom the fate of the great fortress. Before the leaves fell, Cobb was back in the Bay of Fundy, sailing *York* up the Saint John River and mercilessly harrying remaining Acadian settlers. He paused in 1760 to build a new family home at Liverpool, Nova Scotia, then sailed off again in British service to the attack on Havana, Cuba, in 1762. There, fate at last caught up with Sylvanus Cobb, and he died of yellow fever in Havana harbour, almost literally with his seaboots on.

With the coming of the American Revolution, from 1776 to 1783, the furious energy that the English had put into battling the French on land and sea was turned inward. With the population of Nova Scotia being almost four-fifths in origin from the New England colonies of Rhode Island, Connecticut and Massachusetts, the conflict took on aspects of a civil war, and eruptions of rebellious behaviour in Nova Scotia became almost as serious as those in New England, if ultimately unsuccessful. The coastline of the rebelling colonies, as it would be in 1812–14, was the roaming ground at will of the Royal Navy. The enormous length of that coastline, and the relatively few ships that the Royal Navy could congregate at any one time, as well as their frequent preoccupation elsewhere, meant that New England and Nova Scotian waters were the open hunting grounds of privateers, both loyal and rebel. As Marsters observed, "The nature of privateering gave the rebels many advantages over the big, powerful ships of the Royal Navy throughout the [Revolutionary] war. Royal Navy frigates were busy escorting convoys to and from the main theatres of war to the south, leaving the Nova Scotia coastline poorly defended."

The rebels were quick off the mark sending privateers northward to attack Nova Scotian settlements and shipping, even though George Washington attempted to halt such depredations in hopes of eventually recruiting the northern colony to the rebel cause. The town of Liverpool, near Nova Scotia's southern tip, came in for particular attention almost as soon as the musket smoke had cleared from Lexington and Concord. In October 1776 a Liverpool schooner was captured by a cousinly schooner out of Marblehead, Massachusetts, and in March 1777 similar vessels sent crews ashore to carry off guns meant for Liverpool's defence, adding another schooner capture in October 1777. The little town rallied its defences under the energetic Simeon Perkins, and Nova Scotia began to issue its own letters of marque, such as that given to John Fawson's 10-gun schooner *Revenge*, which had a mixed career of success. Larger fish had been swimming on Nova Scotia waters, however. John Paul Jones, later to be a founding hero of the United States Navy, captured several ships off Cape Breton and mainland Nova Scotia with impunity in November 1776, and the advantage seemed always to be with the more numerous rebels.

After three years of relative calm, the waters of Nova Scotia once again heard the thump of privateer guns and were obscured by the smoke of burning buildings. Privateers out of Salem, Massachusetts, swept in on the long-suffering town of Liverpool in 1780, attacking its small fort and taking townsfolk hostage. In August 1781 two rebel privateers mounted a serious raid on Annapolis Royal, capturing the blockhouse and indulging in widespread looting before carrying away hostages. A similar raid took place in July 1782, when four rebel vessels landed their crews at Lunenburg, where they looted shops and homes and burned a blockhouse. This last raid marked the high-water mark of rebel activity in Maritime waters; Yorktown had fallen the year before, and the war was for all practical purposes at an end. The final peace treaty would come the following year, 1783, and gradually the normal semi-fraternal relationships of trade and interchange began to reassert themselves between the newly independent American colonies and the Maritimes, which had narrowly remained loyal— and had paid for it in life and property.

With the coming of peace came also a sudden increase in the population of Nova Scotia, as Loyalists in their thousands were evacuated from New York and carried north. Most would move on, but a new level of energy and sheer force of numbers changed the dynamics of life—two new colonies, Cape Breton and New Brunswick, were created—and this new state of affairs was soon reflected in the region's activities at sea. There was a marked increase in the fishery and general trade, aided by the new charts of J.F.W. DesBarres and his *Atlantic Neptune* compilation as well as the charting work of James Cook. Then, when war broke out with revolutionary France in the 1790s, Nova Scotians and New Brunswickers turned again to privateering.

Once again the feisty little town of Liverpool, Nova Scotia, became a home port for adventurous crews that eagerly seized letters of marque issued at Halifax and sailed off to the Caribbean to prey on Spanish and French shipping. Heavily armed privateers such as the *Charles Mary Wentworth*, the *Fly*, the *Lord Nelson*, the *Duke of Kent* and the *Lord Spencer* brought a fear of "Bluenose" fighting qualities to Iberian and French ships plying to the West Indies. In 1800 one such privateer, the *Rover* under Captain Alexander Godfrey, sailed to hunt prizes off Puerto Rico then turned her jib-boom toward the coast of South America, the fabled Spanish Main. There, *Rover* fought off every vessel sent against it, whether naval or otherwise. The culmination of this extraordinary foray was a desperate battle between the outmatched *Rover* and a powerful Spanish vessel, the *Santa Rita*. The Nova Scotians fought with such redoubtable courage in their defeat of the larger Spaniard that an impressed Royal Navy offered Godfrey a King's Commission in the navy in tribute.

As Britain's naval might gradually swept French shipping from the seas, particularly after Horatio Nelson's defeat of the combined French and Spanish fleets off Cape Trafalgar in October 1805, the opportunities for Maritime privateers became few and far between, and the ships and their crews turned to more mundane pursuits. But looming on the horizon was the pinnacle of privateering for vessels sailing out of what would become Canadian ports: the deadly struggle of the War of 1812.

When war came in 1812, it was welcomed neither in the Maritime colonies nor in New England. Bound by birth, interest and familiarity, the eastern neighbours undertook quietly to avoid the impact of the war as far as possible. As the perceptive historian Faye Kert has observed:

> The War of 1812 proved that while governments could make war, they could not make enemies. Despite the best efforts of both the British and American authorities, trade continued throughout the war of 1812. Whether smuggled or licensed, goods moved over borders and across the ocean because the merchants who engaged in this trade refused to allow politics to interfere with profits. Longstanding business and family ties between New England and the Maritime Provinces proved more persuasive than either maritime grievances or annexationist dreams . . .

The effort to minimize the effect of the war led to the British issue of over five hundred "licences" to American ships, freeing them to trade with impunity to Nova Scotia, New Brunswick and Spain in support of the British war effort against Napoleon. At the same time, however, the Royal Navy, with no interest in the cousinly agreements between Maine and Nova Scotia, mounted such an effective blockade of the American coast that, as shipping dried up, American owners and crews had but three options: smuggling, licensed trade with the British or privateering against British shipping. Notwithstanding the generally good relations between New England and the Maritimes, many out-of-work seamen and shipowners were forced to opt for privateering. As Kert drily relates:

> Soon the American coast was bristling with privateers ranging from heavily armed ships of several hundred tons carrying more than 150 men to open whaleboats manned by a few men armed with muskets. Some were so small that, in one case, the privateer was carried home on the deck of her prize. Ironically known as "shaving mills" these small open boats, mostly from the coast of Maine, were rowed by up to thirty or so scruffy-looking men with little regard for either shaving or the finer rules of private armed warfare, especially those that prohibited attacks on land. Vessels such as the *Weazel* of Castine terrorized inhabitants along the Fundy coast with frequent raids on shore and thefts of food, fishing gear and even women's clothing.

The American ships would not find the waters to the north empty of equally aggressive and capable privateers, of various stripes and ability. From New Brunswick, Cape Breton, Prince Edward Island and, above all, Nova Scotia, armed private vessels of war put to sea looking for Yankee prizes. During the period 1812 to 1814, over thirty-seven such vessels would be engaged in privateering, with twelve others issued letters authorizing them to attack an enemy prize if one appeared during a trading voyage. This sizable fleet was very effective: one-third of all British captures at sea off the American coast were accomplished by Maritime privateers, which also made a material contribution to the shutdown of American coastal trade that by 1814 had reduced the United States Treasury to virtual bankruptcy.

These Canadian privateers sailed under many names, some adventurous, some prosaic. Among them were the *Retaliation*, *Wolverine*, *Retrieve*, *Shannon*, *Comet*, *Broke*, *Dart*, *Sir John Sherbrooke*, *General Smyth* and the delightfully named *Saucy Sixteen*. But perhaps the most successful of these ships was a comparatively small schooner with a fifty-foot waterline, the *Liverpool Packet*. It had been bought for £420 by a partnership of John and James Barss, Benjamin Knaut and Caleb Seeley, all of Liverpool, Nova Scotia, and Enos Collins of Halifax. The marine historian C.H.J. Snider lyrically described her:

> A lean-lined thing she was, straight as a gunbarrel, with bold bows, undercut stern and raking keel, and two taunt spars, long as she was, slanting back so sharply they seemed to be falling over her narrow stern. Fast as a gull, perhaps; she had all the signs of one of those Virginia pilot boats which were coming into fashion as "Baltimore Clippers"; but cut away at stem and stern and sides until she was nothing but a wedge, held upright by her pig-iron ballast.

Wedge though it was, the little *Liverpool Packet* put to sea on its first privateering voyage on August 30, 1812, loaded to its channels with the supplies and stuff of war:

> . . . victualled for sixty days, with 200 rounds of canister and 300 of roundshot in her magazine, four hundred-weight of gunpowder, two anchors, two cables, 300 lbs. of spare cordage, and twenty-five muskets and forty cutlasses for her forty-five men. She had five guns, one 6-pounder, two 4-pounders, and two 12-pounders.

Over her extraordinary career the little ship—known also at various times as the *Black Joke*, *Young Teazer's Ghost* and the *Portsmouth Packet*—sailed under three captains, Joseph Barss, Caleb Seeley and Lewis Knaut. Barss proved the most successful, and *Liverpool Packet* would bring in no fewer than fifty American prizes, and damaged more. Her hovering presence off Boston led to the planning of the Cape Cod Canal, and she even survived capture and recapture before completing a career that brought in a formal figure of $264,000 in prize money, but which actually may have totalled over $1,000,000, a staggering sum for the era.

In December 1812 alone, the *Liverpool Packet* took eight schooners and a brig within sight of Cape Cod. The *Boston Messenger* was livid:

> That an insignificant fishing schooner should have captured and carried home eight or nine sail, valued at from $70,000 to $90,000, within twenty days of the time she left Liverpool, N.S., is shameful. A few weeks ago she captured, within ten miles of Cape Cod, vessels with cargo worth $50,000 . . .

By March 1813 the newspapers had grown apoplectic:

> The evil genius of our coasting trade has of late changed her cruising ground from Cape Cod to our north shore. About five o'clock on Saturday afternoon she took, near the outer harbour of Gloucester, the schooner *Fanny*, bound from Boston to the eastward, having on board a cargo of corn, tar, cordage, etc. On Saturday morning she took a sloop with wood, and sent her in to Gloucester with prisoners. The privateer continued off the harbour until Sunday afternoon, when the inhabitants, provoked at seeing their port thus blockaded, sent out the brig *New Orleans*, manned with smart and experienced men, in pursuit of her, on which the privateer made off. But the brig chased until she got within a mile and a half of her, when it fell calm, and the privateer, by the sweeps (from the *Defiance*'s cargo!) and night coming on, escaped . . .

The saga of the Maritime privateers of the War of 1812 is a riveting one, and it led to several great fortunes, of which a number of buildings in the restored quarter of Halifax's historic waterfront remain as testament. When the war ended and normal relations resumed with the Boston States to the south, the privateers that had sailed out of Maritime ports not only had established a reputation for audacity and seamanship, but had also contributed materially to the disappointment of American war aims and a return to peace in the status quo that had existed before the war. The building blocks of the future nation of Canada would not be swallowed up by the burgeoning republic to the south, in part due to their service.

The astonishing success of the Canadian privateers led indeed to personal wealth for many. But more important was the substantial upward jolt it gave to the Atlantic Canadian economy, even with the disruption of normal trade with New England. The capture and auction of literally hundreds of ships and their equipment and cargoes at Halifax and other prize ports injected capital into the colonial economy that went on to fund important businesses that flourished in the protected world of the postwar British Empire and the Atlantic trading system. Samuel Cunard's first ships were captured American vessels of the 1812 conflict, and the privateer owner Enos Collins earned so much from the sea war that he was able to found the Halifax Banking Company, Nova Scotia's first bank and one of the most important in early Canadian history. When, in 1871, Collins died at age ninety-seven, he was the richest man in the Atlantic provinces, and indeed in any part of the new Canadian confederation. And it had been the ship's guns of his privateers, banging out over the waters of the Atlantic Ocean, that had won the beginnings of this early Canadian fortune. Again, a major building block of the evolving Canadian nationhood and society had been moulded on, and by, the sea.

11

The Rush
to the Pacific

Great is Ne-Kil-stlas, the Raven,
Loftiest and mightiest of Chiefs!
Sun, moon, water and this cold clay of Earth,
He made them—Ne-Kil-stlas, the Great Raven.
Eagle, wolf, beaver and all the birds that fly and sing.
Killer whale, seal, sea otter, and all
The silver salmon that swim the seas.
Cedar, spruce, salmonberry, and the green leaves
That rustle in the wind.
He made them all.
And the people of the four ways of this round, flat world.
High is Ne-Kil-stlas,
The greatest of Great Chiefs!

THE WORDS RELATE how it was created, for the first inhabitants: a coastline of incomparable beauty, marked by limitless inlets and sounds flanked by towering rainforests and cloud-hung mountains, its stunning panorama still breathtaking today after two centuries of civilization's inroads and termite-like attack. As we have seen, the Pacific coastline of what would later become British Columbia may well have been the first land in Canada to know the tread of human feet, as seaborne migrants fringing the edge of the great glacial sheets voyaged in skin boats from Asia to Alaska and on southward. There, as the glaciers retreated, they stayed and prospered, creating sea-dependent cultures of depth and complexity, marked by beautiful art forms in the working of the rich natural resources of the coast and a seagoing ability in pursuit of whales and other prey in large cedar canoes.

As the millennia passed, the oral remembrances of the great sea trek from Kamchatka and Siberia passed away, to be replaced by no less vibrant, if more fanciful, tales of the people's coming to the Evergreen Coast. Pacific scholars George and Helen Akrigg, who collected the legend of Raven's creation of the world, also found one tale of that coming:

> First there was a god named Qua-utz. And Qua-utz created a woman and left her to live alone and lamenting in the dark forests of Yucuatl [Nootka Sound]. And with her in the forest were deer created by Qua-utz, but they had as yet no antlers. And there were dogs, but they had as yet no tails. And there were ducks, but they had as yet no wings. Then Qua-utz took pity on the loneliness of the maiden. He came to her over the ocean in a gleaming canoe made all of copper. Swiftly the copper canoe came towards the shore, with young men plying copper paddles. One of the handsome young men spoke to the desolate maiden from the copper canoe and told her that Qua-utz, to whom all things are possible, had come to supply her with company of her own kind. At these words the maiden wept, and her tears fell upon the ground. Then Qua-utz himself bade her look where her tears had fallen, and she saw they had formed the body of a tiny baby. And Qua-utz told her to place it in a small seashell and then, as it grew in size, in a larger shell, and still later a larger shell. Then Qua-utz extended his bounty to the deer, the dogs, and the ducks. The deer sprouted antlers, the dogs wagged tails and the ducks, growing wings, soared into the air. Qua-utz and his men departed in their great canoe of copper, but the little baby remained. He grew into a sturdy boy and then into a strong young man. Then he took the maiden to be his wife and they begat children. From their first-

born son descended the tyees [chiefs], and from their other sons the common people.

For the Mo'achaht and others, their existence on the British Columbia coast would develop unhindered for perhaps ten thousand years, until the coming of another people from another part of the world ended their ancient way of life forever. Questing west and south out of their remote and gloomy peninsula in search of gold, conquest and the propagation of their faith, Europeans came upon the Americas again in the late 1400s, four centuries after their first attempt at North American settlement was defeated by distance and the resolute hostility of the skraelings. In 1492, Christopher Columbus made the first fully announced contact with the New World, even though he still thought it to be a part of the Old. Then, in 1497, Giovanni Caboto confirmed for England the location of Newfoundland, and within a few years men such as Verrazano were travelling the coasts of America, finding to their initial annoyance that it was a continent standing in the way of their reaching the riches of the Orient. In 1519, Ferdinand Magellan made the dramatic first entry into the Pacific, around the American barrier. As the pre-eminent Canadian maritime historian Barry Gough has observed:

For four centuries beginning with the sixteenth, Europeans came to chart and exploit the vast waters and shores of the Pacific Ocean. They rounded the Cape of Good Hope or Cape Horn in their small, gun-carrying sailing ships whose home ports were in far-off Portugal, Spain, England, France, or Holland. Some, including Russians, Spanish, Americans and Canadians, made their way to the Pacific overland. As these men entered into commercial and political enterprises, they found themselves at times dependent on support from their respective governments—support that could only reach them over long, tenuous, and vulnerable seaways. The fact that the British were able to establish a firm and lasting foothold on a large part of the Northwest Coast of North America was owing in no small measure to their commercial enterprises by sea and the presence, strength, and explorations of the Royal Navy.

The first arrival of a European vessel on the coast of British Columbia was likely that of Sir Francis Drake, although Chinese junks may have visited its shores as early as 1421, before China gave up deep-sea exploration. Drake had sailed from England with five ships, but after a twenty-month voyage round the Horn only one was left, Drake's 100-ton flagship, which he renamed the *Golden Hinde*; the remainder had either been lost at sea or turned back. Drake had pressed on, raiding the Spanish settlements on the Pacific coastline and then capping the raids with the spectacular capture in Nicaraguan waters of the silver-laden galleon *Nuestra Señora de la Concepción*, inbound from Manila. Groaning under a new ballast of twenty-six tons of silver and other plunder, the *Golden Hinde* turned northward on a voyage whose northern extremity remains a mystery. By June 1579, Drake was somewhere off the coast of either California, Oregon, Washington—or British Columbia. The reasons for his heading north are fairly clear. A map of 1574 drawn by Abraham Ortelius had shown a passage from the west coast of North America to Hudson Bay, titled the "Strait of Anian." Drake, it would appear, was looking for this strait as a means of getting the *Golden Hinde* and its cumbersome cargo home. Drake ran in too close with the North American coast, remarking of the event:

The land in that part of America, bearing farther out into the West than we before imagined, we were nearer on it then when we were aware; and yet nearer still wee came unto it, the more extremitie of cold did sease upon us. The 5 day of June, wee were forced by contrary windes to runne in with the shoare, which we then first descried, and to cast anchor in a bad bay, the best roade wee could for the present meete with, where wee were not without some danger by reason of the many extreme gusts and flawes that beate upon us, which if they ceased and were still at any time, immediately upon their intermission there followed most vile, thicke and stinking fogges, against which the sea prevailed nothing . . .

Where exactly Drake found his "vile, thicke and stinking fogges" has never been clear, the usual assumption being that his farthest point of northern advance was the Washington coast. In 2003, however, the writer Steven Bawlf suggested in his *The Secret Voyage of Sir Francis Drake* that the explorer may have reached as far as 50° north, and that his "bad bay" was on the Pacific coast of Vancouver Island. Bawlf goes on to claim that fear of unduly alarming the Spanish, who saw the Pacific and its shores as their possession, led Queen Elizabeth I and her court to suppress the knowledge of Drake's actual track. In the event, Drake returned southward away from the "extremities of cold," refitted the *Golden Hinde* at a bay north of San Francisco, and sailed off west on a circumnavigation back to England, after having named the territory he had visited New Albion.

The contact Drake and the English may have had with the indigenous people of the coast is unknown, but an intriguing hint is found in a tale collected by historian George H. Griffin relating the experience of a Nootka sub-chief named Stello-Walth.

The moon had just risen. Her silvery disk was halfway over the rim of the horizon, and the ripples on the broad swells of the ocean glittered and glinted in the radiance. Stello-Walth paused, a solitary figure, and contemplated the beauty before him. With preoccupied thoughts he stood perfectly still and let his vision wander outward across the waters, following the pathway of light. Suddenly he started, and passed a hand across his eyes. He looked again. There, moving slowly across the face of the moon, was a great canoe. Now it was framed within the lunar semicircle, and Stello-Walth saw that the canoe had wings. He could hardly credit his senses, but there it was. Ever so slowly the vessel passed out of the screen of light, and he observed that it carried with it a part of the moon, which showed like pin-pricks just below the billowing wings. He waited no longer, but hurried to the lodges clustered under the brow of the bluff upon which he stood. Arriving in the village, he told them of the vision he had seen.

Stello-Walth is met by skepticism in the village until the next morning, when the great canoe is revealed at rest in a nearby cove. Stello-Walth argues that a canoe of selected villagers must go out and meet the "Children of the Moon." A party of astonished warriors paddles out to the great canoe, where Stello-Walth makes a long speech in which he welcomes the strangers they can see aboard the great canoe. With gestures, they are invited aboard the huge vessel.

The Moon Chief came up to them and spoke to them in a strange tongue. Like the hissing of snakes, it sounded to the warriors. Stello-Walth gazed intently at the white face and the eyes the colour of the blue sky and the hair that looked like grass when it is yellow after the drought of the summer. The Moon Chief made signs for them to be seated, and when they had done so, slaves appeared who also had white faces and placed before them on the deck shining white disks, hollow in the centre and containing dark blood and bleached bones. The Moon Chief signified that they should eat. Stello-Walth turned to his warriors and saw the look of dismay on their faces. Solemnly he shook his head in disapproval. Never before had they feasted on raw blood and bones. At last, one of the Moon Children placed some of the vile stuff in his mouth and ate it. A warrior, younger than the rest of his companions, followed his example. Spurred on by this, Stello-Walth began to eat. How crumbly the bones were, and how sweet the dark blood!

As Stello-Walth and his companions were introduced to molasses and ship's biscuit, they may have been marking again the closure of the circle of contact between humanity coming to Canada from the east and from the west, six hundred years after the first closing in Vinland by the skraelings and the Norse.

The Spanish at this point were fifty years on from their conquest and destruction of the Aztec Empire, and were well established in the lands to the south of California. Where their own voyaging up the Pacific coast in the 1500s had taken them is uncertain, but in the 1590s a Greek seaman named Apostolos Valerianos—known also as Juan de Fuca—told an English seaman who encountered him in Venice that he had found an eastward-leading strait north of California. In the late eighteenth century, sometime after Captain James Cook visited Nootka Sound, another English mariner, Charles Barkeley, found de Fuca's strait where he said it would be; Cook had missed it. The most northerly exploratory efforts of the Spanish seem, however, not to have gone beyond San Francisco Bay to any degree for the next century, until, in 1774, their interest revived. The viceroy in Mexico determined to send an expedition north along the coast in response to rumours and stories of Russian fur trade "intrusions" from the north, particularly the voyage of Vitus Bering in 1741. In a little vessel selected for the expedition, an officer named Juan Pérez sailed as far north as latitude 51° 42' north, visited the Queen Charlotte Islands and Nootka Sound, and then turned back. The following year, 1775, the Spanish sent out two ships, Pérez's little *Santiago*, under the command of Bruno de Hezeta, and the equally diminutive *Sonora*, commanded by a man of more notable qualities, Juan Francisco de la Bodega y Quadra. Hezeta had been ordered to sail as far as 65° north but declined to do so. Bodega y Quadra, made of sterner stuff, pressed on to reach Alaskan territory at 55° 17' north, marking the farthest known northern penetration of Spanish exploration to that date.

Two years later, in 1778, the English returned to the British Columbia coast in a manner that formed the basis, along with Drake's voyage, for the claim of English rights on the shores north of Spanish America. That Spanish America in the eyes of the Spanish extended as far as Alaska meant that a future of conflicting claims lay ahead. James Cook's third Pacific voyage had as its goal the same aim as Drake's two hundred years earlier: the finding of the Northwest Passage or Strait of Anian as an ice-free navigable channel back to the North Atlantic. Cook's two ships, *Resolution* and *Discovery*, had paused at Hawaii after revealing those islands to European awareness before closing with the North American coast. Cook, as noted, missed entirely Juan de Fuca's strait, saying with uncharacteristic dismissal "we saw nothing like it, nor is there the least probability that iver any such thing existed." By Sunday, March 29, Cook's ships arrived in the latitudes of Vancouver Island, and Cook once more closed with the foggy, mountainous coast. He entered a large bay, naming it Hope Bay, and found an inlet that would become known as Nootka Sound:

> Monday 30th March. In the Morning I sent three armed boats under the command of Mr. King to look for a harbour for the ships and soon after I went my self in a small boat on the same service. On the NW side of the arm we were in and not far from the ship, I found a pretty snug cove.

The sound they entered was inhabited by the Mo'achaht people, who helpfully directed the English around the spit that forms the village site of Yuquot (ancient Yuquotl) and soon established a shrewd bargaining relationship with the men of Cook's ships, a mutually respectful one in the end, which lasted until Cook had repaired a mast, charted the waters of the sound, and sailed on April 26 to Arctic exploration and eventual death in Hawaii.

If Cook's visit provided a pretext for English claims to the region, it was a far more significant event from another standpoint. The men of *Resolution* and *Discovery* had paid modest prices to the Mo'achaht for lustrous sea otter furs. After Cook's death, the expedition returned home by the Chinese port of Macao, and there the men of the ships were astonished at the staggeringly high prices the Chinese were willing to pay for the sea otter pelts. There must have been few men amongst the crews who could not see that a for-

La Entra da de Nutka, 1792   *C 117914*

tune awaited the first ships that could return to cull the animals and sell their furs in China. It was the beginning of the single most important motivation in the early development of Canada's west coast, until the coming of settlement and the rise of other commodity pursuits: the fur trade. As one of James Cook's marines, the American-born John Ledyard, later related: "We purchased while [at Nootka] about 1500 beaver besides other skins, but took none but the best, having no thought at the time of using them to any other advantage than converting them to the purposes of clothing, but it afterward happened that skins which did not cost the purchaser sixpence sold in China for 100 [Spanish] dollars . . ."

On the return of Cook's ships, the word spread like wildfire through English and American seaports and houses of commerce. The first vessel dedicated solely to the pursuit of the sea otter arrived on the coast in 1785. It would be the harbinger of thousands more, until the plentiful sea otter was hunted to the edge of extinction. Even the French, until now largely absent from the North Pacific, sent out an expedition under Jean-François de Galaup, Comte de La Pérouse, with instructions, as the Akriggs relate, to examine that part of the coast of northwest America which had not been seen by Cook:

Early in August [of 1786] La Pérouse's ships, *Astrolabe* and *Boussole*, arrived off the northern end of the Queen Charlotte Islands, discovering Dixon Entrance a year before Dixon himself. Coasting down the Queen Charlotte Islands, La Pérouse rounded their southern tip and gave to Cape St. James the name of Cape Hector. After sailing eastward, he ranged the mainland coast from Millbank Sound southwards. Later, from Kamchatka, he sent to France his journal for this part of the voyage.

La Pérouse was later to disappear with all his men in the South Pacific, the wrecks of his ships being found years later on the reefs of Vanikolo.

If the English were quick off the mark to exploit the potential of the sea otter trade, they also put in place a mechanism to control the profits. The South Sea Company had control of licences that allowed trading on the west coast of North America, and any trade with China required a similar licence from the East India Company. As British and American ships began to flock to the northwest coast, as many arrived illegally as did with proper licences in hand. One of the first fur traders to establish himself was John Meares, who built a trading post on the beach at Yuquot, Nootka Sound, and in 1788 launched the first small ship ever built on Canada's west coast, the *North West America*. Far to the south, the Spanish became alarmed at these incursions into their claimed realm, and in 1789 sent a substantial expedition north that landed at Nootka Sound. The Spanish hoisted their own flag, confiscated any British vessels they could get their hands on and sent them off under guard to Mexico. The so-called Nootka Crisis that almost led to war between Britain and Spain was nominally resolved by a treaty, the Nootka Convention of October 28, 1790, which gave British traders free access to the coast except within thirty miles of Spanish settlements. But for the Spanish and English at Nootka and elsewhere on the coast, the signing of a faraway treaty hardly settled matters.

In 1790, to enforce and formalize the terms of the Convention, the British government sent out an expedition of two ships, HMS

Discovery and a support vessel, HMS *Chatham*. Both were initially under the command of Captain Henry Roberts, but Roberts was succeeded by his first lieutenant in *Discovery*, George Vancouver. The expedition's orders were twofold: a survey and charting of the coast from 30° north to 60° north latitude, and the receipt at Nootka of the British post and properties, being restored as per the terms of the Convention. As Lieutenant Vancouver made his way toward the coast, the viceroy of Mexico—who was ignorant of the signing of the Convention—ordered an enlargement of the Spanish post at Nootka and the installation of a permanent garrison. Further, he sent off an exploratory expedition in the ship *Princesa Real* under Manuel Quimper and Gonzalo López de Haro to probe Juan de Fuca Strait. This they did to a degree, landing to erect large wooden crosses along the shores of the strait, including just west of the modern site of Victoria.

Seventeen ninety-two would prove to be a turning-point year for the British Columbia coast, as it was in that year that the Spanish made their last efforts to retain Nootka, the number of British and American fur-hunting ships suddenly increased dramatically, and George Vancouver began his meticulous survey of the coastal waters. It was the year that marked the end of the rainforest coast's remoteness, and the beginning of a relentless exploitation and development that continues to the present day. The Spanish now were hoping to claim the Strait of Juan de Fuca as their northern boundary, if all else failed. But the pressure of the fur trade and eventual American immigration were going to make that claim impossible.

In the meantime, Vancouver entered the strait and then the waters of what are now Puget Sound and the Strait of Georgia. Having learned the surveying and charting techniques of Captain James Cook, Vancouver used Cook's wide-ranging longboat voyaging to explore and chart the myriad coves, bays and inlets. After extensive surveying, during which Vancouver met, and even for a time sailed in company with, exploring Spanish vessels, he finally arrived again on the outer shore of Vancouver Island and put in to Nootka Sound to carry out the terms of the Convention. At Nootka he was dealing with a gentleman of admirable character and efficiency, Don Juan Francisco de la Bodega y Quadra, who as we have seen first arrived on the coast in the little *Sonora* as a lieutenant. Although the English and the Spanish rapidly developed an amicable relationship, they could not accept each other's interpretation of the Convention's terms. Agreeing to disagree, they would refer the matter to their home governments for resolution, and parted as friends.

The next year, 1793, saw the first overland link with Canada take place, as Alexander Mackenzie, a fur trade employee, arrived on the coast at the mouth of the Bella Coola River after an extraordinary canoe, horse and foot trek from inland. Narrowly missing Vancouver's own presence in the area, Mackenzie would paint on a large rock

> Alex Mackenzie from Canada
> By land 22nd July 1793

Never knowing how close he had come to meeting the courageous young Scot, Vancouver sailed off to Hawaii for the winter, to the delight of his young crews, and then returned in 1794 to complete his surveys, from Cook Inlet to Port Conclusion. Having carried out his orders to the best of his ability, circumnavigated the island which would come to bear his name and left a chart folio that would open British Columbia waters to reasonable navigation for the first time, Vancouver sailed for home. He left a coast dominated by ruthless American fur-hunting vessels and a sea otter population almost wiped out. But the American wave of activity on the coast was just beginning; it was not going to be a Spanish or a British preserve, in either fact or law.

Alexander Mackenzie went on to a successful career with the North American fur trade, but the publication of his journals, in which he argued for the establishment of a continent-wide fur trade system, stimulated interest in a place he may not have expected. Along with George Vancouver's own book, *A Voyage of Discovery to the North Pacific Ocean* (1798), Mackenzie's journals planted in the mind of the American president Thomas Jefferson the notion that the young United States should reach for just such an empire. Accordingly, he dispatched a cross-continent expedition under the command of Merriwether Lewis and William Clark, charged to reach the Pacific coast and establish a formal American fur trade presence at the mouth of the Columbia River. The most immediate rival to the Americans was the Canada-based North West Company, which merged with the short-lived XY Company in 1804. The North West Company's Simon Fraser countered the threat of the Lewis and Clark expedition by beginning the establishment of fur trade posts up in the vast interior drained by the Columbia, the great swath of land known as New Caledonia. It would take some years for Jefferson's vision of an American post on the Columbia to materialize; meanwhile, the Canadians were pushing through to that same coast, determined that the profits to be had from the country would flow to Montreal and London, not New York.

One by one, the men under the Union Jack strove to establish themselves on the northwest coast. In 1807, David Thompson found his way through the Rockies and set up a post at Kootenay House. In the next year, 1808, Simon Fraser led a canoe expedition down what he thought was the Columbia, only to find it to be another river, the Fraser. David Thompson attempted to reach the sea itself, but turned back before succeeding. The efforts would continue.

Two years later, in 1810, Alexander Mackenzie's feat and his journals inspired an energetic German immigrant to New York, John Jacob Astor, to pursue Mackenzie's dream of a continent-wide fur trade system. Knowing their superior skills, Astor decided to hire the Scots and French Canadians who might otherwise have been his competitors. In that year Astor sent off two groups to build a fur trade post on the Columbia: a seaborne party, in the supply ship *Tonquin*, sailed off around Cape Horn to the Columbia, while an overland party of Scots, Iroquois and French Canadians set off by canoe from Lachine, in Lower Canada. David Thompson was ordered to beat Astor's men to the Columbia, but in the event he failed. The *Tonquin* made it safely to the mouth of the Columbia River, and the fur trade post of Astoria rose on a river-edge clearing, the Stars and Stripes floating over it. The overland party soon arrived, but then ill luck struck. The *Tonquin*, searching out sources of furs to the north, blew up spectacularly when her magazine detonated during an attack by warriors from a coastal village. The Astorians were still dealing with this blow when—at last—David Thompson tried again and succeeded in reaching the Columbia River. Alexander Ross, an employee of Astor's newly minted Pacific Fur Company, recorded the moment:

> On the 15th of July we were rather surprised at the unexpected arrival of a north-west proprietor at Astoria, and still more so at the free and cordial reception given to an opponent. Mr. Thompson, northwest-like, came dashing down the Columbia in a light canoe, manned with eight Iroquois and an interpreter, chiefly men from the vicinity of Montreal.

Astor, however, had won the race to the mouth of the Columbia, Thompson's dash notwithstanding, and the Pacific Fur Company's presence would form the basis for American claims to the territory.

Very rapidly, the Pacific Fur Company began to expand its activities north and east toward Okanagan Lake and beyond, buoyed by the successful arrival of several more ships sent round the Horn from New York by Astor to replace the ill-fated *Tonquin*. Then, in 1813, news arrived of the outbreak of the War of 1812 a year earlier, which put the mostly British and Canadian employees at Astoria in a quandary as to loyalty. The issue was somewhat resolved by the arrival in October 1813 of ten canoes bearing a large party of Nor'westers down the Columbia. They had come to take possession of Astoria, and the Pacific Fur Company, never forgetting their business concerns, sold the post's assets to the Nor'westers. The transfer was completed when the sloop of war HMS *Racoon* arrived from South America, and its captain, William Black, staged a formal ceremony in which Astoria was renamed Fort George, the Union

Jack was raised, and the "establishment and the country" were taken possession of in the name of His Britannic Majesty.

Within a year and a half, the British and American governments had signed a peace treaty that provided for "joint occupation" of the Oregon territory and restored matters as they had been before 1812. The American government wanted Astoria marked as an *American* settlement, and this was accomplished finally on the occasion of the visit of another Royal Navy vessel, HMS *Blossom*, in 1818. The American government now had a more demonstrable case to make as to territorial claims on the northwest coast. Their argument, in fact, was that Great Britain had no claim at all to *any* part of the coast, while London claimed rights to everything not claimed by the Spanish to the south and the Russians to the north. With a civility edged with the threat of naval confrontation, the period 1818 to 1846 would be an unsettled time of conflicting American and British claims to the Pacific coast.

The fur trade, with the virtual annihilation of the sea otter, had other pelts to pursue, and it did not wait for the niceties of diplomatic negotiation to determine who had a right to trade where. The transfer of Astoria to American ownership in 1818 provided for the North West Company to continue trading from the post, regardless of what flag flew above the stockade walls. But the Nor'westers soon had more to think about than flags: in 1819 the Hudson's Bay Company's agents arrived in New Caledonia, intent on competing for Pacific furs. By 1821 the bitter competition abruptly came to an end with the amalgamation of the two companies under the Hudson's Bay Company name. The Company was now the principal agent for trade, commerce and development on what would become Canada's west coast. It lost no time in making arrangements for efficient trade and the integration of the Pacific furs into the main Company system reaching back to Great Britain.

The northern part of the New Caledonia country would have a chief factor at Fort St. James, and a new, southern trading area to be named Columbia would be headquartered at Fort Vancouver, a new post eighty-five miles up the Columbia River, which was then linked to the faraway post at York Factory on Hudson's Bay by an astounding canoe and York boat waterway known as "the Communication." Supporting these posts and becoming virtually the only ships plying the coast was a growing fleet of HBC supply vessels, which gradually squeezed out the freebooting American trading schooners. In 1825 the posts welcomed the arrival of the *William and Anne*, the first Hudson's Bay vessel wholly devoted to the Pacific fur trade.

As historians, George and Helen Akrigg saw the coming of the Hudson's Bay Company as a positive development for the coastal tribes.

> Whereas the American trading ships by their outrageous tactics had filled the Indians with hatred for the "Boston men," every Indian knew that, though the Boston men were bad, the "King George men" were good. Visitors to British Columbia, right through to the latter part of the nineteenth century, were impressed by how consistently and relentlessly the Indians held by that distinction.

Furthermore, according to the Akriggs:

> When the Americans launched their wars against the Indians in Washington Territory, no HBC man was ever attacked by the embattled Indians. In consequence, terrified American settlers presented themselves at the HBC posts, seeking to purchase as safe disguises the [blanket coats] which were, in effect, the uniform of the HBC . . . No episode could bear more eloquent testimony to what the HBC had achieved by fairness and firmness.

The regular arrival of the Company's ships on the Pacific coast was the only element of stability, beyond the occasional visits by Royal Navy vessels, for the next decade or more. Though growing, the coastal villages still faced the unprincipled behaviour of freebooting American schooner crews, and had to cope with the beginnings of cultural and physical collapse under the effect of the white man's firearms, alcohol, disease and frequent criminality, a story that had been played out in eastern North America a century earlier.

With the 1825 arrival of the little *William and Anne*, the Hudson's Bay Company was launched into the west coast maritime fur trade that had begun with the offhand purchase of sea otter pelts by James Cook's men fifty years before. After arriving at the mouth of the Columbia River and navigating the very dangerous sandbars at its entrance to offload supplies, the *William and Anne* sailed to the Queen Charlottes and Nootka, and then returned to enter the Strait of Juan de Fuca in order to fix on the chart the mouth of Simon Fraser's river. Within two years two more ships had arrived to join in this sort of work, the schooners *Cadboro* and *Vancouver*, each of about sixty to seventy tons, and the Company had established a key post on the lower Fraser River, known as Fort Langley. The dangers of this new navigation, particularly at the mouth of the Columbia, soon took their toll. The intrepid little *William and Anne* was wrecked there in 1829, and a replacement, the *Isabella*, survived a voyage round the Horn from Great Britain only to be wrecked itself on arrival. The *Cadboro* and *Vancouver* sailed on, joined by other vessels including the *Llama*, the *Dryad* and the *Eagle*, all of which had so many near disasters that one observer was led to comment that the Company "seemed to have an uncanny knack for finding alcoholics to command the Company's ships bound for the North-West Coast."

As the 1830s opened, the Hudson's Bay Company found itself under pressure from two sources. The Russian government, still ineptly intent on a North American presence, objected to any northward activities of the Company, while the American government objected to any activities of the Company at all. With American settlement increasing on the Columbia River, the pressure on the Company to leave its southern operating area based at Fort Vancouver began to grow, particularly after 1836, when there arrived from a perilous Cape Horn voyage a Hudson's Bay Company

View of Esquimalt Harbour, 1870   *PA 124052*

steamship, rigged as a brigantine, destined for a half-century or more of fame: the *Beaver*.

In 1837, as rebellions convulsed the Canadas to the east, the Hudson's Bay Company took stock of the building American settler pressure that was more interested in having the fur-trapping tribes simply go away than in trading with them. Adding to the mix the difficulties of the navigation on the Columbia, the Company determined to move its operations north from the Columbia River area. The *Beaver* was given the task of sailing off and finding a suitable location for a new and important post on the *north* side of the Strait of Juan de Fuca. Her side wheels churning, *Beaver* set off on her voyage, and before long had come upon the inlet of Camosun, the site of modern Victoria. *Beaver*'s captain was pleased at having found "an excellent harbour and a fine open country along the sea shore, apparently well adapted for both tillage and pasturage."

As the Company pondered the move to Camosun, the overall lawlessness of the coast was eased, at least temporarily, by the return of the Royal Navy in the form of HMS *Sulphur* and HMS *Starling*, up from Valparaíso, Chile, under the command of Captain Edward

Belcher, RN. The arrival of these two warships highlighted the fact that the principal, and often only, police and deterrent presence on the coast until well along in the nineteenth century would be the ships and bluejackets of the Royal Navy. That state of affairs would last until the coming of colonial status and proper government in place of fur trade posts surrounded by an ungoverned wilderness.

With American settlement continuing apace, the Company moved to protect its holdings between Puget Sound and the Columbia River by forming the quaintly named Puget Sound Agricultural Company, in 1839. America's pursuit of its perceived destiny was continuing, however, evidenced by the arrival in 1841 of the United States Exploring Expedition, comprising the American warships USS *Vincennes* and USS *Porpoise*. The two vessels cruised impressively through the islands of Puget Sound under the command of Commodore Charles Wilkes, USN, and made a de facto claim of influence in the region. Both the Americans and the nervous HBC officials were aware that, thousands of miles to the east, British and American negotiators were establishing the disputed American-Canadian border but leaving its actual line in the west an uncertainty. What was certain was that the HBC wanted the Columbia River as a possible future border with American territory while the Americans wanted a line far to the north—or none at all.

The Webster–Ashburton Treaty, when it came in 1842, left the western border unsettled, and the Company read the portents in the clouds. The next year, Fort Vancouver on the Columbia was replaced as the prime Pacific depot of the HBC by the new post at Camosun, which was to bear the name Fort Victoria. The sturdy *Beaver* arrived there on March 14, 1853, with the founding party, including the chief factor, James Douglas. Behind them, the cries grew louder from American settlers for the ejection of "Queen Victoria's men" from the disputed territory.

The Royal Navy did what it could. In 1844, HMS *Modeste*, 18 guns, put in briefly to show the flag, and then in 1845 a somewhat more impressive vessel appeared in the form of the aptly named HMS *America*, 50 guns. The *America*'s arrival marked the beginning of a regular Royal Navy presence in what would become British Columbia waters. It came none too soon, as the newly elected President Polk in Washington had campaigned on a platform of not only outright takeover of the Oregon Country and rejection of any British claims, but at the very least a border demand of 54° 40' north—"or fight!"—which would have put the eventual Canadian border almost at the level of Alaska.

Determined not to give in to so extreme a demand, the British government and the Admiralty sent off Rear Admiral Sir George Seymour to the Strait of Georgia and Puget Sound with Her Majesty's Ships *Fisgard*, 42 guns; *Herald*, 26 guns; *Pandora*, 6 guns; and even a side wheel steamer, *Cormorant*, 6 guns, to add to *Modeste* and *America*. These hung about grandly in the islands—disturbed only by the sudden defection of *America* back to England—while Seymour waited to find out what the politicians would come up with. What the politicians produced was a treaty signed June 15, 1846, that continued the 49th-parallel border all the way to the Pacific coast. Britain would not have to fight over the ludicrous 54° 40' north boundary, but neither would she keep the lush Columbia River territory. The modern boundary between the United States and what would become Canada was virtually established, with the exception of the exact line through the Gulf Islands separating British territory (Vancouver Island) and the mainland to the south. The island of San Juan was claimed by both sides, as the supposed border of 1846 ran through the "channel" but the Americans and British could not agree on which side of the island the channel actually ran.

A crisis was reached when a pig belonging to the small Hudson's Bay Company post on the island wandered off and was shot dead by an American settler who found it rooting up his garden. Tempers escalated beyond common sense, and soon armed camps were developing at either end of the island, with attendant naval support. An appalled administration in Washington saw a major war looming with Great Britain over a shot pig even as conflict with the Southern states was worsening. A hero of the War of 1812, General

Winfield Scott, was told to defuse the situation, his orders observing that "it would be a shocking event if . . . two nations should be preoccupied into a war respecting the possession of a small island." Not to mention the pig.

Scott managed to keep a straight face and resolved the conflict by chastising the more belligerent American officers involved, and by working out with the British that, as with the Spanish at Nootka, the home governments would decide the issue. The tension lessened, and both sides agreed to live and let live until the actual borderline was established.

With the trauma of its civil war behind it, the United States set about resolving a number of issues with London to put an end to the recurring pattern of crises that stood in the way of natural British-American trade and co-operation. One of these issues was the question of the borderline in the Gulf Islands. The issue was referred to the German kaiser for arbitration, and he awarded San Juan Island to the United States, the border being declared as lying through Haro Strait. In the early 1900s the northern border of Canadian territory would be resolved by another British-American treaty— to the detriment of the Canadian claim—and the long struggle was largely over. The Treaty of Washington of 1871, the comic-opera adventure of the potential Pig War on San Juan, and the Alaska boundary settlement had marked the end of the great race to claim the beautiful coast that had first revealed its dark allure to Francis Drake three hundred years earlier.

Through the whole tumultuous story, it had been the sea that had shaped events—as a path of discovery, as the source of the sea otters and the fishery, and as both barrier and highway to the spread of indigenous and then European settlement. Even more than is generally acknowledged, the sea and the human relationship to it shaped the founding, growth and character of the Canadian Pacific coast and its people. The great mountains to the east silently block the flight of imagination over their white-shouldered peaks. Instead, the hearts and minds of Pacific coast Canadians were, and remain, turned to the north, the south and the west, shaped and drawn by the great sea that washes their shores. The sea has created a world that retains their commitment, and steadily draws thousands from less fortunate places to join them.

12

The
Northwest
Passage

We still made our way north-west, meeting sometimes with ice, and then again clear water. Thus, proceeding betwixt ice and ice, we see a great island of ice tumble over, which was a good warning to us to not come near them. The next day we had a great storm and were driven to put in amongst the ice and there to lie. Some of our men fell sick; I will not say from fear, though I saw no other symptoms to explain their sickness. The storm ceasing, we stood on to the west as the sea and the ice would suffer us . . .

THE CANADIAN AUTHOR Farley Mowat, writing in 1960, used these words from the account of Abacuk Prickett, a survivor of Henry Hudson's 1610 voyage in search of the Northwest Passage, to illustrate the mixture of fear and determination that marked European efforts in search of a northwest route to Asia. From the moment the first Crusaders returned to gloomy, rain-sodden Europe with tales of—and a taste for—the riches, spices, fruit and other wonders of that sunlit East, the seed of desire was planted in European minds to find a route to the Orient, to the ultimate source of all that Europe seemed to lack. With the rediscovery of the New World that came with the European explosion out onto the open ocean in the late 1400s, itself a product of Renaissance awakening and Turkish limitations on trade access to the East, that desire reached its full power. The spectacular discoveries by the Spanish of the Aztec and Inca empires, the

Portuguese success in reaching India, and the wealth from both that began to flow back to the Iberian continent filled the men of the wet north with a longing to partake of these riches. The Spanish and Portuguese retained a jealous monopoly on the new trade routes around Africa to India and beyond, and across the southern Atlantic to America, and were prepared to defend those routes against the interloping French, Dutch and English. To these last, the challenge was clear: a northerly, preferably westerly route direct to China and the Indies out of reach of the Iberians was the key to opening northern Europe's own river of gold and silver, and the wealth of Cathay and the Indies.

The discovery of land in the west in the 1490s suggested to the European imagination that outlying islands of Asia had in fact been reached; it would only require a further bit of coastal voyaging westward before the fabled cities of China would be in sight. That dream died hard: 150 years later, French explorers in Canada brought along dress robes in their birchbark canoes in case the court of the Great Khan was stumbled on somewhere west of the Mattawa River.

Of all the early North American explorers, it may have been Sebastian Cabot, son of Giovanni Caboto who had found either Newfoundland or Cape Breton in 1497, who first realized that the Americas constituted a separate continent, and one that would have to be got around if China were to be reached. The Canadian classicist L.H. Neatby, writing in 1958, observed that Cabot had said as much to the Spanish scholar Peter Martyr in 1502, theorizing to him that "there should be certain great open places" to the north of America "whereby the waters should flow from the East unto the West." In that same year of 1502, Cabot may have made the first attempt at the Northwest Passage to China. Martyr's account relates that

> hee therefore furnished two ships in Englande at his own charges, and first with 300 men directed his course so farre towards the North Pole, than even in the moneth of July he found monstrous heaps of ice swimming in the sea, and in a

manner continual daylight, and yet hee saw the land in that tract free from ice, which had been melted by the heat of the sunne.

Where Cabot actually sailed is not known, and he did not return to the northwestern Atlantic—if he had been there at all—devoting himself instead to a "Muscovy Company" intent on reaching Russia via the top of Norway.

The pressure on the English and other Europeans to brave Arctic waters in pursuit of the wealth of the Indies lay in the Treaty of Tordesillas of 1494, handed down by the Pope to the Spanish and Portuguese, and which, as we saw in chapter 4, essentially gave Spain claim to all of the Americas except Brazil. With the Portuguese dominating access to the Indian Ocean, the Spanish gaining in their conquest of the Netherlands and set to control English access to Europe, and the Spanish and Portuguese crowns about to unite, the English virtually had nowhere to go but northwest or northeast. The latter would prove unproductive, with death in the ice off Spitsbergen or Svalbard awaiting those who attempted to reach the modest if exotic riches of "Muscovy." The choice, then, was either to raid as an outlaw the huge world ocean empire the Iberians were claiming, or to try for the Northwest Passage. The issue was compounded after Magellan's 1519 passage through the strait named for him by the Spanish "closure" of it to all but their own shipping. It was with this as motivation that the sixteenth-century voyages of Frobisher, Davis and others were mounted, and that of Hudson in the early seventeenth. Beneath it all, of course, was far less a thirst for geopolitical knowledge than a simple greed for gold.

The first known significant voyage that had as its direct goal the finding of the Passage was mounted by Thomas Button, who sailed in May 1612 with Hudson's *Discovery* and another vessel, the *Resolution* (Cook's expedition in the 1770s would echo these names). With him was the taciturn and acquitted survivor of Hudson's voyage, Robert Bylot. Button's backers had given him orders that were simple enough: besides looking for Hudson—a search that was soon abandoned—he was not to come back "without either the good news of a Passage, or sufficient assurance of an impossibility." Making a safe crossing of the Atlantic, Button went through Hudson Strait then continued sailing west until he arrived at its western shore. Appropriately naming this place Hope Check'd, he turned south to about latitude 57° north, near the mouths of the Nelson and Hayes rivers. There he overwintered, remarkably successfully as it turned out. In the next year, 1613, Button voyaged north up Hudson Bay's west coast until he reached 65° north, then turned for home. He reached England safely, having found the mouths of the Nelson and Churchill rivers, and having proved that Hudson Bay, at least, was not the sea route to Cathay.

Robert Bylot soon found himself back in Canadian waters, when merchant backers sent the redoubtable *Discovery* west again, this time with Bylot commanding, assisted by a veteran Greenland whaler, William Baffin. Their 1615 voyage was unremarkable; they entered Hudson Bay, turned north and were almost immediately blocked by ice. But on the return to England the observant Baffin suggested that the next direction in which to look would be northward up the open waters of Davis Strait. The merchants agreed, and in 1616 Bylot and Baffin returned in *Discovery*. The voyage came closer to succeeding than might be imagined as, rounding the southern tip of Greenland, *Discovery* worked her way up as far as 78° north, or the later Smith Sound, before turning back because of ice and cold, an astonishing achievement. Coasting down the west side of Davis Strait, Bylot and Baffin saw Lancaster Sound—the mouth of the true Northwest Passage—but were certain it was a large bay due to heavy pack ice. From there, *Discovery* steered for Greenland and home. Of the odd and mysterious Bylot nothing more is heard, while Baffin died in a trade war in the Persian Gulf. Had ice, visibility and other factors been different, their names might have had a far greater posterity.

The end of the 1616 voyage marked the beginning of a long hiatus in the search for the Passage, as Europe became embroiled in other matters. There were a few exceptions to this general lack of interest. As described in chapter 5, the Dane Jens Munk visited Hudson Bay in 1619; and in 1631 there were two merchant-backed expeditions, one under Luke Foxe and the other under Thomas James. Thereafter, as Neatby relates, "for a generation after the voyage of James, [the English] gave up the northwestern enterprise and forgot the bay of Hudson as completely as that of Baffin, until a chance quarrel in New France revived their interest and perhaps altered the history of the entire continent."

The "chance quarrel" was the argument between the administration of New France and the fur traders Radisson and Des Groseilliers. That dispute, as we have seen, led to the establishment of the Hudson's Bay Company in 1670 and renewed English interest in the Arctic. But with that renewed commercial interest in the fur trade into Hudson Bay came once more the elusive goal of finding the Northwest Passage. And this had a new urgency, as the mercantile system that pitted the newly emerging European nations against one another in worldwide economic competition made easy access to China and India of increasing importance. Fundamental to the English search was the idea of the Strait of Anian, the mythical waterway leading from Hudson Bay to the Pacific coast of North America.

First off the mark after the long pause was Hudson's Bay employee James Knight, who in 1718 set off up the west coast of Hudson Bay in search of both the strait and rumoured gold deposits. He found neither, but instead was wrecked and died with all his men, stranded on Marble Island. It would be twenty-three years after this grim event before someone would again seek the strait. In 1741 the Admiralty sent out a sloop of war under a Captain Middleton to search for the Strait of Anian, at the urging—and with the healthy support—of a wealthy merchant, William Dobbs. To Dobbs's disappointment, Middleton competently got himself to Hudson Bay, briefly explored the promising Chesterfield Inlet, and sailed home with no result other than survival.

There was another gap of thirty years. Then the land treks of fur trade employees Samuel Hearne, in 1771–72, and Alexander

First Communication with the Natives of Prince Regent's Bay, 1818 C 119412

Mackenzie found no intervening strait leading west, and brought them to the shores of the Arctic Ocean, where they discovered only an ice-choked sea that seemed entirely unnavigable. In 1778 the third voyage of the intrepid Captain Cook arrived on the Pacific coast from Hawaii, intent on finding the Passage from the west side, if it existed. Cook's two ships worked their way from Vancouver Island—he had missed the Strait of Juan de Fuca, as we have seen—up the Alaskan coast into the Bering Sea. There, the ships "turned the corner" across the top of Alaska and began to work eastward across the roof of North America—only to be stopped by pack ice off the appropriately named Icy Cape. Cook's ships turned away, to his death in Hawaii, a second fruitless attempt to probe the Arctic ice and, finally, the sad return of the expedition to England. The wars against the rebellious American colonies and Napoleonic France, and the War of 1812, halted English naval exploratory interest in the Northwest Passage, and only the fragments of Arctic sea shoreline revealed by Hearne and Mackenzie suggested what the sea road to the Orient might actually look like.

In 1818, with the Congress of Vienna having restored order in Europe, with Napoleon sealed off like a plague bacillus on the faraway island of St. Helena, and with the young United States a rea-

sonable if not yet amicable trading partner, Britain turned its attention once again to the Northwest Passage. Captain John Ross was
sent out, seconded by Lieutenant William Parry, to survey Baffin
Bay and probe for a passage westward. Ross's survey of Baffin's coast
was useful, but he incorrectly identified Lancaster Sound as an inlet,
an observation with which Parry disagreed. Their Lordships of the
Admiralty disagreed as well, as Parry was sent back the next year,
1819, to try his luck in Lancaster Sound. There would be a difference with Parry's effort, however, in the form of the addition of a
simultaneous land-based exploratory thrust into the Arctic, one
that would add the most famous name to the story of the Northwest
Passage: Sir John Franklin.

For the 1819 effort, the Admiralty ordered then lieutenant John
Franklin, who had been to Spitsbergen, to voyage to Canada and
trek overland to the mouth of the Coppermine River, found by
Hearne in the eighteenth century. From there, Franklin was to use
canoes to chart the coast east to Hudson Bay. It was a daunting and
almost fatal assignment, in which Franklin reached the mouth of
the Coppermine, found the canoes that had been so laboriously
carried there to be useless in the ice-jammed waters, and only made
it back southward with a few survivors due to timely Indian help. It
was 1822 before Franklin finally regained the safety of England.

His counterpart at sea, William Parry, had a far more productive
experience. On May 20, 1819, Parry sailed with HMS *Hecla*, a full-
rigged ship of 375 tons, and a little 180-ton brig, the *Griper*. His
orders were clear: achieve the Northwest Passage by Lancaster
Sound, if possible. To encourage the crews, the ships' companies
would share in £10,000 if the Passage was found and £5,000 if the
ships managed to reach 110° west longitude. It was a powerful
incentive, and Parry was favoured with good winds and an easy
transit of the North Atlantic, as well as light ice conditions in Lancaster Sound. Their spirits rising with each westward nautical mile
reeled off, the expedition pressed on until, on September 1, 1819,
off the shores of Melville Island, they achieved the first goal of
110° west longitude. Abruptly encountering heavy pack ice soon

thereafter, Parry ordered the ships to prepare for winter at a cove on Melville Island's south shore, known thereafter as Winter Harbour. Thanks to the thoroughness with which Parry had prepared the expedition, and his leadership of it, the crews survived the long, dark winter well.

The next year, it took until August 1 to hack the ships free of the ice and attempt to sail west again. Open water beckoned for a time, but finally the ships came up against permanent pack ice originating in the Beaufort Sea. Ahead in the distance, Parry could make out land he christened Banks Land, after Sir Joseph Banks, the semi-legendary president of the Royal Society. The ships were at 113° 4' 43.5" west longitude, and Parry had come within an ace of reaching the Beaufort Sea itself, completing the Passage. It was not to be, however, and the ships turned for home, reaching England safely. It was the most successful voyage of Parry's career. In 1821–23 he returned with two ships, HMS *Hecla* and *Fury*, spending fruitless months trying to find outlets from Hudson Bay. Parry returned again in 1824–25, losing *Fury* to the ice but bringing all safe home in *Hecla*, a commendable achievement in itself.

As Parry returned to a deserved hero's welcome, John Franklin prepared to confront again the land that had almost killed him, and certainly had claimed the lives of many of his shipmates. Travelling with an astonishing display of endurance overland to the Arctic Ocean again, he carried out a survey of portions of its westward stretch of coastline to which a later land expedition led by George— later Sir George—Back would add much more information. The perimeter of the northern mainland was becoming known; but the passage by sea still eluded discovery.

A new expedition was mounted in 1829, led by John Ross, Parry's commander in 1818, but funded privately this time by businessman Felix Booth. Ross sailed his ship, the *Victory*, into Lancaster Sound and then down into a dead end in the Gulf of Boothia. The *Victory* was trapped and destroyed in the ice there, but Ross would earn a knighthood by the fortitude with which he kept his freezing, starving men alive through months of struggle, then led them north in the ship's boats, sailing and rowing north and then east along Lancaster Sound until they reached the open waters of Davis Strait, where astonished Greenland whalers rescued them. It was 1833.

Three years later, as the Canadian colonies were about to explode in open rebellion, the navy tried once more to crack the nut of the Passage, sending into the hunt this time HMS *Terror*, 340 tons, under the command of the redoubtable land explorer George Back. Back achieved little and returned with no new knowledge, but earned the admiration of all for his leadership in extracting his damaged ship and crew from the ice and getting them home safely after a year's entrapment. Back's return voyage marks the beginning of a second major hiatus in the maritime search for the Northwest Passage. During that period, roughly 1836 to 1844, the principal achievement in Arctic exploration was the surveying by land of large portions of the Arctic Ocean coastline by Hudson's Bay employee Thomas Simpson. Simpson would die in mysterious circumstances in the United States while on his way to New York in 1840, but not before a journal of his discoveries had been made available.

In 1844, the Royal Geographical Society urgently appealed for a final resolution of the Northwest Passage mystery, with Simpson's journal being the catalyst. As L.H. Neatby effectively summarized, it led to the last—and ultimately successful, if also tragic—chapter of the story:

> The publication of Simpson's journal . . . had extended the map of the continental shoreline in an easterly direction to longitude 95 degrees, overlapping by eighteen degrees Parry's westerly penetration to longitude 113 degrees, and had narrowed the problem of the Northwest Passage to the gap of something over three hundred miles which separated Barrow Strait and Melville Sound from the continental shoreline. There

was a general feeling that this obstacle could easily be overcome, and in 1844, shortly after the return of Ross and Franklin from [posts in] the Antipodes, the Royal Geographical Society requested the Admiralty to make the attempt. Their Lordships consented, and ordered the *Erebus* and *Terror* to be refitted for this purpose.

In command of these ships was the veteran Arctic land explorer Sir John Franklin, no stranger to conditions in the Canadian Arctic. Franklin sailed in May 1845, with orders to attempt to find the Northwest Passage to the *south* of Lancaster Sound. The *Erebus* and the *Terror* were steam-assisted sailing vessels, specially rebuilt to survive Arctic navigation and pack ice conditions. Franklin had 129 chosen officers and men, and supplies to last four years, including new forms of canned rations. As the Canadian author Farley Mowat observed, writing in 1960:

> It was accepted as a certainty that Franklin would succeed. Yet, after speaking to some whalers off Greenland in July of 1845, he, with his two ships and all their people, vanished from the known world. During the succeeding fourteen years the attempt to solve the mystery of their disappearance resulted in an assault upon the Arctic which was not to be equalled in weight or intensity until the late 1940s brought the US Navy steaming north to take *de facto* possession of Canadian waters.

It would later be learned that Franklin had entered Lancaster Sound and then, in obedience of his orders, had turned south down what became known as Franklin Strait, to the west of King William Island. His way blocked there by impenetrable ice, Franklin lost his ships, and he and his men would all die attempting to march out pulling boats, possibly poisoned by faulty canning methods in their food supply.

The year 1848 brought the first serious expedition in search of Franklin, beginning a process in which Lady Franklin would

Abandoning Franklin's Vessels, by Sir Julius V. Payer PA 147986

expend most of her private fortune paying for three expeditions. On the first one, Sir John Ross sailed with HM ships *Enterprise* and *Investigator*. With him was a remarkable young lieutenant, Francis M'Clintock, who established a name for himself by pioneering and carrying out new methods of shore exploration. Mowat relates:

> As a young lieutenant in the Navy, M'Clintock had first gone north with the earliest Franklin "relief" party, the [Ross] expedition of 1848–49, during which he did considerable sledge travelling in the then-fashionable manner, with sailors pulling heavily overladen sledges while the officers kept themselves aloof from work; and where there was little or no reliance upon living off the land. M'Clintock at once recognized the basic stupidity of this procedure, and during his next Arctic voyage, with Captain Austin's [Franklin search] expedition in 1850, he began to experiment, not only with new and lighter sleds and equipment, but with the general possibilities of adapting himself and his material to the real nature of the country.

M'Clintock's innovations, and the need to examine a great deal of country in a very short time, meant that the previous methods of exploration, which kept the explorers trapped aboard ship, were set aside. The new ways provided the naval explorers with the means not only of eventually finding the remains of Franklin, but of solving at last the riddle of the Northwest Passage itself. M'Clintock would later have a key role in determining what had happened to Franklin.

That moment was about to arrive. On January 20, 1850, two vessels, HMS *Enterprise*, under Captain Richard Collinson, and HMS *Investigator*, under Commander Robert John Le Mesurier McClure, sailed from England bound for Cape Horn. Their intention was to attempt resolution of the question of the Northwest Passage from the *west*. They safely rounded Cape Horn, paused at Hawaii and then sailed for the Bering Strait. The two ships became separated, and McClure in *Investigator* crossed the Arctic Circle alone on July 29, 1850. From that point, as James Cook had done seventy-two years previously, McClure "turned the corner" eastward across the top of Alaska and began to work his way through the ice toward the distant Canadian archipelago. Neatby related the climactic moment:

> On October the 21st, McClure and Court left the ship with a sledge crew, and on the 26th reached Point Russell, the NE extremity of Banks Land, so proving the waters of [McClure] Strait continuous with the open sea [of Viscount Melville Sound] beyond. Though the autumn twilight hid Melville Island from their view, observations made it certain that the coast trending NW from Point Russell was the very "loom of land" to which Parry had given the name of Banks Land thirty years before. The ocean passage from Atlantic to Pacific was complete.

McClure and his men very nearly did not survive to receive the £10,000 prize for the finding of the Northwest Passage. *Investigator* had to be abandoned in the ice, and its haggard crew were rescued by other ships.

The first successful passages of the route were still far in the future, with the first—if lengthy—transit westward of the Northwest Passage being achieved by a small Norwegian herring boat, the *Gjoa*, captained by Roald Amundsen, between 1903 and 1905. Later, be-

Skulls of members of the Franklin Expedition before burial

tween 1905 and 1911, the waters sailed by virtually all the explorers who had sought the Passage were visited by the sturdy steamer *Arctic*, under the command of a legendary Canadian seaman, Captain J.E. Bernier. The final footnote to the search for the Passage came in the Second World War, when the little wooden RCMP schooner *St. Roch*, under the command of Sergeant Henry Larsen, made a double passage of the route, once in each direction. It was an extraordinary achievement, yet treated matter-of-factly by Larsen and his crew. The ice, if not beaten, had at last given up its secrets.

As historian George Thomson observed, writing in 1975:

For hundreds of years, daring men in fragile ships challenged the Arctic wastes of what would become northern Canada in search of the route to all the fabled riches of India and Cathay—the Northwest Passage. From a merely commercial proposition—the quest for wealth to gratify the dynastic dreams and to fill the empty coffers of the Elizabethans—the search became the obsession of a steady stream of colourful and dauntless adventurers, each of whom pitted his imagination, strength and cunning against the mysterious and unyielding land of ice and snow.

With the disappearance of that unyielding ice and snow, the waters of the Northwest Passage are entering a dramatic and uncertain new chapter in their history. The Passage, and the northern archipelago through which it tracks, has become a matter of international contention. The islands to the north of mainland Canada were transferred by the British government to Canadian control in 1880, and since that time Canada has considered the waters surrounding the vast island group as "archipelagic waters" as defined by the United Nations Convention on the Law of the Sea, and, as such, completely under Canadian control. Led by the United States, nations that maintain substantial seaborne traffic disagree with this designation, and insist that the waters of the Northwest Passage, amidst the Canadian islands, constitute international waters in which vessels of all nations have a right of transit, and in which Canada cannot deny vessels such passage.

As the Arctic warms, the great concern for Canada is to demonstrate and maintain sovereignty over the Arctic archipelago and its waters, to ensure that any development there is undertaken in Canada's interests, and particularly that the environmentally fragile Arctic waters are subject to the protection of enforceable Canadian pollution regulations. There is a sense of urgency to this debate now, but it was not always so, as Canadian Arctic mariner Captain J.E. Bernier bemoaned in a 1909 speech to the Empire Club of Canada:

> In 1880 the Imperial Government gave to Canada this immense territory in the North, but nobody made any efforts, not even the Canadian people, to use what England had given us. What they gave us cost them nearly two million pounds, and the British exploration of the North cost seven hundred and fifty lives; and one hundred and fifty different expeditions were sent to search for one of the greatest men of that time—Sir John Franklin—who gave his life to find the Northwest Passage.

The transfer of responsibility to Canada handed over a vast territory and seas that were imperfectly known. The Canadian government declared ownership of all lands, discovered or undiscovered, as far north as the Pole, but had neither the resources nor the apparent inclination to establish a permanent Canadian presence in the North. Leading up to the Second World War and the groundbreaking voyage of the little *St. Roch*, there had been only two really noteworthy Canadian bursts of activity into the Arctic. One was the remarkable sovereignty voyages of the Canadian Government Ship *Arctic*, under the command of Captain Bernier, in the years 1904 to 1911, and the other, the mercurial and controversial career of the Icelandic-Canadian explorer and northern enthusiast Vilhjalmur Stefansson, who led among other activities the Canadian Arctic Expedition of 1913–18 into the western Arctic. Stefansson was not without his detractors, but a particularly astute biographer, D.M. LeBourdais, writing in 1963, bemoaned the fact that Stefansson's message urging greater Canadian involvement in the North had been largely ignored, with consequences that ring particularly true in the resource-hungry twenty-first century:

If, during the twenties and thirties, Canadians had been aware of the value of their North, thousands of men who sat in idleness through the Depression might have been engaged—for the good of the country and for their own good—in a far-reaching project of integrating it into the rest of Canada. If the millions spent in next-to-worthless schemes had been devoted to this purpose, Canada today might have been at least a generation further advanced . . . When it is realized that since 1958 it has been known to geologists that islands discovered by Stefansson in 1915–16 (and ignored until recently) constitute a portion of what some day may be known as one of the chief oil-concentration areas of the world, some idea may be gained of the great cost to Canada of the wasted years.

If Bernier's energy and commitment left any legacy in the North, it was in the sovereignty that he declared on Canada's behalf, at least to the lands. The seas would be another matter.

We have planted our flag on Baffin's Land, Violet Island, Griffith's Island, King William Island, and many others. On the first day of July last year [1908], on Confederation Day, I had a slab made and on that slab I wrote, "This memorial is erected here today to commemorate the taking possession of all the Arctic archipelago." I was doing a wholesale business, taking possession for Canada of all lands and islands to the eastward of the international line between Alaska and Canada on the 141st meridian as far north as 90 degrees north. The Pole was not mentioned because it is an invisible point, but 90 degrees north, that is a quarter of the globe, and I claimed all that land for Canada as a whole. It seems that the United States has agreed to that, because she says we are mistress of all the lands to the North.

With the realization in the 1950s that Canada's Arctic would be a resource-rich hunting ground for anyone able to exploit it, the debate began in earnest as to whether the waters between the Canadian islands were Canadian, as Canada insisted, or waters of international passage, as the Americans and others claimed. The American government was anxious to secure easy transportation of oil from newly discovered oil fields on Alaska's North Slope to the southern forty-eight states, and it would have been useful if the American claim that the Canadian waters were straits with right of free passage could have been backed up by actual passages made without reference to Canada.

An attempt was made in 1969 to demonstrate the feasibility of Northwest Passage commercial traffic, when the American super-tanker *Manhattan*, with a specially ice-strengthened hull, attempted to voyage through the Passage and return. Canada was "informed" of the voyage, but no permissions were sought. It would have strengthened the American depiction of Canadian Arctic waters as international ones had the *Manhattan* managed the voyage on its own. However, only the presence of a Canadian icebreaker, the *Sir John A. Macdonald*, and some help from an American coast guard vessel allowed the great tanker to complete its voyage. As Arctic historian Ross Coen, writing in 2004, observed, the *Manhattan*'s voyage simply posed even more questions beyond those of contested national jurisdictions:

> The voyage of the S.S. *Manhattan*, an icebreaking tanker that traversed the Northwest Passage, proved commercial use of the Canadian Arctic as a marine transportation route was feasible, but difficult and prohibitively expensive. However, as global climate change reduces [the] coverage of circumpolar sea ice, an increase in trans-Arctic shipping and offshore oil exploration [is certain]. The *Manhattan*'s experimental, data-gathering voyage was predicated on the belief that scientific [research] and technological innovation could overcome any challenge posed by the Arctic environment. [This conclusion] occurred largely to the exclusion of meaningful consideration of how such industrial expansion will affect the north itself. The voyage of the *Manhattan* provides an historical baseline of sorts indicating that industrial development in the Canadian Arctic will similarly depend on the application of science and technology on a massive scale; yet such scientific endeavours must be placed in an appropriate context where social, economic, political, and environmental impacts are considered.

It is ironic that these northern Canadian waters, once explored at such human and material cost simply because they might serve as a route to riches elsewhere, are about to be contested for because of the riches they themselves retain. The battle for control and development of the Northwest Passage, and of Canada's Arctic legacy, has only just begun.

13

The
Inland
Seas

The beauty of the shore of that sweet sea! Here we saw fishes of divers
[sorts], some like the sturgeon & have a kind of slice att the end of their nose
some three fingers broad in the end and 2 only neere the nose, and some
8 thumbs long, all marbled of a blakish color. There are birds whose bills
are two and 20 thumbs long. That bird swallows a whole salmon, keeps it
a long time in his bill. We saw also shee goats very big. There is an animal
somewhat lesse than a cow whose meat is exceedingly good. There is no
want of Staggs or Buffs. There are so many Tourkeys that the boys throw
stones att them for their recreation . . .

WHEN EUROPEANS like Pierre Radisson gazed
out over the Great Lakes, they were astonished
to realize that their waters were not salt, but
fresh. Gradually their understanding grew that these five enormous
bodies of water were not an arm of the western sea that led to
Cathay and India, but a system of independent freshwater lakes of
a startling size. Together, Lakes Ontario, Erie, Huron, Michigan
and Superior make up the largest group of freshwater lakes on the
planet, and, with the St. Lawrence River that drains them into the
Atlantic, the largest freshwater system. An early explorer on their
waters wrote in his journal that the Lakes were "as wide and terrible
as any sea," and they are in truth inland seas, offering to navigators
all the challenges of an ocean save that of tidal flows.

With 20 percent of the world's surface fresh water held in them, the Great Lakes are dotted with over 35,000 islands and have a total coastline of some 12,500 miles. The Lakes are deep enough to hold a total volume of 5,500 cubic miles, or enough to cover most of mainland Canada with a shallow sea between six and ten feet deep. A remnant of the last great ice age, which ended some ten thousand years ago, the Great Lakes are the remaining deposits of glacial meltwater and of a much larger inland sea that once covered a good deal of eastern North America.

For the First Nations, the Great Lakes were resources for fishing during the summer months and a highway for coastal travel in birchbark and dugout. Having not developed open-water craft like the west coast nations, the eastern woodlands peoples did not navigate on the Lakes as such; that would await the coming of the French. Even after the French began their serious westward exploration out of the St. Lawrence River valley in the 1600s, the extent of the Great Lakes was not learned for some time. Samuel de Champlain crossed Lake Ontario in his 1609 expedition with the Huron, but French canoe-borne explorations went north from Montreal along the Ottawa River to the Upper Lakes; ironically, Lake Erie was one of the last lakes to be found by the French.

The French gradually extended their fur trade posts and trading routes westward, following initially the Ottawa River route because of the access it gave to Georgian Bay and the rich fur lands of the Northwest, but also because the Native societies encountered there were less hostile. The St. Lawrence River and Lake Ontario marked the northern boundary of the lands of the Iroquois, who from 1609 until the Great Peace of 1701 were in an almost permanent state of war with New France. It was not until the mid-1600s that French posts were established on the Lower Lakes, and the first appearance of masts and sails on Lake Ontario likely occurred on July 12, 1673, when Governor Frontenac voyaged from Montreal to meet the Iroquois at Cataraqui—now Kingston—in a flotilla that included bateaux with square sails emblazoned with insignia to impress the Iroquois delegates. In the next year, 1674, René-Robert, Sieur de

La Salle, was granted a seigneury—a form of feudal land hold-ing—at Cataraqui, and serious boatbuilding began there soon after. Finally, in 1678, La Salle formally established a shipyard at Cataraqui, imported shipwrights to man it, and declared his inten-tion to build vessels for the expansion of the fur trade on Lake Ontario, Lake Erie and the Mississippi River. The yard at Cataraqui soon began to turn out multi-purpose open or partially decked boats of between twenty-five and forty tons—about the size of modern sailing yachts—of which the two-masted *bugalet* the *Frontenac* may have been the first example.

Before long, the French were voyaging to the upper end of Lake Ontario, at the mouth of the Niagara River. The journey of Father Hennepin, described in chapter 5, is the first recorded voyage by a true sailing vessel on the Great Lakes. That account related as well the appearance of La Salle's pioneering *Griffon* in 1679, the first ves-sel built on the Great Lakes above Niagara Falls. Its shipyard was located on the east bank of the Niagara River, across from Grand Island, at the mouth of the Cayuga River in modern New York State. The *Griffon*'s pioneering career was brief; she was lost return-ing from the head of the Lakes with a valuable cargo of furs, her resting place never to be found. Father Hennepin's account of the *Griffon*'s loss was quoted by Great Lakes historian Donald Bamford, writing in 2007:

> The ship came to an anchor to the North of the Lake of the Illi-nois, where she was seen by some Savages, who told us that they advised our Men to sail along the Coast, and not toward the middle of the Lake, because of the Sands that make the Naviga-tion dangerous when there is any high wind. Our Pilot, as I said before, was dissatisfy'd, and would steer as he pleas'd without harkening to the Advice of the Savages, who generally speaking, have more Sense than the Europeans think at first: but the ship was hardly a League from the Coast, when it was toss'd up in a violent Storm in such a manner, that our Men were never heard of since; and it is suppos'd that the Ship struck upon a Sand, and

was there bury'd. This was a great loss for M. la Salle and other Adventurists; for that ship, with its Cargo, cost about sixty thousand livres.

Through the first half of the eighteenth century, the French continued to maintain a small fleet of vessels, usually of the schooner variety, on the Lower Lakes, with one or more vessels operating on the Upper Lakes. These vessels were primarily concerned with carrying trade goods and trading post supplies up the lake system and returning large quantities of furs downstream. These ships complemented the canoe brigades passing along the Ottawa River to and from the Upper Lakes. Both the canoe and ship flotillas supported the flow of furs from the West and the Ohio valley back to Canada, as the French established their arc of posts from the St. Lawrence round the Great Lakes to the Mississippi and south to Louisiana. The principal seaport, if that is the correct term, remained at Cataraqui and Fort Frontenac, and by the time the last and definitive struggle for North America broke into open warfare in 1754, the French had a competent little squadron of armed vessels based at Cataraqui that, backed by a flotilla of open flatboats, constituted a substantial lake navy. The key vessels were *La Marquise de Vaudreuil*, a square-topsail schooner of 120 tons, with 20 guns; *La Hurault*, another square-topsail schooner, 90 tons and 14 guns; *La Louise*, a gaff-rigged schooner, 50 tons and 6 guns; and the little *Le Victor*, a sloop or cutter of 40 tons, which carried 4 small guns. This fleet, which had been built between 1749 and 1756, gave the French a considerable resource with which to dominate Lake Ontario, the posts on its shores and the shipping route up past Fort Niagara to the Upper Lakes.

The English were not about to allow uncontested French control of Lake Ontario, however. As the English pressed north and west from the Atlantic seaboard, they reached Lake Ontario at the mouth of the Oswego River. There they established a post and began to build a flotilla with which to challenge the French, and if possible siphon off the fur trade to the Mohawk River valley

Boats in ice, Lake Superior *C 25922*

and on to Albany and New York. By 1755 the English had launched
two 100-ton sloops of 5 guns each at Oswego, the *Oswego* and the
Ontario, and soon added to them two schooners, the *Vigilant* and
the *George*. Donald Bamford relates:

> [The schooner's] dimensions are unknown, but they were prob-
> ably not much larger than the earlier sloops, for they could be
> moved by sweeps (oars) if becalmed. They were armed the same
> as the *Ontario* and *Oswego*. Altogether eleven ships were built
> between the years 1755 and 1759. One hundred whaleboats,
> pinnaces and galleys were added to the small fleet, all in readi-
> ness for an assault on Fort Frontenac and Niagara.

As Bamford observes, the creation of this fleet at Oswego was a
remarkable feat, given that the English did not have the relative ease
of shipment of supplies by water up the St. Lawrence. However, the
fleet engaged in only one tentative clash with the French squadron,
on June 27, 1756. Led by *La Marquise de Vaudreuil*, the four French
ships encountered the English flotilla on the open lake and closed in

for a fight. The English flotilla chose to beat a hasty retreat, losing a vessel in the process and earning the scorn of the French, including that of the newly arrived Louis-Antoine de Bougainville, aide-de camp to the French military commander, the Marquis de Montcalm-Gozon. Bougainville's journal entry read:

> Received news of the taking of an English shallop, armed with nine swivels, on Lake Ontario, our armed craft met those of the English on their first reconnaissance. The English manoeuvred to give chase, but, seeing us advance instead of turning tail, they fled. Maxim of the English at sea: avoid combat when only on equal or slightly superior terms on the same principle that one gives one's purse to any thief that demands it, even in a public place and within reach of help. The crew, to a number of sixteen men, has been sent to Quebec. A petty victory like all achieved in this country, but interesting because of the impression of superiority that it gives our Indians.

This "petty victory" was an omen for the future, as, in the pattern of bold success that characterized French strategy in North America from 1754 to 1757, a French force under the command of Montcalm arrived unexpectedly off Oswego on August 14, 1756, and carried off an assault landing that captured the post—and the English Lake Ontario fleet—at one stroke.

France now had control of Lake Ontario. The British, however, then mounted the climactic, three-pronged campaign of 1758–60 that was aimed at the heartland of Canada. The British didn't attempt to rebuild a Lake Ontario fleet, but instead returned north to retake Oswego by land, and then quickly moved their huge force by bateaux and longboats to Cataraqui, which they promptly captured and destroyed. Fort Niagara soon followed into English hands. All but two of the French fleet were burned at Cataraqui, and new English vessels were built for Lake Ontario, facing no serious challenge. Lake Ontario, and all above it, was essentially in English hands.

The French still controlled the St. Lawrence, and in the spring of 1759 they launched two armed vessels on the river near modern Maitland, Ontario: the brig *L'Outaouaise* and the ship-rigged (three-masted) *L'Iroquoise*. Each vessel, regardless of rig, was what the French called a corvette, a kind of small frigate or sloop of war. They carried anything up to 18 guns each, and were the principal French means remaining afloat of repulsing an English descent of the river.

The capture of Cataraqui had been carried out by Colonel John Bradstreet in 1758; now, in 1760, the British pincer was closing on Canada. A column from Quebec, taken in 1759, was moving up-river toward the French last stand at Montreal; a second column was ascending Lake Champlain; and the major force, thousands of men in hundreds of flatboats escorted by newly built small warships, was descending the St. Lawrence under Major General Jeffrey Amherst, with Montreal as its goal. In the way stood a gallant little garrison in the island fort of Lévis; a few small gunboats; and the guns of *L'Iroquoise* and *L'Outaouaise*. For *L'Iroquoise* the end came ignominiously: she ran aground in the St. Lawrence, was deemed unfit to serve and was sunk a few days later by the advancing English flotilla. *L'Outaouaise* was brought to bay off modern Prescott, Ontario, by a swarm of British gunboats armed with heavy long guns in their bows. Outmanoeuvred in the windless waters by the rowing boats and pummelled by their guns, *L'Outaouaise* struck her colours at midday. After a gallant defence Fort de Lévis fell to the English, and Amherst's army rolled on unchecked to Montreal.

L'Outaouaise survived the campaign, entering into British service as His Majesty's Provincial Vessel *Williamson*, only to be wrecked in Lake Ontario in 1761. As she sank, she carried with her the last surviving physical evidence of the French naval presence on the inland seas. A small flotilla on Lake Champlain, built on the Richelieu River, had been scuttled in the lake ahead of an advancing British flotilla.

As the Seven Years War drew to a close, the British consolidated their hold on Canada and began to establish a small fleet of government ships on the Upper and Lower Lakes, initially under the command of Royal Navy officers. This led to the construction of four schooners on the upper Niagara River above the Falls, for use on Lake Erie and above: the *Royal Charlotte*, *Victory*, *Michigan* and *Huron*, all built on the appropriately named Navy Island. On Lake Ontario, the British established a naval base and shipyard on Carleton Island, in the St. Lawrence River. Initially this post, and the vessels built and operated from it, was under navy control as well, but in 1777, with the American Revolution well under way, the British turned over control of all vessels on the Lakes to a branch of the Quartermaster Corps of the army, the Provincial Marine.

Under the Provincial Marine, a substantial little fleet was created that gave Britain essential control of the waters of Lake Ontario, the St. Lawrence and the Upper Lakes. A number of the vessels it launched, such as the 220-ton *Ontario* of 1780 and the *Limnade* of 1781, sailed Lake Ontario with little threat other than weather—which nonetheless sank the *Ontario* the year she was launched. On the Upper Lakes, the establishment of Amherstburg on the Detroit River in 1796 provided a base for the Provincial Marine. Through the years 1783–12 the Provincial Marine, quasi–shipping company, quasi–naval force, became manned almost entirely by Canadians, and in some respects was Canada's first indigenous naval force, an ancestor of the modern Canadian navy. Sailing alongside the workhorse vessels of the Provincial Marine during this period were a growing number of small trading, lumber and fur trade schooners and sloops that had begun to ply the Lakes as soon as the proscription against private shipping was lifted in 1788. One of these was the packet schooner *Lord Nelson*, which would prove to be one of the first American captures of the War of 1812, taken as it ran a cargo of flour between Kingston and Newark—now Niagara-on-the-Lake—Ontario.

It was under the aegis and with the assistance of the Provincial Marine that the Loyalist settlement of much of Ontario took place, not counting the refugees from the American Revolution who trekked by land to the Niagara, Detroit or Lake Champlain frontiers. Sailing from the Loyalists' assembly point at Sorel, Quebec, the refugees moved inland up the great river in a scene captured well by the Canadian historian A.R.M. Lower, writing in 1946:

> We can picture the procession of barges that set out in the spring of 1784: Settlers, animals, supplies, tools, all piled in together, for the attack on the wilderness in the new townships surveyed between the last French settlements and the Bay of Quinté. The convoy would move slowly along, sailing, poling, rowing, and as it came to the spots decided on, some of the barges would drop off, leaving their occupants to face the woods that were henceforth to be their home.

The full story of the role of the Provincial Marine in the settlement and development of early Upper Canada is a tale still waiting to be told.

The War of 1812, and its breaking of thirty years or so of peace on the frontier and the Lakes, has been touched on elsewhere in this narrative. But one story was not mentioned that deserves to be: the adventure and fate of the government Upper Lakes schooner *Nancy*. The *Nancy* was a beautiful sixty-foot double square-topsail schooner that had been built in 1789 for the fur trade at a boatyard located just south of Fort Detroit, on the later American side of the river. Until 1812 the schooner was in the service of fur trade companies based at Montreal, trading to the Upper Lakes. When war broke out, the schooner was signed into the Provincial Marine but remained essentially a supply ship for the fur trade. With the arrival of the Royal Navy's authority at Amherstburg in 1813, the vessel became HM Schooner *Nancy* and was employed carrying supplies from Matchedash, a port just east of Penetanguishene, Ontario, at the head of a long supply route from York—now Toronto—to the Upper Lakes posts at Mackinac and elsewhere.

In the year 1814, an American squadron had sailed north up Lake Huron to recapture the fortified post at Michilimackinac, and on the return voyage it spotted the *Nancy* lying hidden up the

Nottawasaga River, at modern Wasaga Beach, Ontario. The *Nancy* was destroyed by a bombardment, but her commander, Miller Worsley, exacted a dramatic revenge from the Americans. Still in possession of some supplies desperately needed by Fort Mackinac—which had repulsed the American squadron's attack—Worsley and his men took two bateaux and a large fur trade canoe and rowed and paddled almost 450 miles up to the head of Georgian Bay. There, they spotted two schooners from the American squadron, the *Tigress* and the *Scorpion*, that had been left behind to blockade the Upper Lakes posts. In a daring boat action, Worsley and his men captured both schooners by boarding them. Renamed the *Confiance* and the *Surprise*, they entered British service, and after the War of 1812 were based at Dunnville, Ontario, until 1831.

The War of 1812 had brought into sharper focus the fact that, with Baltic timber difficult for Britain to obtain for its shipbuilding programs, Canadian timber had become more and more significant as a resource. The hunger for these vast stands of timber opened the door to the third great industry of Canada after the fishery and the fur trade: the timber trade. As A.R.M. Lower wrote in 1946:

> [In 1810] the attack on the Canadian forest began. Since then it has never ceased, and year by year timber of every type has gone over to Great Britain . . . It had served its immediate purpose and had created a large forest industry in Canada devoted to the production of square timber and to a lesser extent, of "deals" in sawmills erected for the purpose. The new forest industry . . . was to be the colonies' salvation for it gave to them the only means of growth they could have had, their third staple, timber. Timber could support far more people than the other two, fish and fur. Canada, in many senses, has been hewn out of her forests.

As settlers flooded into Upper Canada after 1812, they landed from the schooners, barges and bateaux that had brought them to the forested shores and launched into the progression of jobs that marked the assault on the wilderness, thereby creating the first cargoes for the ships to carry back down the Lakes and the great river. The settlers would log off the land, building crude cabins but also providing timber to sell, once cut. The stumps were then pulled and burned for potash. The potash served as fertilizer and also allowed the purchase of seed for the first crops of wheat, barley and oats—all of which eventually could be carried by horseback, wagon or ox cart to the lakeshore and embarked for shipment in the schooners.

Between 1815 and 1850, before the coming of the railway, as the shores of Lakes Ontario, Erie, Huron and Michigan were being settled, water transport remained the cheapest and swiftest means of getting people and goods where they had to go, as roads were little better than mud-choked cart trails. Settlements on the Canadian side grew largely because companies had been formed to create them, and gradually a number of ports developed on the Lakes that could handle schooners and provide them with cargo. Port Stanley, Goderich, Southampton, Port Dover and a host of other port towns arose as thousands of British and American settlers came up the Lakes. Their route was a tested one: by riverboat, flatboat or bateau to Lake Ontario, then by schooner to Niagara, a crossing of the Niagara portage trail, and re-embarkation on Lake Erie for the passage onward.

The smoke of the battles of 1812–14 had barely cleared when smoke of another kind appeared over the Lakes, that of the steamship. Donald Bamford relates the moment:

> In 1815, a company of merchants at Kingston, Ontario, was formed to finance the construction of a steamship. In October of that year a contract was let to Messrs. Teabout and Chapman, both of whom had been shipwrights at [the USN base at] Sackets Harbor under Henry Eckford. The engines of the new ship came from the Birmingham firm of Boulton and Watt. The new vessel, the SS *Frontenac*, was launched at Finkles Point [near Bath, Ontario] on September 7, 1816, and thus started

the steam age on the lakes. The SS *Frontenac* was a resounding success.

Even as the steamers began to grow in numbers on the Lakes, the sailing vessel fleet expanded at an equal rate, carrying settlers up the system, bringing them supplies and carrying down their produce. Centres of shipbuilding developed, notably in the Bay of Quinte area on Lake Ontario. Eventually the fur trade vessels gave way—particularly after the collapse of the fur trade in 1821, when European men's hat fashions changed from beaver to silk—to the merchant schooners. The fleet grew apace with settlement, until by 1870 there were some two thousand sailing ships operating on the Great Lakes. The majority of them were jack-of-all-trades schooners, as Bamford describes:

> Every conceivable cargo, from the early shipments of furs, fish and grain, through ore and stone, copper, iron and limestone, lumber, manufactured articles, farm machinery, furniture and much, much more, was carried by sail in the early days. Gradually [steam] carriers took over the trade for high volume cargos, but sail continued to carry the package goods.

Schooner in full view *PA 60751*

The schooner was the generic lake boat—the term "ship" was never used on the Great Lakes by the seamen themselves; they were always "boats"—as it was a safer design than the square rig. The best designs were meant to be sailed by only a handful of men, two to a mast plus a helmsman in extreme conditions—far fewer than the labour-intensive square riggers.

Paralleling the growth on the Lakes of the general-purpose schooner—often marked by a distinctive triangular topsail, on the

THE INLAND SEAS | 231

foremast called a "rafee"—were smaller fishing boats that proliferated as the rich stocks of whitefish and other catches became
known. In Canadian lake ports whole classes of gaff-rigged fishing
smacks, never more than fifty feet in length, were built and sailed
out of ports that gave them their names—Huron boats, Mackinaw
boats and Collingwood boats among them. These stately and graceful little fishing craft lasted longer than the big cargo freighters as
steam overtook them, but as the twentieth century opened they
were vanishing, to be replaced by slab-sided, engine-driven "fish
tugs" of far more capacity but far less grace and beauty.

Some of the lake vessels carried only heavy raw materials, such as
the so-called "timber droghers" that carried down the vast cuts of
timber from the rapacious logging that denuded the Michigan and
Canadian shores to feed the eastern hunger for wood. Sailing with
them were "stone hookers," which carried down cut stone from
northern quarries for the new stone buildings of towns and cities
from Cleveland to Toronto, Hamilton and Rochester. After 1870
they and other sailing vessels on the Great Lakes slowly began to
vanish as side-wheel and then propellered steam vessels gradually
took over the navigation of the Lakes, beginning with the settlers'
passenger trade. The great schooners one by one had their rigs cut
down, and they became barges towed ignominiously in long lines
behind squat steam tugs that belched their way sootily up lakes
that had once known only the beauty of white sails spread before
the wind. The life of the Great Lakes sailing fleet had been brief:
by 1890 it was virtually over, although some small cargo schooners
were working well into the twentieth century.

The coming of steamboats to the Great Lakes after the War of
1812 meant that a parallel process of ship development took place,
in effect an expansion and development of both the sailing and
steam fleets until 1890, and then the gradual ascendancy of steamboats, which reached their final flowering in the years 1890 to
1929. As the renowned Great Lakes marine curator Maurice Smith
put it, writing in 2005:

A well-placed and timely technology, the steamboat was able to fully exploit the canal system and a natural highway of lakes and rivers that reached into the interior of the province. Although sailing vessels continued to carry low-value bulk cargo into the 20th Century, steamboats introduced, probably for the first time in history, the idea of regularity in transportation for the average traveller. Overcoming the limited manoeuvrability of sailing ships, steamboats moved directly into the wind and waves, making predictable progress—most of the time. Passengers could depart from Kingston and travel directly to York, exactly as advertised. It was the steamboat that helped power the transmission of new ideas, political and technological.

The post-1812 settlement wave westward produced competition within the Canadian and American business and governmental communities to see who could ship more people and goods into the Great Lakes region, and more cargoes out to the Atlantic seaboard or the St. Lawrence. This soon took the form of a canal-building race to get around the major obstacle of Niagara Falls, between the various incarnations of the Erie Canal in New York State, running from Albany to Buffalo, and similar versions of the Welland Canal, between Lake Ontario and Lake Erie. That competition lost some of its impetus in the 1850s, with the proliferation of railways, but canal development continued as a route for the steam cargo ship. No fewer than four Welland Canals were built, each an improvement on the other, until finally competition gave way to co-operation with a spectacular climax in 1959: the opening of the St. Lawrence Seaway, ironically at a moment when Great Lakes shipping was already in decline and international shipping beginning to resort to coastal container ports rather than the long inland voyage to lake ports.

The impact of the Great Lakes steamboat shipping industry remains, however, inasmuch as the great metropolitan centres that were initially established as ports to receive the growing nineteenth-century sail and steamboat traffic established land communication patterns that were mirrors of the waterborne links. As Carl Muhlenbruck and Robert Stuart wrote in 1959:

> The transition from major commodity shipments by water to those by rail in the nineteenth century led to major rail centres in many of these port cities. Commercial centres developed at rail and highway centres while other port cities in many cases reached the zenith of their development. The orientation of the Great Lakes has established travel patterns that exist to this day.

Powered shipping on the Great Lakes can be said to have passed through four distinct phases: the growth and development period, 1816 to 1890; a heyday between 1890 and 1929; paralysis and then uncertainty caused by the Depression and the Second World War; and a slow decline since the end of the war to the modern day.

From 1816 until the 1850s the predominant steamboat design was the sidewheeler, with large paddlewheels at the side of the hull propelled by simple steam engines such as the "walking beam" type. Then the introduction of the screw propeller placed the power plant deeper within the hull, freeing the sides of the boat for passenger cabins or greater cargo-carrying capacity. The next major shift in Great Lakes steamboat design came in the period just after the American Civil War, when the explosive development of the timber industry in Minnesota, Michigan and Wisconsin, and expanding iron ore shipments, led to a revolutionary hull design change that introduced the classic look of the traditional Great Lakes freighter. The first of these new vessels was built in 1869 by Cleveland shipowner E.M. Peck. His new vessel, the *R.J. Hackett*, was characterized by

> navigating cabins at the bow and the engines and crew's quarters at the back of the hull, leaving a long, open deck broken by hatches to provide access to the vessel's holds. The high bow

Ottawa River steamer SS *Empress* *C 3718*

and stern cabins protected lumber cargoes stored on deck from
the wind and waves, and provided ready access to the holds for
other bulk cargoes.

The design of the *R.J. Hackett* lives on as the template of Great
Lakes cargo vessel design. Passenger and cruise ships soon set their
own design patterns after the passing of the sidewheeler, with passenger quarters placed on the upper decks, cargo and vehicles on
the lower decks, and large ports let in the sides of the vessels to allow
easy loading and unloading.

The first practical Canadian steamboat on Lake Ontario, the
Frontenac of 1816, was in fact meant for service on the St. Lawrence
between Prescott, Ontario, and Kingston. It was only after the vessel struck bottom on the river that it was moved to the safer waters
of Lake Ontario, where it began regular service to York, which it
continued until 1827. Following the *Frontenac* came a steadily growing flotilla of boats that plied between the rapidly growing Canadian ports. The first Canadian steamboat on Lake Erie, the *Adelaide*,
began operation in 1833, dwarfed by an already-existing American

flotilla of thirty steamboats. Until the coming of the American Civil War these ships were kept busy carrying an endless stream of European immigrants to the new lands to the west.

On the Upper Lakes, the dip in shipping activity caused by the sudden slump in the fur trade in 1821 ended when the timber industry, mining of iron ore deposits and the opening of a small American canal at Sault Ste. Marie in 1853 set in motion the growth of steam shipping in remote waters where formerly only fur trade canoes had ventured. A Canadian canal to Lake Superior opened only in 1895. Meanwhile, the expansion of the railways filled in a spiderweb of movement and supply behind the growing steam fleet. Many new Canadian communities were created, dependent upon lake shipping and linked railways for their survival. In one such case, as Maurice Smith notes,

> the port of Collingwood had a near monopoly on the passage of freight by ship for about a decade after the rail line arrived from Toronto in 1857. Steamships extended the connections north and west; Chicago had an insatiable need for lumber and sent agricultural goods back east; small settlements along the remote shores of Georgian Bay and into Lake Superior depended on the steamer to bring manufactured goods and essential supplies from Toronto.

Disaster always stalked the "boats" of the Great Lakes, and many were the tragic tales of steamers carrying settlers that went down in horrendous, sudden gales or were destroyed by grounding, fire or collision. The great storm of November 1913 sank many vessels and killed hundreds. And fire imperilled the great cruise ships that had developed on the Great Lakes right to the end: the ghastly deaths of over one hundred men and women in the burning cruise ship *Noronic* at a Toronto dock in 1949 essentially marked the end of large-scale Great Lakes passenger cruising, although some vessels carried on until the 1960s.

If steam-powered cargo and passenger vessels enjoyed their golden age on the Lakes between 1890 and 1929, the Great Depression marked the end of that era, with two-thirds of the bulk carriers, many of the smaller freighters and almost all of the passenger vessels that had cruised in glory from Chicago to Toronto tied up and unused. The Second World War would see many vessels leave for the Atlantic, never to return; and the completion of the St. Lawrence Seaway in 1959, as noted, provided at last an unhindered highway for Atlantic-to-Lakehead navigation. Some five thousand wrecks now lie on the bottom of the Great Lakes, mute testimonials to a feverish century and a half of voyaging under steam and sail for profit, and for the grander and more lasting purposes of nation building.

It was not for want of human effort that so many lives and ships were lost to the Lakes; very early in their history as navigable seas, both French and English had attempted to end the dreadful toll of wrecks by the erection of lighthouses. But this process did not get seriously under way until after the War of 1812. Representative of this effort was the program to build lighthouses on Georgian Bay, which ushered in the era of hardy lightkeepers and their families struggling to keep both themselves and their lights alive, winter and summer, on one of the most challenging and unpredictable bodies of water on earth.

The expansion of the iron ore industry on Lake Superior and the opening in 1855 of a larger ship canal at Sault Ste. Marie turned Collingwood, Ontario, into the eastern end of a shorter shipping route, via the North Channel to the "Soo" and on to Lake Superior. While this high northern route was short and practical, it passed along a sailor's dreaded "lee shore" to its south when storms appeared out of the northeast, and it was menaced as well by many iron-coasted islands on either side that were able to trap and destroy any vessel straying from the safe track northwestward. To remedy these dangers, a builder named John Brown was contracted in 1855 to begin the construction of major lighthouses and attendant build-

Steamers in Kingston Harbour *PA 61431*

ings on six of the most lovely—and, in the cold seasons, some of the most forbidding—spots on Georgian Bay: Point Clarke, Chantry Island, Cove Island, Griffith Island, Nottawasaga Island and Christian Island, where the decimated Huron had taken refuge from the war parties of the Iroquois two hundred years earlier.

The building process was an agonizing one, with the failure of a supply ship meaning hunger and exposure, the blackflies and mosquitoes an unending torment, and the fierce and sudden storms awesome displays of nature's power. Brown and his workmen persevered, and in 1858 the first light was lit on Cove Island. Along with the other five, the Cove Island light, manned by hardy and long-suffering keepers and their families, served navigation on the Upper Lakes until well into the twentieth century, when the limestone towers fell dark, replaced by self-tending metal latticework towers. Of the men, and their equally brave families, who endured the life of a Georgian Bay lightkeeper far too little has yet been written, but it is one of the great stories of courage and endurance in Canada's maritime history.

Like lighthouses on the east and west coasts, the Georgian Bay lights were typically maintained by keepers who were accompanied by their families, and who lived a windswept existence in small, exposed houses adjacent to the light tower. It was a grim and tenuous life, dependent upon the coming of infrequent supply ships and the strength of the small houses to weather the wrath of fierce storms. The oil-fuelled lamps had to be tended year-round, each hour of the day and night, and all members of the family were usually involved. Foghorns were hand-operated, and days of fog could mean tedious and exhausting shifts at the horn bellows for even the littlest child of the family. Happy was the lightkeeper who served out his contract and brought his family back to communal life intact and unharmed. There were many instances, however, of lightkeepers and their families risking their lives on the rocky shores, and even in small boats, to save mariners and passengers of ships that foundered in storms within sight of the lighthouse.

It was a hard and demanding world they lived amidst, and with the passing of the manned lighthouses in the mid-twentieth century a chapter in human fortitude and in the story of Canada and its seas was closed, the event going largely unnoticed—except by those who remembered loved ones saved, or disaster averted, by the steady, rhythmic gleaming of distant lights, maintained tirelessly by dedicated hands.

Every effort to keep ships and crews from falling into the grip of the deadly inland seas sometimes came to nothing, however, as some five thousand wreck sites tell. Even in the modern era, radar, depth sounders and powerful engines have not saved hulls and men from watery disaster. Two disasters in particular have come to symbolize the power of the Great Lakes to claim any ship they choose, of any size and of any era, as easily as might an ocean.

One is the loss of the *Edmund Fitzgerald*, one of the largest ore carriers ever to sail the Great Lakes. Built at River Rouge, Michigan, by the Great Lakes Engineering Works in 1958, the huge vessel was named, in an ultimately bitter irony, after the chairman of the Northwestern Mutual Life Insurance Company. Its gross weight was 13,632 tons, and fully loaded its weight exceeded 40,000 tons—more than a Second World War aircraft carrier. Its length was an astonishing 729 feet, and it was fitted with a full suite of navigational and communications gear, carried twenty-nine men and was driven by powerful engines. On November 9, 1975, the *Edmund Fitzgerald* sailed down Lake Superior with a load of iron ore pellets. The next day, November 10, beset by huge waves and enveloped in a furious white squall, the *Edmund Fitzgerald* was overwhelmed by the swells, broke in two, and went down suddenly with all twenty-nine of her crew aboard. It was an appalling loss that stunned the shipping world like the loss of the *Titanic* had decades before.

The other tragedy involved the *Algoma*, one of three first-class steamers built by the railway to transport passengers in comfort from Owen Sound to the Lakehead in the nineteenth century. Richly furnished and fitted with an auxiliary sail rig as well as its powerful main engines, the *Algoma* soon became a well-known and respected fixture on the Upper Lakes, along with its sister ships *Alberta* and *Athabasca*. But in November 1885, Lake Superior's power claimed the *Algoma*, as it would later claim the *Edmund Fitzgerald*.

Great Lakes historian Mark Bourrie, writing in 2004 in a fine compendium of Great Lakes history, quoted the account of the tragedy given by the *Algoma*'s first mate, John Hastings:

> The seas was running mountains high, and the boat was tossed around like a cork. Fifteen minutes past four o'clock [a.m.], the order was given to take in all of the sails and put the wheel hard a-starboard to bring the ship about and head out on the lake again, because of the storm and the darkness. While the ship was coming about, we struck Greenhouse Point, on Isle Royale, about fifty miles from Port Arthur and one mile from Passage Island lighthouse, which had been abandoned since the first of the month. After striking the first time, the boat forged ahead, driven by the wind. A second shock occurred shortly after the first. The vessel struck the reef violently, and immediately started to break up.

It would all end in an appalling loss of life. Hastings went on:

> Screams of women and children were heard above the fury of the storm. The crew hurried hither and thither, doing what they could in the darkness to render assistance; but their efforts were of little avail, for in less than twenty minutes, the entire forward part of the boat was carried away, together with her cargo and human freight. Several clung to the rigging and lifeline the captain had stretched along the deck, but were soon swept away and swallowed by the angry waves. The stern of the boat was steadily pushed up on to the rock, and those who were not too exhausted with the fatigue and benumbed by the cold crept to the after steerage and sought its shelter. Less than an hour after striking, all was over.

Out of more than sixty crew and passengers, a mere fifteen survived, of whom only two were passengers. The Great Lakes had proven, as they would again, that they were indeed "as wide and terrible as any sea." They remain so to this day.

14

The Windjammer
Fleets, 1860–1914

The "Bluenose Bucko Mate" was soon the villain of a thousand yarns in seamen's taverns around the globe. Sometimes he deserved it, and more often not. His job was to sail the ship by the captain's orders and to keep her like a Dutch housewife. A cargo badly stowed, a smear on the shining deck, or a rope's end flying loose meant disgrace for the mate and torment for the crew. The sight of an idle hand sent him roaring for paint pots or polishing rags. On the tougher ships a man who loafed on the halyards or showed an inclination to stay below in a gale was helped along to his station by a boot or a belaying-pin or a length of rope. The "hobo" or "sojer" who wished to stand and argue got the bare fist sometimes enclosed in the brass knuckle.

The second mate was a younger copy of the first, and both were made in the image of the captain. The three of them together were the brains and heart of the ship. Out of these triumvirates, multiplying on all the seas, grew the reputation of the Bluenose windjammers. "Floating hells," reported the bums as they reeled ashore after a voyage to recover in the shoreside taverns. "Better than your limey hard-scrabble packets," retorted the good sailors. If you knew your trade and did your work, you were all right with the Bluenoses. There was no nonsense about them. When they shipped a man they had paid out good money in advance wages for an able seaman, and an able seaman he was going to be.

THERE IS A SPARE, austere beauty to the coastline of Canada's Maritime provinces, the homeland of the vanished breed of seaman that Joseph Schull, author of the words above, wrote about in 1957. In some places it is a shoreline of densely packed evergreens above iron rocks, in others a gentle, tree-clad land of tidy farms and reddish mud flats. Its harbours and coves were renowned for their heritage of hard work in the face of scarcity; as a land where one had to keep a level head; a land whose most lasting product was fine men and women. Once, these shores teemed with every variety of sailing vessel that put to sea, carrying the British ensigns under which they sailed to every corner of the globe. Of that vast fleet little remains but memories, artwork, faded documents and photographs, and the traditions kept alive by subsidized vessels such as the Nova Scotian government's *Bluenose II*. For a painfully brief period the Maritime provinces held their own as one of the world centres of shipbuilding and ocean commerce. As Charles Armour and Thomas Lackey wrote in 1975:

> In 1773, the Maritime provinces of Canada were, for the most part, a vast wilderness of trees with only a few scattered settlements along the coast. Less than one hundred years later Canada had developed a vast shipbuilding industry that during the peak years of the 1860s supplied nearly one-third of all British shipping. By the end of the century over 26,000 vessels had been built in the Maritimes. While many of these were built for direct transfer to British owners, many Maritime merchants owned and operated their own vessels. In 1878, the peak year in Canadian ownership, Canada stood fifth on the list of ship-owning countries of the world, and 7,469 vessels totalling 1,333,015 tons were on the registry books. Of this number, 4,467 vessels representing 943,583 tons were registered in the Maritime provinces.

The great drama of the Canadian "windjammer" fleet began in earnest after the start of the seemingly endless war against revolutionary and then Napoleonic France, which lasted from 1792 to 1815. It received its strongest boost in 1809, when the British government favoured British North American timber with a protective tariff that would last for thirty years and give rise to a shipbuilding surge in Nova Scotia, New Brunswick and Prince Edward Island based on the endless stands of timber. As New Brunswick historians Robert Elliot and Alan McNairn put it succinctly in 1987, "the exploitation of this natural resource, motivated by political and economic circumstances abroad, led to the growth of an economy based on lumbering and the construction of vessels to carry timber."

The eighteenth-century settlement of maritime Canada was accomplished by Europeans who looked primarily for farmland on which to reproduce the wheat-based ordered parkland of Europe, and this required clearance of the forests. Only if the climate or soil made farming impossible did the settlers turn, as they largely did along the harsher Atlantic coast of the provinces, to fishing and maritime trade for their livelihood. Prior to 1749 the principal Nova Scotian settlement was the small community of Annapolis Royal, which also served as the colonial capital. With the founding of Halifax in 1749, followed by the German settlement of Lunenburg from 1750 to 1752, the first sizable populations were established along the rugged Atlantic coast, which soon proved difficult to farm in abundance, leading Halifax to rely on shipping and government for survival, and Lunenburg the fishery. The colonial populations continued to grow with the arrival of New England farmers in 1760 and the coming of Scots in 1773 to the Pictou area aboard the *Hector*. However, it was not until the American Loyalists flooded north after the Revolution, in 1783, that real form came to the Maritime colonies, as with a stroke the colonial population was quadrupled.

Although prosperous farms could be achieved, particularly in the river valleys, by dint of hard work and dogged endurance, few of the town-bred Loyalist settlers could muster these qualities. Many moved on, but those who stayed in large part turned to the fishery or to commerce upon the sea. The felling of the forests for the farmer, and the building of ships to take that lumber to Britain, gradually evolved toward the building of ships for a Maritimes-based trade and not merely for sale in Britain.

Beginning in the 1770s, with the publication of J.F.W. DesBarres's landmark *Atlantic Neptune* and the charting work of Samuel Holland, James Cook, Michael Lane and others, the feasibility of safer navigation in Maritime waters was established. The sudden growth of the colonies with the Loyalist influx soon had vessels of all kinds operating on the colonial coast, and along with the creation of a separate colony of New Brunswick in 1784 came the Navigation Act of 1787, which sought to regulate the new shipping in the colonies and required the establishment of Ports of Registry for these vessels. Five such ports were established initially: Halifax; Saint John; St. John's Island (later Prince Edward Island); Sydney, in the then-separate colony of Cape Breton Island; and Shelburne, Nova Scotia, also known as Port Roseway.

With the registry established and the burgeoning of the population, Maritime waters were soon busy with not only the growing fleet of the inshore and Grand Banks fishery, but schooners, brigs, snows, sloops and brigantines employed between the new ports and the American ports of Boston, Philadelphia and New York, and increasingly Europe and the West Indies. By 1800 over seven hundred vessels had been built and registered in the Maritimes. The return to all-out war with France that followed the short peace established by the Treaty of Amiens in 1802 produced an expansion of Maritime shipbuilding. While the War of 1812 led to losses in Canadian shipping, there was an equal gain in the taking of American prizes, many of which through sale or operation established the first major business fortunes in the Atlantic colonies.

The early colonial vessels were revealing studies in both workaday vessel rigs and eclectic cargoes. Armour and Lackey offer an example:

> The *Osborn Gally*, a brig of 100 tons, was built and registered at Halifax in 1751 and owned by John Graham. A contemporary port list gives an interesting example of the cargo carried by a colonial ship. The vessel cleared Halifax on July 8, 1751, with "Sam'l Appleton" as master and a crew of six men, bound for London with a cargo of ". . . 80 tons of Black Birch Timber, 313 oars, 240 Hand Spikes, 70 spars, 3136 QT. Blubber, 3 tons pitch pine and 20 QT fish."

Gradually, the nature of Maritime shipping changed from the creation of ships that were meant to be sold abroad, along with their raw-materials cargoes, to Maritimes-based shipping carrying a range of cargoes. This process was particularly evident at Halifax where, after the War of 1812, fortunes earned in the privateering war against the Americans were applied to the development of true shipping companies that retained their fleets. Leaders in the field were men such as Enos Collins and Samuel Cunard. Cunard got his start in 1813, using captured American prize vessels to trade to the West Indies. In later years his business would evolve into the Cunard Steamship Company, the giant of North Atlantic shipping whose vessels ply those waters still.

After a brief postwar depression, rebounding timber prices and a demand in Britain for Maritimes- and Quebec-built vessels led to sustained activity in Maritime shipyards from 1820 to 1845, particularly in Nova Scotia and New Brunswick. There would be a number of other "boom" periods, tied to events elsewhere, including 1844, when free trade with the United States was established; 1849, the year of the California gold rush; 1851, the year of the Australian goldfields; and 1854, with the outbreak of the Crimean War. The great apex of wooden shipbuilding in the Maritimes took place between 1846, the year the tea trade to China began to draw investors, and 1865, the end of the American Civil War. In that latter year Maritime shipyards produced no fewer than 660 ocean-going merchant vessels. The output had been astounding: Bluenose full-rigged ships, barques, barquentines and schooners roamed the world. "Bluenose" came to be a term used worldwide for a Maritime-built colonial vessel, even though it now refers to Nova Scotians and their vessels. The total number of vessels built in the Maritime colonial shipyards over those twenty years reached some ten thousand hulls.

The end of the American Civil War in 1865 also marked the end of the golden age of Maritime shipbuilding, as for three years a deep worldwide depression cut sharply into the demand for Maritime-built ships. As the Atlantic colonies debated Maritime Union, and

Schooners at dock at Quebec, 1918 *PA 71207*

then finally agreed with some reluctance to political union with Canada in 1867, the great heyday of the Maritime shipbuilding and shipping industry was already drawing toward a close. The production of wooden sailing vessels did recover to a degree after the depression, but by 1874 it was clearly in decline as steam propulsion and iron-hulled ships gradually began to replace the wooden-hulled sailing vessel in the world's commercial fleets, notably that of Great Britain, where Bluenose ships once counted for one-quarter to one-third of *all* worldwide tonnage of the British Empire. It was an extraordinary period of achievement for the Maritimes, eclipsed only by the coming of heavy industrialization that made redundant the skilled shipwright with his chisel and adze, or the sailmaker whose acres of snowy canvas once drove cargo-packed ships cleanly and beautifully round the world on wind power alone.

From the moment of Confederation, the star of Canadian merchant shipping was in decline. The change was not immediate, however. In 1878, as Armour and Lackey document, the numbers of operating Canadian-registered commercial vessels were considerable: New Brunswick listed 1,142, Nova Scotia 3,003, Prince Edward Island 322, giving a total for the Maritimes of 4,467. The total for Canada was 7,469, which included the Great Lakes. It is a poignant and sobering thought, in an era when virtually only a handful of vessels beyond naval or government ships show the Canadian flag in foreign ports, that Canada's flag was once carried around the globe by ships in the thousands.

The transition to iron and steel hulls was beyond the industrial capacity of most Maritime ports, the strength there having been the army of skilled shipwrights, caulkers, riggers and sailmakers who had produced the great ships of the past. By 1890 these men were aging, and it proved difficult to find young men willing to apprentice in these older trades that were not applicable except in a secondary way to the building of the new iron ships. In addition, while it had been possible to build wooden sailing vessels at moderate cost, the financial support and beginning capital needed for the construction of iron and steel vessels were beyond the means of most Maritime business communities. With the turn of the twentieth century, yards which had once turned out towering square riggers with hundred-foot masts that had raced to China for tea were building modest little coastal fishing boats. Of the "tall ships," the only remnants into the 1900s were undermanned, multi-masted cargo schooners in dwindling numbers and the swift fishing schooners such as *Bluenose* that sailed out of Lunenburg and other Atlantic ports. The story of the fishing schooners deserves to be told on its own (see chapter 15), but by the end of the 1930s they too had folded the glory of their shining white canvas wings and were cut down to motor vessels, or were left to rot away on tidal flats, the grey bones of their forlorn hulls marking the end of a grand and valuable tradition.

The ships produced by that Maritime tradition were some of the finest ever built in the world, and some became legendary. One such vessel was the full-rigged *Marco Polo*. A "full-rigged ship" means a vessel normally fitted with three masts, and setting square sails on all three. The *Marco Polo* was such a ship, a "clipper" in the manner

of the great American tea clippers—designed more often by Nova
Scotians such as Donald McKay—like *Sea Witch*, with sharp bows,
long and narrow hulls, and a towering skysail rig that could drive
the lean greyhound hulls at up to twenty knots in the powerful
winds of the open ocean. *Marco Polo* was launched on April 19,
1851, at Courtney Bay, Saint John, New Brunswick. Its owner and
builder was James Smith, and the vessel was built at his yard by New
Brunswick shipwrights. When launched and rigged, the *Marco Polo*
was an impressive sight. Its length was 184 feet, and it was registered
at 1,625 tons. Below decks it had three complete decks running
fore and aft, and on its high masts it carried the full clipper suit of
courses, topsails, topgallants—pronounced "t'gallants"—and royals,
with a lance-like jib-boom arrowing ahead of a sleek, black-painted
hull marked with white "gunports," a paint scheme fashioned to
frighten away pirates or belligerent islanders who might mistake
the vessel for a warship.

When *Marco Polo* sailed on May 31, 1851, its maiden voyage, it
carried a prosaic cargo of timber and scrap iron. Another unremarkable crossing followed, from Liverpool to Mobile, Alabama,
for a cargo of cotton. On the ship's return to Liverpool, however,
it was set on a new course away from bulk cargo mediocrity into
the demanding passenger trade, being converted to carry emigrants
from Britain out to Australia. It was the moment that opened the
door to greatness and legend for the New Brunswick ship. Conversion for the immigrant trade meant fitting the lower decks with
tiers of wooden bunks and creating other spaces for the immigrants'
wash places, baggage stowage and other needs, including a sufficient galley to feed hundreds of mouths beyond those of the crew.
For the time, the ship was converted to very high standards—some
immigrant ships were hellish prisons for their wretched passengers—and it was bought by the Black Ball Line, a renowned packet
line on the North Atlantic run.

Finally, on July 4, 1852, *Marco Polo* put to sea, outbound for
Australia with 930 emigrants and the ship's crew of 60 on board.

Driving the vessel—and that was the operative word—was Captain James N. Forbes, known as "Bully" Forbes for his ferocious manner in pushing a ship and its crew to their limits, the latter by force of his fists as well as his personality. The *Marco Polo* proved tough enough to withstand Forbes, and the ship made a blistering passage round to Australia, arriving there on September 18, 1852, after sixty-eight days at sea, fully a week ahead of the steamer *Australia* that had taken the same route. It was an extraordinary achievement, and the passengers were loud in their praise for the ship and its tough captain. Not content with that success, Forbes sailed for England on October 11, 1852, vowing to complete the round trip in under six months. *Marco Polo* arrived in England on Sunday, December 26, after a seventy-six-day passage. Forbes had lived up to his vow: the round trip had taken five months and twenty-one days, and *Marco Polo* now had a reputation as the world's fastest sailing vessel.

The proud ship sailed continuously in the immigrant trade until 1870, always making fast passages and rarely empty thanks to its reputation for speed and the conditions provided for its passengers. Then, in 1870, the ship was sold into general cargo work; its glory days were over. In 1880 *Marco Polo* returned to Canadian waters under the Norwegian flag as a timber ship trading out of Quebec. Perhaps age had caught up with the flying clipper, as on July 22, 1883, its hull leaking badly, *Marco Polo* was pounded to pieces on the broad beaches of Prince Edward Island's north shore.

Its passing marked the end of significant Canadian large-vessel sailing ship construction. That construction left a remarkable legacy, from the littlest trading sloop to the largest of them all, the 2,458-ton *William D. Lawrence*, a full-rigged ship 220 feet on the keel and with a 46-foot beam. Like *Marco Polo*, the *William D. Lawrence* ended its days in the hands of Norwegians, lasting until 1898.

If the ships of the Maritimes' nineteenth-century sailing fleet were an important basis for the seacoast economy, work in those ships—sailors always said "in" a ship rather than "on"—was a major source of employment. The labour historian Eric Sager, writing in 1989, noted its importance:

> In 1870 the fleets of Atlantic Canada employed in mid-summer almost as many workers as the entire forest products industries of Nova Scotia and New Brunswick. Shipping employed about three times as many workers as Maritime shipbuilding yards. In winter employment fell, especially in small coastal and fishing vessels.

Even so, Canadian interest in the work slowly began to evaporate. Sager goes on to note that toward the end of the great Canadian sailing ship era, a growing proportion of the crews of Maritime ships were foreign in origin and residence, and that "a man could work in this colonial industry without ever setting foot in Atlantic Canada."

It is difficult from the perspective of the twenty-first century and a highly mechanized lifestyle to appreciate the hardships and sheer daily rigour that constituted the life of an Atlantic Canadian seaman in an ocean-going vessel; a life that men from Nova Scotia, New Brunswick and Prince Edward Island once embraced in their thousands as they shipped in Bluenose hulls outbound to Britain, the West Indies, Cape Horn and the Pacific, or to the Boston States of New England. Equally difficult to grasp is the mental toughness that such a life required, and which goes far to reveal the qualities that were bred into, or called forth from, the men of the cold northern shores. Sager relates an event when a typical Nova Scotian seaman in a full-rigged ship was compelled by pride to do a job rather than obey an order meant to preserve him:

> We had taken in the mizzen royal, topgallant sail and crossjack course, the main royal and topgallant sail and the fore royal when the foretopgallant sheet parted and unrove out of the topsail yard. As the clew swung forward, the frazzled end of the

sheet flew aft and caught around the fore royal stay. We lowered the topgallant sail down, but, with the sheet caught, we were unable to haul up the weather clew, which was slatting away out of reach, ready to split at any moment. I went up to the royal masthead and got out on the stay. It shook so from the surging of the sail that I was afraid to go down.

Mr. Fields was watching me. Seeing me start down the stay he yelled, "Come back, Dan, don't go down there— Down on deck with you, I say . . ." I pulled out my sheath knife, got my legs around the stay, and slid down. The stay was shaking so that though my teeth were well rooted I had to clench them to keep them in my mouth. The mate kept hailing, "Hold on, boy, hold on." I sawed away with the sheath knife on the rope until it was cut through, and then slid down the stay to the jib-boom. When I came on deck the mate shook me by the shoulders and said, "What a man you are, Dan. I never expected to see you come down alive. Why didn't you come down when I told you to?" "Well," I said, "I was afraid you'd send somebody else up there, and if he did what I didn't dare do, I'd be forever ashamed of myself."

The character of Canadian sailing ship seamen had its roots in the small sea-edge Maritime and Quebec communities from which most came, and the self-reliant values those communities instilled in their young people, both men and women, simply by virtue of the daily difficulty of life by a northern ocean. As Sager goes on to note, fishing and farming communities encouraged a self-reliant attitude that placed a man's success or failure squarely in his own hands, and not in those of others. This gave the seaman of Atlantic Canada what Sager identifies as a "small boat mentality" of self-advancement and responsibility for one's actions, a kind of wintry integrity that saw these young men and women grow to strength and ability in a world of mutual trust and interdependence, able to fight for a family's survival or drive a wind ship through the open ocean simply by being responsible, without blame, for their own actions and relying on others to act similarly. A few lines from the 1937 memoirs of Captain John W. Froude have been quoted by Sager and others as revealing this thinking in its simplicity:

> In battle or business whatever the game
> In law or in love, it is ever the same
> In the struggle for power or the scramble for self
> Let this be your motto: rely on yourself
> For whether the prize be a ribbon or throne
> The victor is he who can go it alone.

To the landsman unfamiliar with the world of a sailing vessel at sea, the above lines may seem to reflect a sociopathic self-absorption and selfishness worthy of the best Ayn Rand novel. Yet, paradoxically, it was a philosophy that allowed men to work as a mutually reliant team in the demanding and unforgiving world of the open-ocean sailing ship. The ethos of self-reliance meant that each man came to trust the others at sea with him, knowing that they would do their jobs and ensure their collective survival because the "small boat mentality" would keep each man true to his own sense of duty and responsibility even if unsupervised, and thus not allow him to let down either the rest of the crew or the ship itself. It was an environment and a social philosophy that bred fine men and women who were an ornament to the Maritimes they sprang from and the Canada to which they belonged. But their world, and the white-canvassed, towering ships that were its icons, has vanished with few traces, leaving little to mark the courage of their lives, or the scale of its achievement.

Gradually, the movement to steam-powered vessels of iron and steel, and the shift toward the vast industrial bases of Europe and America that supported them, took the capacity to maintain commercial shipping out of the hands of ordinary Atlantic Canadians, with few exceptions. Other factors were at work as well that spelled the end of the great ships and the clink of the shipwrights' hammers that built them. As Elliot and McNairn wrote of New Brunswick:

> Most marine entrepreneurs, reacting to a decrease in freight rates which began in the mid 1870s and to Canadian government policies promoting landward development, redirected their capital away from the sea to enterprises they expected to be more lucrative. By the turn of the century, New Brunswick's significant role in international shipping and shipbuilding existed only as a memory.

The story would prove to be the same in Nova Scotia and elsewhere in Atlantic Canada. The men in the boardrooms and head offices largely turned away from the sea, leaving only proud old men who had once achieved something magnificent to look out on the largely empty waters and remember what they had put there.

15

The
Great
Schooners

THEY are largely vanished now, perpetuated in a few harbour cruise vessels and a treasured provincial ambassador: the tall, fleet schooners that sailed out of Maritime ports to the North Atlantic fishery within living memory, or steered north from Victoria to the frigid sealing grounds of the Aleutians. In their passing they ended an adventure under sail on the North American coast that began half a millennium earlier. As we have seen, it was the lure of the seemingly inexhaustible fishery that drew Europeans to sail to North America in the 1400s, and there are men living still who as boys sailed as their ancestors did centuries before, under white canvas and on wooden decks, to fish for the once never-ending cod.

For the most part the fishing vessels of England and France that would have been found off Canada's east coast in the seventeenth and early eighteenth centuries were of traditional square sail rigs, much as were employed in commercial shipping. Gradually, however, the growing English colonies of New England and their northern extensions in Nova Scotia began to employ an indigenous type of working sail rig that was highly suited for the broad-reach coastal sailing in the colonies, or the long tack up to windward against the westerlies, going home from the Grand Banks: the fore-and-aft schooner. Virtually all of the rig could be set and handled from the deck, and without the need to go aloft a schooner could be sailed by very few men, as few as two to a mast. In the cost-conscious world of colonial shipping, this made the schooner rig an attractive option. Also of major importance was the schooner's ability to tack: to work to windward in a series of zigzags that the square-rigged ship performed with difficulty if at all. The double value of low labour intensity and handiness on any point of sailing made the schooner the ideal craft for coastal North American trade—and the fishery.

It was around 1850 that Nova Scotian and New Brunswick fishing schooners began to use the ship-borne dory. The corklike dories were stacked on deck and launched over the side with tackles (pronounced "taykles") rigged from aloft. With hands tailing onto the "falls"—the lengths of line leading from the tackles—the dories were hoisted clear of the deck and then levered out over the rail with long wooden beams called spoons. Once in the water, they rowed off from the mother ship with one or two fishermen aboard, equipped with fish tubs and fishing gear, a simple spritsail, a water jug and a bag of hardtack biscuit.

With the introduction of the longline, a French invention, the dorymen would lay out a long pattern of individual longlines anchored to the bottom and bristling with baited hooks along their length, ending at a buoy marked with numbers or colours for identification. The dorymen would lay out the pattern then row back along it a few hours later and haul in the individual lines, collecting the catch as they went. The fish were then taken back to the schooner for splitting and salting. This process went on until the schooner's holds were full or the salt expended.

Thus, the colonial fishermen developed their industry off Canada's east coast, one which lasted in that form well into the twentieth century. But as with commercial shipbuilding and shipping, the fishery in Canada, with its reliance on essentially a pre-industrial model based on the wooden sailing schooner, began to decline with the changes in Canadian society and the economy, the coming of steel and iron vessels, and the shift in investor interest into manufacturing, railways and the demands of an inland economy. The fishing schooner of the Canadian Maritimes and New

Part of sealing fleet laid up in Victoria Harbour, 1891   *C 86451*

England reached its apex of power, beauty and efficiency at the turn
of the twentieth century, just as technology, money and the changing economy had effectively written out its death sentence. Even
on the west coast, the far more concentrated salmon fishery and
halibut fishery made the transition to powered vessels scant decades
after the assembly of a formal fishing industry, giving the sailing
fishing vessel a short life indeed before it was superseded.

Following the First World War and the immediate postwar slump,
the Atlantic communities of Canada such as Lunenburg, Nova Scotia, that were reliant on the offshore fishery for economic survival,
but which lacked the sheer capital to equip themselves with steam or
diesel trawlers and longliners, had recourse only to the one technology they had mastered, and which was still within their financial
means: the construction and operation of fast wooden schooners and
dories able to catch enough fish and speed the catch to shore in sufficient bulk and with sufficient speed to make the business pay. By 1920,
Lunenburg and similar American communities such as Gloucester,
Massachusetts, were still making a precarious living sending to sea

dory-equipped wooden schooners of astonishing beauty, speed and seakeeping ability. In almost all respects they were perpetuating a technology unchanged from the nineteenth century, and by the 1920s it was apparent to most that the era of the great fishing schooner would last little longer than the softwood planking of their sleek hulls. The last great, incandescent moments of existence for these magnificent working schooners would come not as a simple disappearance before new ranks of steam trawlers or an ignominious, cut-down conversion into engine-driven hulks, but in a series of tremendous races inspired by, of all things, yachting.

The America's Cup was a trophy for which sailing yachts in North America and Britain had competed since it had first been won by the schooner *America*, which in 1851 had sailed to Britain and shown her heels to British yachts in a series of races. By the turn of the 1900s the race was being run by huge, delicate vessels of light scantlings and vast clouds of canvas that were as fragile as they were attractive, and which could only sail in moderate winds. In 1920, the attention of the hardbitten schooner men of Nova Scotia and Massachusetts, who drove their big working vessels out to the Grand Banks in horrendous winter gales, was caught by that year's America's Cup competition, in which one race was cancelled because the wind—slightly over twenty knots—was considered too risky for the competing yachts to venture out in. The fishermen began to discuss with each other and their owners the idea of a separate race that would have little fear of wind and seas. Further, the idea was that such a race would not be between delicate, purpose-built yachts of only recreational value, but between ocean-capable working schooners able to complete a full fishing season on the Banks. The idea of such a race took hold in both Nova Scotia and New England; rules were drawn up specifying limits to the hull and the sail plan; and it was made clear that any competing boat had to be a genuine working fishing schooner, not a yacht. The races were assured finally when the publisher of the Halifax *Herald* put up a trophy, which became known as the International Fishermen's Trophy.

The communities involved were Lunenburg, Nova Scotia, and Gloucester, Massachusetts, each of which regularly sent large fleets of fishing schooners to sea. There were important differences between the ships of the two communities, however, as historian Scott Flinn observed in 2004:

Although Lunenburg and Gloucester supported similar fleets, there was an important difference in the type of fishing they did that makes the achievements of [the Canadian schooner *Bluenose*] even more remarkable. The Lunenburg fleet was engaged in salt fishing while Gloucester was more interested in the fresh fishery. The Lunenburg vessels were therefore constructed to carry large amounts of salt to the Banks where they would stay for extended periods of time, salting and storing fish as it was caught. For this purpose the ships had to be both large and sturdy. The Gloucester ships, in contrast, were built for speed so that small catches could be hastened ashore while still fresh. That their ships be proven faster was therefore a matter of particular pride for the Gloucestermen.

On October 11, 1920, the elimination races to select a Canadian contestant for the trophy were held, and the schooner *Delawana* won over its closest rival, the *Gilbert B. Walters*, whose captain was Angus Walters. The Americans having had their own elimination races, which selected the schooner *Esperanto* as their contestant, the first trophy race was scheduled off Halifax for October 30, 1920. The Nova Scotians were shocked when *Esperanto* lived up to Gloucester's expectations and won the first two out of a planned three races, one by a twenty-minute margin and the second by seven minutes. As the Americans triumphantly carried the trophy off to Gloucester, the decision was made in Lunenburg to build a new contestant. It would still be a working vessel, but it would be *fast*.

The youthful Halifax naval architect William J. Roue was hired to design the new vessel. The trophy regulations called for a vessel

Schooner *Bluenose* under sail off Nova Scotia *PA 41990*

no longer than 145 feet overall, with a waterline length of 112 feet or less. Roue produced a design for a sleek, powerful schooner that fully satisfied the working-vessel requirements but promised to be fast and capable, particularly in heavy winds. Christened *Bluenose*, the big schooner was launched on March 26, 1921, at Lunenburg's Smith and Rhuland yard, the 121st vessel to be launched there. The losing captain in the 1920 eliminations, Angus Walters, had a share in the vessel's financing, along with a consortium of Halifax businessmen. The first part of the race requirements were handily satisfied when *Bluenose* and her dories had a successful summer fishing season on the Grand Banks. Then the trials for the 1921 race had to be overcome, but *Bluenose* showed her heels to seven competing Lunenburg schooners with ease. The question now was whether the big northern vessel could hold its own against the speedy Gloucestermen.

In late October the race was held off Gloucester, with *Bluenose* paired against the American schooner *Elsie*. Nova Scotia and much of Canada held its breath as the vessels surged over the start line, but Roue's design skill and Walters's skippering soon ended the suspense. *Bluenose* thundered ahead, winning the first and second races handily. The trophy was back in Lunenburg. The next year, 1922, the American challenger *Henry Ford* salved Gloucester pride by winning one race, only to have *Bluenose* win the other two and retain the trophy.

In 1923, the competition began with *Bluenose* narrowly winning the first race against the beautiful American challenger *Columbia*, and then controversy arose. In the second race, which *Bluenose* appeared to have won, the Canadian schooner passed a buoy on the wrong side, and the race committee awarded the race to *Columbia*. Walters protested what he felt was an unfair decision and took *Bluenose* home to Lunenburg, opening a seven-year period during which no races took place and the arguments appeared insoluble. Then, in 1930, the wealthy Englishman Sir Thomas Lipton put up a separate cup for a match between the American and Canadian schooners, and *Bluenose* returned to the world of competitive sailing. Seven years of hard work and punishing storms may have wrought their toll on the big vessel, as the American entrant, the *Gertrude L. Thibaud*, won two out of three races and claimed Lipton's cup. Angus Walters would later claim that it was his mistakes that cost *Bluenose* the cup, not the qualities of the ship.

Enthusiasm for a renewal of the International Fishermen's Trophy races was reborn in New England as a result of *Gertrude L. Thibaud*'s victory, and a new series was scheduled for October 1931, ten years after *Bluenose* had won her first victory. A decade of hard work was usually all that could be expected from the softwood-built schooners, and *Bluenose* may have looked her age as she came up to the start line. Nonetheless, the big schooner and Walters proved equal to the task, as *Bluenose* won over the *Gertrude L. Thibaud* in two uncontested races.

Those eight years between the controversial 1923 series and the races against the *Thibaud* in 1931 had been hard on *Bluenose*, as working life was on all the fishing schooners. At one point the schooner was aground for four days in Placentia Bay, Newfoundland, as heavy seas tore her dories from her deck. In April 1926, while anchored on the Northwest Bar on the southwest side of Sable Island, the "Graveyard of the Atlantic," *Bluenose* was enveloped by a sudden rising gale and blizzard. *Bluenose*'s anchor line snapped, and the great seas and wind began to drive the big schooner toward certain death on the shore of Sable Island. Stanchions, rails and deck gear were smashed, and the battle seemed to be a losing one. With only a few bar-taut storm trysails set, the schooner fought for its life, Angus Walters gripping the helm the whole time. Authors Phil and Brian Backman, writing in 1965, quoted Walters as marvelling later: "She kept heading up, biting her way into the gale. Don't know as any other vessel could have done it!" A year later, in August 1927, a hurricane swept north from the West Indies and smashed six Lunenburg schooners on Sable Island, but *Bluenose* somehow survived, sailing home to join the mourning for over one hundred men lost in that dreadful storm. The tragedy revealed to all who learned of it the appallingly difficult and risky work of fishermen in the big schooners, a way of life that had changed little since the eighteenth century even as inland citizens were going about their business in the excitement, security and technology of the twentieth century.

Bluenose kept working as a fishing schooner through the hardscrabble years of the 1930s, as the Depression deepened and the vessel's age made uncertain whether it could carry on. But it had become firmly fixed in the hearts and minds of Canadians, and in 1933 *Bluenose* took some respite from the gruelling fishery to sail up the St. Lawrence to the Great Lakes and the Chicago Exposition, where her decks were tramped over by thousands who came to the waterfront to see the fabled vessel.

In 1935, the big schooner received its greatest honour when it was invited to Britain for the Silver Jubilee of King George V and Queen Mary. *Bluenose* made a speedy passage to Plymouth as an official Canadian representative vessel, and found itself invited to Spithead for the Grand Review of the British fleet. The king was aboard the royal yacht *Victoria and Albert* during the review, and Angus Walters was invited aboard to meet the king, remarking, as Brian and Phil Backman noted, "He was a very nice, ordinary sort of fella, though if I may say so, he looked a little frail." The *Bluenose* was invited to take part in the annual yacht race around the Isle of Wight. The weather-beaten old schooner surprised the yachtsmen with her speed, coming in third after two sleek racing yachts. An impressed George V presented Walters and the *Bluenose* with the mainsail of the royal yacht *Britannia* in tribute.

The visit to the United Kingdom almost brought *Bluenose* to her doom, as on the return voyage to Nova Scotia the schooner ran headlong into another hurricane in the open Atlantic, barely a day after leaving Falmouth. For three days the *Bluenose* was beset, with Walters trying to keep some storm canvas on the vessel, finally lying hove to under bare poles as the storm did its worst. Then a blow came that almost finished the ship. As the Backmans relate, a huge sea appeared that struck *Bluenose* broadside:

> For the first time in her life, *Bluenose* heeled over on her beam ends—her below decks flooded with tons of water. In the blow, the ocean had smashed both boats, the deckhouse engine box, the foreboom and the mainboom jaws; the galley was uprooted and in shambles, and her port bulwarks had vanished. During the minutes she stayed under, Angus gave up hope she could ever survive. But the mangled champion painfully and slowly righted herself. [Said Angus,] "I was never prouder of her."

After a refit in Britain, the schooner returned to Canada, where financial pressures forced Walters to install diesel engines as he tried to keep the old vessel profitable amidst the grim realities of the Depression and the coming of modern trawlers. It appeared that *Bluenose*'s days of glory were now truly at an end.

Then, in 1938, when most of the fishing schooners were vanishing off the seas, or plodding out to the Grand Banks with cut-down masts, ugly deck houses and thumping engines, the Gloucestermen unexpectedly issued another challenge: race *Bluenose* once more against her equally elderly old rival, the *Gertrude L. Thibaud*, for the Fishermen's Trophy. Walters and his partners were not sure. The old schooner's hull had been permanently weakened by the British hurricane, and it was "hogged," which is to say that it had lost its beautiful curving sheer and now sagged at bow and stern. The schooner was eighteen years old at a time when softwood schooners, worked hard, barely lasted ten years. And the hated engines would have to be removed, but Walters had installed them so that would be possible. Finally, the Nova Scotians agreed to the race.

The final confrontation took place off Boston and Gloucester in October 1938, and it was not without its tense moments as the Americans tried to create a situation in which their *Gertrude L. Thibaud* would win. But in an extended and bitterly fought series of five races, *Bluenose* won three, including the exciting final race that gave the trophy permanently to Walters and the big schooner. As the Backmans relate it, it was a historic moment:

> Surging toward the finish line, the magnificent Lunenburger stood under way [as a tumultuous ovation from the American audience] burst forth in unrestrained salute to the greatest schooner of them all. The greeting echoed back and forth across the bay. It could not have been more resounding had it issued from the realm of her own home waters. Americans, for all their erstwhile sweat and tears, knew a champion when they saw one; they could not, would not begrudge her one whit due in this moment of supreme triumph.

That race marked virtually the end of the era of the big wooden schooner in the Canadian fishery, and the end of *Bluenose*'s days in the limelight. The war began the following year, and Walters was forced to sell the schooner to the West Indian Trading Company in 1942. With her masts cut down and her once-proud lines marred by a deck house and the funnels of the diesels, *Bluenose* toiled in obscurity in the Caribbean until January 28, 1946. On that day her unwatchful crew let the sto-

The Starboard Lookout, by W.R. Macaskill PA 123637

ried old ship run aground on a reef off the Île à Vache, on Haiti's south coast. The crew abandoned her, and slowly she was pounded to pieces by the blue-green swells until nothing was left to mark her passing. It was a sad end for a vessel of legend, and Angus Walters mourned as if he had lost a part of his own soul.

The memory of the magnificent schooner lives on in various ways. In 1937 the Canadian government changed the design of the ten-cent piece to show a Grand Banks schooner in its full glory under sail, and in 1963 the Oland Brewing Company built a replica of the schooner, named *Bluenose II*, at the same yard in Lunenburg and crafted by many of the same hands that had shaped the original. Now owned by the Nova Scotian government and fitted out like a yacht below decks, the new schooner suggests much of the speed, power and magic of the first *Bluenose*, although out of respect for the original's record the replica is never raced.

But the magic is still there. In 1967 the author sailed for a time as a green young seaman in *Bluenose II*, and on a passage from Montreal to Halifax had the helm as *Bluenose II* forged along on a broad reach in the Gulf of St. Lawrence north of Prince Edward Island in a heavy October wind, with all working canvas up. The big schooner rushed through the low swells with just under ten thousand square feet of canvas drawing. The mate, a laconic Norwegian, came on deck to stare over the side for a bit and then muttered, "Seventeen knots, I tink. Maybe more. She can fly if she vants, eh?" before going below to leave that helmsman staring aloft in wide-eyed wonder. It was an understatement that said much, akin to the simple, telling observation about the original *Bluenose* spoken by her diminutive, unbeatable captain, Angus Walters, who said, "The wood of the vessel that will beat the *Bluenose* is still growing!"

For Canadians, it is unlikely that any vessel will ever inspire respect and love like that now-vanished champion schooner of Canada's Atlantic fishery—a true champion, to the very end.

16

A Few Adventurers

T HE PAGES of Canadian maritime history teem with the stories of larger-than-life men and women whose adventures, risks, achievements—and failures—make for fascinating reading. At every point in Canada's history, individuals with the stuff of dramatic heroism or with simple, quiet courage can be found. The names are many: Baffin, Davis, Cartier, Hudson, d'Iberville, McClure, Bernier, Larsen, to name a few. Their stories can be as immediate as the astonishing adventure of Victoria resident John Guzzwell, who in the 1950s built a modest little wooden yawl, *Trekka*, and then took her alone around the world in a slow, event-packed odyssey that ended before he was thirty. His little ship, amazingly delicate to have survived so much, rests in the Maritime Museum of British Columbia in Victoria. But besides the Cartiers and the Berniers and the Guzzwells of Canadian history there are also unlikely adventurers: ones who undertook remarkable voyages almost by accident, by force of circumstance or because of the difficulties of life ashore. Three such men are found in Canada's stories of the sea, as unalike one another as might be imagined, but alike in having an inner drive either to do something unique in their lives or to survive unexpected challenges: Robert Stobo, John Voss and Joshua Slocum.

Robert Stobo was a handsome, articulate and talented lowland Scot, born at Glasgow in 1727, the son of a merchant. He had a gentleman's upbringing that ended abruptly at age fifteen when the death of his mother forced him to leave university and enter the family business. Although young Stobo was far more interested in a liber-tine social life, he proved adept enough at clerking to be sent out to Virginia as an agent for not only his family's business but those of several other Glasgow merchants as well. Arriving in the colony, he set himself up at Petersburg, Virginia, where he used his quick wits if not great business acumen to avoid business failure. Between 1748 and 1754, Stobo rapidly became a favourite in the colonial social whirl for his charm, breeding and very evident appreciation of ladies; less appealing to him was the life of the counting house. When, in 1754, rising tensions with the French led the Virginia legislature to send George Washington off to the Ohio valley to challenge French claims to that territory, Stobo determined to go as well. Representing himself somehow as a capable engineer, he was soon commissioned as a captain in the Provincial Virginia Reg-iment, and was sent off with an infantry company to Great Mead-ows, Pennsylvania, where Washington, having unwisely attacked a French party in the Ohio wilderness, was awaiting French retalia-tion. Stobo arrived in time to join the garrison of Washington's tiny, crudely made Fort Necessity and, in a driving rainstorm, took part in the first battle of the French and Indian War—a battle that led to Washington's surrender and, overall, to the beginning of the huge worldwide conflict known as the Seven Years War.

The little fight in the rain lasted four soggy hours, and as part of the terms of Washington's surrender he agreed to provide two hostages to the French, who would be held until French prisoners in Virginia were released. Along with a trilingual Dutchman, Jacob Van Braam, Robert Stobo volunteered to serve as one of the hostages. The two men were soon carried off to the French Fort Duquesne, where Pittsburgh now stands. There, they saw English prisoners and concluded they need not honour the terms of their hostage taking since the French held prisoners they had denied having. Stobo fatefully drew a diagram of Fort Duquesne, with written commentary, which was smuggled out to the English by a friendly Indian.

Stobo was taken to Quebec, where he initially led a quite open and free life as an officer on his "parole," or honourable code of behaviour including an undertaking not to try to escape. He became active socially, particularly with the vivacious young women of Quebec, and even dabbled in business as his fluency in French developed. Then, abruptly, his status changed from guest to felon. His diagram of Fort Duquesne had been found by the French in the papers of the English general Braddock, whose army had been cut to pieces outside Fort Duquesne in 1755. Stobo was branded a spy and sentenced to death—a sentence almost immediately commuted, although he was now treated with great suspicion while the French tried to decide what to do with him.

For his part, Stobo determined to escape the walled town. Still granted some limited freedoms, Stobo had by 1759 made several solo attempts at escape. Realizing he needed support, he assembled a group of English prisoners and other detainees in Quebec—the French definition of "imprisonment" was clearly a loose one—quietly bought some necessary supplies, and even managed to secure several flintlock muskets with powder and shot. Escaping over the walls of the town one night in the month of May, Stobo and his party stole a large, thirty-foot fur trade canoe from the shoreline and began paddling downriver. As Robert C. Alberts wrote in 1965:

> There were nine persons altogether: Major Stobo, in command as senior officer and financier of the enterprise; Lieutenant Simon Stevens, second in command; Elizah Denbo of New Jersey; Oliver Deakin, the prisoner of the Indians; William Clark, the carpenter, the only man who knew anything about boats or navigation; and Clark's wife and three children. Their plan was to paddle down the Saint Lawrence River, through its notoriously difficult and dangerous rocks, tides, whirlpools and currents, across the Bay of St. Lawrence, and out into the ocean to Louisbourg on Cape Breton island. Their goal was almost 1,000 miles away.

Inexperienced as he was, Stobo soon showed an aptitude for handling the craft, and, leaving the mouth of the Rivière St-Charles, the party steered across the turbulent waters of the basin into the South Channel, passing close along the shore of the Île d'Orléans. Realizing the risks of following the main shipping channel, which swung to the north side of the river, Stobo kept the canoe to the south side, passing along the neat rows of farms stretching back to the forest, and trusting that their nondescript dress and his command of French would allay any suspicion. For several days they paddled on, sleeping in the canoe when they could, until finally, just below Île aux Coudres, the wind turned out of the east and they were forced to make a camp ashore. Surprising some Huron at a nearby campsite, Stobo and the other men killed them in desperation, and took their food and supplies. The party ventured on when the wind shifted again, the Clark family huddled miserably in the bottom of the canoe, until after a week of dogged effort they had descended the river some 125 miles, reaching a point where the river was twelve miles across. In a brief moment of terror the canoe was caught in a monstrous tidal whirlpool off the mouth of the Saguenay River, and only frenzied paddling prevented the craft from being overset and sucked under.

By May 9 the haggard little party was suffering intensely from exposure, and their meagre stock of food was gone. They had dragged the canoe ashore and collapsed in a rough camp when they became aware of a four-oared longboat putting in to shore. The overheard conversation of the boat's crew revealed they were French, putting in to refill a water cask. While Mrs. Clark and the children hid in the forest, Stobo and the other men pounced on the longboat crew as soon as they came ashore and took them prisoner. Embarking the Clark family—and gratefully digging in to the food the French had with them in the boat—Stobo and the others put the French to work on the oars and rowed on downriver. Another brief moment of terror occurred at the Île du Bic when a French sloop thought the overcrowded boat looked suspicious and fired at them as it manoeuvred to intercept them. By dint of hard rowing and luck—the French vessel was downwind and could not tack up after them—they managed to escape.

The French prisoners had not proved troublesome, and had been kindly to the Clark children. At Rivière Métis, Stobo put them ashore with some basic supplies and one of the flintlocks. The French were appreciative of Stobo's act in a time of war, and the parting was not rancorous.

The winds now allowed the longboat to set up its sailing rig, and the party pressed on around the curve of the Gaspé coast, passing the hulking shape of Percé Rock until they entered the Baie des Chaleurs. From here, English territory was within striking distance: the Isle of Saint John—Prince Edward Island—could almost be glimpsed to the southeast. It would mean the challenge of an open-water crossing in the longboat, however, not coastal sailing. They continued on along the New Brunswick coast and into the entrance to Northumberland Strait, hoping to lessen the distance of that open passage. The daily routine was one of constant peril and risk, as this entry from the diary of Lieutenant Stevens as recorded by Alberts, reveals:

> 12th [of May, 1759]. Very early this morning we weighed anchor, and set sail with a fair wind; after we had sailed about thirteen leagues we attempted to land on the southern shore, but the wind was so high we dared not venture; we then sailed about a league further, and came to a cove, where we put in. We immediately saw a boat on shore, and a smoke, which caused us to put back. We sailed about a league further, and came to another cove, we put in there, and went ashore, where we tarried all night.

The discomfort to the little party, particularly the children, of "tarrying" without shelter on the harsh, forested shore can only be imagined. But they soon found themselves in greater peril. On May 17 the boat struck hard on rocks off the New Brunswick coast and was shattered beyond repair. Wading ashore into the dark forest, sodden and with their food lost, the party considered what to do. Fortune remained with them, however. While the men were arguing about trying to walk overland to Fort Cumberland on the Chignecto peninsula, a small French schooner coasted along the shore near to them. Stobo used his French to lure the schooner men in to "rescue" his party, then managed to capture the schooner, and even a small French sloop that sailed into the cove shortly thereafter. Cramming the schooner with supplies from both boats, Stobo burned the sloop then set all but four of the French ashore with food.

Within hours they were sailing on, heading eastward along Northumberland Strait for the harbour of Port-la-Joye, now Charlottetown. To their inestimable joy, they tacked up into Hillsborough Bay and saw the Union flag floating over the little settlement. It was May 27, 1759. As Alberts relates:

> The commander [at Charlottetown] received them courteously, entertained them, and when they left provided a ship's guard of a sergeant and twelve privates. They sailed east through the Strait of Canso and up the east coast of Cape Breton island, the British flag flying above the French fleur-de-lys on the ensign's staff as the mark of a prize vessel taken from the enemy. On June 6, thirty-six days from the time they had fled Quebec, they sailed through a narrow passage into the spacious harbour of Louisbourg.

The harbour was empty: the huge fleet of 141 ships, commanded by Vice Admiral Saunders and carrying James Wolfe and his army to Quebec, had sailed shortly before. Stobo was quickly interviewed by the governor and resident naval officers, and within hours he and Stevens had agreed to re-embark in a Royal Navy vessel for the passage back up the river, in pursuit of Wolfe. With new uniforms and orders, Stobo said farewell to his companions in the remarkable adventure down the river. Selling the schooner and its effects without delay, he presented the proceeds to Mrs. Clark and her children. Within a few hours his ship was standing northwest toward the mouth of the great river he had just descended with such courage, determination and innate skill. Historians continue to debate whether it was Stobo who, successfully reaching Quebec before the attack of September 13, 1759, showed James Wolfe the pathway leading up from the Anse au Foulon that gave the British their victory.

Robert Stobo ended the war with honour, and returned to Virginia and a hero's welcome. But then his fortunes turned. He made several bad business deals, and would die a suicide as a penniless military officer in Britain, far from the scene of his heroics, and of an adventurous voyage that remains to this day a legendary story of bravery, willpower and luck on the great river of Canada.

If Robert Stobo was an appealing and attractive character, John Claus Voss was anything but. A short, muscular and gloomily wordless German seaman who only became articulate when roaring drunk, Voss was one of the many odd and misplaced characters who ended up, like the loose contents of a drawer tilted to the west, on the British Columbia coast at the end of the nineteenth century. Voss had been born about 1861 and had gone to sea as a teenager, drifting from ship to ship and to odd shore adventures until he ended up in Victoria in his forties, glumly managing a seedy hotel, dividing his time between easy-riches schemes and drunken homicidal rages.

In 1901, Voss came across a Canadian reporter named Norman Luxton during a Victoria night of hard saloon drinking, and claimed to Luxton that he could convert a west coast Indian canoe into a vessel able to outdo the recent achievement of Captain Joshua Slocum, who had astonished the Maritime community by sailing his little fishing smack *Spray* around the world single-handed, the first man to do so. Luxton took him up on his bet, and Voss bought a thirty-two-foot cedar Nootka canoe on Vancouver Island, which he decked over and rigged as a kind of schooner with three short masts carrying a little over two hundred square feet of sail.

With Luxton as a very seasick crew, Voss sailed away from Victoria in May 1901 on a voyage into the South Pacific characterized by hair's-breadth escapes and an odd relationship between Luxton and Voss, whom Luxton found a competent and determined sailor when sober and a raging, semi-psychotic menace when drunk, which occurred frequently. Luxton took to keeping a loaded pistol handy at all times. They had named the bizarre little craft *Tilikum*, and as they made their way toward the islands of Polynesia, Luxton became, according to Voss's very correct and articulately written account, a fairly capable seaman—when he wasn't trying to keep Voss out of the whisky.

In September 1901, the *Tilikum* reached the Cook Islands and was given a warm welcome by the agreeable Polynesians—so much so that Voss contracted venereal disease from one of the many "island princesses" he seems to have pursued with single-minded vigour. Luxton, far more the gentleman, may have more circumspectly shared in this hospitality, most spectacularly with the legendary Sadie Thompson at Samoa. Between island adventures involving paralytic drinking and the never-ending pursuit of "princesses" Voss nonetheless skilfully navigated the little schooner through the maze of islands—a near shipwreck approaching Tonga was an exception—and made much use of drogue-like "sea anchors," which, when streamed off the vessel's bows, allowed it to ride safely in almost any sea. Luxton crawled ashore at Fiji to regain his health, but agreed to rejoin Voss in Australia for a money-making lecture tour and a chance for Voss to be hospitalized and cured of his venereal complaints. Voss had to deal with other taints to his character as well: a seaman who was signed on in Fiji to replace Luxton as crew vanished overboard en route to Australia, and the suspicion that Voss had thrown him over the side in a drunken fit never quite died away. The case was never proven, however, and Voss managed to secure two other crewmen for subsequent legs of his bizarre voyage, as well as the short-term services of nine others who soon left after the discomforts of the voyage—and Voss's hidden nature—became evident.

As unpredictable and vicious a drunk as he may have been, Voss was a superb and hardy seaman when sober, and he took *Tilikum* from Australia back to New Zealand, then through Endeavour Straits across the vast Indian Ocean to South Africa. From there the little Nootka canoe sailed to Napoleon's place of exile at St. Helena, then up to Pernambuco, Brazil. The final leg of the voyage took *Tilikum* to the Azores and on to England, where Voss arrived in September 1904, claiming to have taken three years, three months and twelve days for the passage from Victoria.

Voss gained some celebrity in Britain for his feat, but it was short-lived, his troglodytic character not contributing to his welcome. And he had failed to equal Slocum's feat, for *Tilikum* almost ended its days on the mud flats of tidal England. Voss's own deepest thoughts and motives were never known, as when he was sober enough to express them he rarely said anything. But he was capable of a simple lyricism about the one thing he knew best, which was sailing:

> I do not like to press a small boat hard when sailing by the wind with a strong breeze and a head sea . . . But it is certainly a pleasure to sail a boat with a free wind, or when she is running before it and has a good large sea in her favour. In running with wind and sea I could sit in the cockpit, with the tiller in my hand, hour upon hour, and watch her going along.

Voss's later life is murky. At one point he was being hunted by the U.S. Coast Guard on a charge of smuggling drugs and illegal Chinese immigrants into the United States. He followed his *Tilikum* voyage with a brief settled period as, once more, a hotel manager in Victoria, only to drift away into obscurity at sea. He is thought to have died around 1922, possibly in California. *Tilikum*, for its part, was rescued from oblivion in Britain and now resides, restored, in Victoria's Maritime Museum.

John Claus Voss was a fine seaman, but there was very little of the gentleman about him. The third adventurer of this chapter was in all respects a true gentleman of the sea, a quiet and unassuming Canadian from Nova Scotia who earned permanent fame as the first man to circumnavigate the globe alone. Joshua Slocum came to his grand adventure almost by force of circumstance, as a "tall ship" captain rapidly being rendered obsolete by the proliferation of steamships, and seeing in the voyage of his little craft a means of demonstrating, if only to himself, his continuing worth.

Joshua Slocum was born in western Nova Scotia in 1844, a descendant of Loyalist Quakers who had come north after the American Revolution. The middle child in a family of eleven children, Slocum grew up in the small community of Brier Island on the Bay of Fundy, where he worked in the shoemaking shop of his father. Seized with restlessness and anxious to be away from the claustrophobic pressures of family and the harshness of his father, he left home in his mid-teens on the death of his mother and travelled to Halifax, where he signed on in a merchant vessel outbound for Dublin, Ireland. This was the beginning of a two-year period as a learning seaman in coal and grain ships operating mostly in the Pacific, during which time he mastered his trade so well that he became a second mate at the age of eighteen. From the 1860s until the 1890s he had a successful career as master, and in some cases co-owner, of no fewer than twelve major sailing vessels. His wife, an American whom he had met in Sydney, Australia, sailed with him for many years, accompanied by their children, and he once brought them safely home to Chesapeake Bay from South America in a 35-foot boat he built himself after the wreck of their ship. Having done some correspondent's work for an American newspaper, he wrote of this experience—a good preparation for the bestselling account of the adventure he finally undertook.

By the mid-1890s, now in late middle age, his career faltering due to the prevalence of steam and with his self-worth at a low ebb, he was at loose ends. About this time someone gave him a boat, a 36-foot fishing sloop in disintegrating condition at Fairhaven, Massachusetts. The donor thought he had played a humorous trick on Slocum, but the canny Nova Scotian took one look at the boat, noted it was called *Spray* and decided to rebuild it. His purpose in doing so, as he later recorded in his account of his world voyage, *Sailing Alone Around the World*, was soon clear:

> I had resolved on a voyage around the world, and as the wind on the morning of April 24, 1895, was fair, at noon I weighed anchor, set sail, and filled away from Boston, where the *Spray* had been moored snugly all winter. The twelve o'clock whistles were blowing just as the sloop shot ahead under full sail. A short board was made up the harbour on the port tack, then coming about she stood to seaward, with her boom well off to port, and swung past the ferries with lively heels. A photographer on the outer pier of East Boston got a picture of her as she swept by, her flag at the peak throwing her folds clear. A thrilling pulse beat high in me. My step was light on deck in the crisp air. I felt there could be no turning back, and that I was engaging in an adventure the meaning of which I thoroughly understood.

It would prove to be every bit the memorable adventure Slocum anticipated.

He had rebuilt *Spray* from its original configuration as a working fish sloop, adding bunks and stowage, always with an eye to the demands of the voyage he was about to undertake. It was perhaps inevitable that a man of Slocum's background would come to this adventure. Family seemed not to be a factor and, as he related,

> Mine was not the sort of life to make one long to coil up one's ropes on land, the customs and ways of which I had finally almost forgotten. And so when times for [sailing ships] got bad, as at last they did, what was there for an old sailor to do? I was born on the breezes, and I had studied the sea as perhaps few men have studied it, neglecting all else . . . Thus the voyage [was] a natural outcome of my love of adventure, but also of my lifelong experience.

Spray was originally rigged as a gaff-rigged sloop, with a deep keel and projecting bowsprit and jib-boom. Later in the voyage Slocum would add a small mizzen to allow him to sail the boat under jib and mizzen. Slocum was adept at shipbuilding—"Next in attractiveness, after seafaring, came shipbuilding. I longed to be master in both professions, and in a small way, in time, I accomplished my desire"—and *Spray* as he rebuilt it was sea-kindly and able to weather almost any conditions. In addition, he could "balance" the sail rig so that the boat would sail itself on any heading relative to the wind, without a hand on the tiller. On long passages Slocum would routinely set the vessel on its course and go below to sleep, an extraordinary comment on his seamanship—and on his trust that *Spray* would not run into something, or be run into, while he was below.

Slocum soon demonstrated to himself and to others that both he and *Spray* might have the qualities the voyage required, as he entered the harbour of Gloucester, Massachusetts, to lay in stores for the voyage:

> The bay was feather-white as my little vessel tore in, smothered in foam. It was my first experience of coming into port alone, with a craft of any size, and in among shipping. Old fishermen ran down to the wharf for which the *Spray* was heading, apparently intent upon braining herself there. I hardly knew how a calamity was averted, but with my heart in my mouth, almost, I let go the wheel, stepped quickly forward, and downed the jib. The sloop naturally rounded in the wind, and just ranging ahead, laid her cheek against a mooring pile at the windward corner of the wharf, so quietly, after all, that she would not have broken an egg. Very leisurely I passed a rope around the post, and she was moored. Then a cheer went up from the little crowd on the wharf. "You couldn't a' done it better," cried an old skipper, "if you weighed a ton!"

Leaving Massachusetts, Slocum took *Spray* across the Atlantic to Gibraltar via the Azores. After a stay at the British naval base, he turned *Spray* southwestward toward the Canary Islands and the Cape Verde Islands, steering for the coast of South America. Off the North African coast *Spray* was pursued by Moroccan pirates, and was saved when a providential squall swept over the sloop and the pursuing Arab felucca, dismasting the latter. From North Africa, *Spray* crossed the Atlantic and made landfall at Pernambuco, Brazil. With stops at Rio de Janeiro and Montevideo, Slocum worked his way down to the Strait of Magellan, making a near-incredible passage of that forbidding waterway single-handed and under sail. He defended himself against a raid by Indians intent on looting *Spray* by littering the boat's decks with tacks, which literally stopped the barefoot Indians in their tracks.

Entering the Pacific, Slocum took *Spray* northwest for a month, to the towering beauty of the Marquesas Islands, then pressed on to the north of Tahiti before finally arriving at Samoa, having spent seventy-two days at sea without touching port. From Samoa, Slocum sailed on to Australia, where he had the happiest moments of the voyage, sailing down to Sydney and Melbourne before working his way up to the Great Barrier Reef. Passing successfully through the Reef and Endeavour Straits, Slocum sailed on to Christmas Island and the Cocos Islands, then went on across the Indian Ocean to Mauritius, Réunion and Durban, South Africa. Another pleasant stay was followed by re-entry into the Atlantic, and a long voyage up from Cape Town to St. Helena, Ascension Island and finally Trinidad in the West Indies. From Trinidad, *Spray*'s track took it up the Leeward and Windward islands to Antigua, and then a long, final passage to Massachusetts. "So on July 3 [1898], with a fair wind, she waltzed beautifully round the coast and up the Acushnet River to Fairhaven, where I secured her to the cedar pile driven in the bank to hold her when she was launched. I could bring her no nearer home."

The great voyage of *Spray* was the high point of Slocum's life. His account of the exploit became a bestseller, and Slocum enjoyed popularity as a lecturer for some years, respected and admired for his achievement but equally for his unpretentious and pleasant character and natural dignity. Slocum was never entirely comfortable ashore, and each winter he took *Spray* on an extended voyage to the Grand Cayman Islands.

In 1909, at the age of sixty-five, Slocum once more put to sea in *Spray*, intending to sail to the mouth of the Orinoco River in South America. *Spray* vanished at sea without a trace, and it was thought that Slocum had gone below to sleep, as was his custom, and the vessel had been run down by one of the steamers that now proliferated on the seas. It was a Viking-like end to his life, and some would say it was a poignantly fitting one for a man only comfortable when away on the deep.

Slocum had commented, at the end of his account of *Spray*'s circumnavigation, that "to face the elements is, to be sure, no light matter when the sea is in its grandest mood. You must then know the sea, and know that you know it, and not forget that it was made to be sailed over." Joshua Slocum's life was an embodiment of such thinking. And it led him to one of the grandest adventures ever experienced by a Canadian.

17

Far Distant Ships:
Canada's Navy
is Born

Once clear of the harbour, the watch closed up to begin the seagoing routine which would last until we berthed on the other side of the Atlantic; one-third of the ship's company manning the engines, boilers, wheel, asdic, wireless, and lookout positions, the other two-thirds below trying to catch what sleep they could before their own four-hour stint began. It is my watch until eight, but the captain lingers anxiously, worried about the rising wind and sea. A green one crashes aboard; peering over the dodger we can see its dark shape engulf our foredeck, and we crouch for shelter as the ship plunges thunderously into it. A wall of water, tons of it, sweeps across our fo'c'sle to hurl itself against our bridge structure with a resounding thump. Water sweeps overhead, even in the shelter of the dodger we are drenched, and from below comes a series of bangs and crashes, from mess decks and galley and upper deck, where a hundred items, big and small, have bumped and smashed and clanged and rattled under the impact of the heavy sea. A great murmur of protest, of oaths and groans and bitching, rises from the ventilators and voice-pipes, and from the wheelhouse we hear the bosun's mate, loud and clear: "This effing bucket! Roll on, our refit!"

The captain grins, catches my eye. "Hearts of oak!" he grunts.

To UNDERSTAND the story of Canada and the sea is to look into the mirror of the Canadian national character: the enduring qualities of practicality, common sense, endurance in the face of adversity, and an unassuming, wintry integrity. Nowhere is this more evident than in the story of Canada's navy, the navy that came of age in experiences like that related above by Second World War veteran James Lamb.

In the first decade of the twenty-first century, Canada possesses a navy of which any middle power could be proud. With intelligent, worldly-wise leadership, with well-trained and professional personnel equal to those of any world navy, and with capable ships equipped with state-of-the-art communications and computer technology and modern weaponry, the Canadian navy—or, more properly, Maritime Command of the Canadian Forces—is a flexible instrument of great value to the Canadian government as it selects options on matters of international policy, territorial sovereignty assertion or the protection of Canada's environmental, alliance or trading commitments. There is little debate on the value to Canada of such a navy, although the navy's traditional reticence to promote itself, in the truest traditions of the "silent service," often prevents the message of its value from reaching the Canadian public. Incredibly, lack of information or interest about navies and what they do almost prevented Canada from ever having one at all. As the historian John Clayton, writing in 1985, observed, "Few countries have ever adopted a naval service with as much reluctance and heated debate, in spite of a deeply rooted maritime tradition and the longest coastline in the world." Reluctant naval power or not, Canada has sent to sea no fewer than five hundred warships under a naval ensign since the navy was created by the Naval Service Act of May 4, 1910.

In the colonial era, naval protection of the Canadian colonies was the responsibility of France's *marine royale* and then, after 1763, of Britain's Royal Navy. As we have seen, the inland waters of Canada were policed, if that is the correct word, by the Provincial Marine, an agency of the army's quartermaster department, until it was replaced by the Royal Navy in 1813. British naval officers commanded the small naval units that were raised on the inland waters at the time of the Rebellions of 1837–38 and during the Fenian Raid alarms of 1866–71. With the coming of Confederation in 1867, the continuing responsibility of the RN for Canadian maritime defence was assumed, but it soon became evident to Canadian politicians

Dominion Government cruiser *Canada*, Shelburne   *PA 42011*

that, declarations of imperial solidarity notwithstanding, Great Britain's overriding interest was maintaining good relations with the United States for mercantile and other reasons, and Canadian concerns were likely to be of secondary importance.

The resolution of many long-standing irritants that had existed between the United States and Great Britain before 1871, and the perceived lack of a maritime threat in the mind of the Canadian public, meant that interest in a home-grown naval service of any kind was minimal. It was not until 1881 that the first fisheries patrol was established on the east coast, and to its credit the Canadian Department of Marine and Fisheries operated a fleet of some thirty-two vessels until 1910 that, if not a navy, did the job of a small one. Eight of the fisheries cruisers were armed, the most noteworthy of which was the CGS *Canada*, and these armed vessels were operated in all respects as warships.

The growing threat seen in imperial Germany after 1900, and the difficulty the British government was experiencing in paying for a sufficiently powerful and modern battle fleet in the face of ambitious German shipbuilding, led the British to call an Imperial Conference in 1902, at which they requested financial contributions from the independent dominions to build warships for the RN as a counter to Germany's battleship construction program. The Canadian delegation listened politely but declined to agree to the British proposal. Again in 1907, the increasingly worried British called an Imperial Conference and repeated the request for shipbuilding money. The Australians and New Zealanders agreed to look at funding a "local squadron" of RN warships in the South Pacific, thereby freeing British funds for the fleet in European waters, but Canada again declined to enter into a support scheme.

By 1909, the armament race between Britain and Germany had become alarming, as the expenditures to produce heavily armoured "dreadnoughts" spiralled upwards out of sight. In Canada, the national debate over the battleships issue became heated. Conservative and western Canadians, and those with a strong attachment to Britain as the mother country, argued for Canadian financial support for Britain; while those with a more nationalist focus and less concern for imperial solidarity argued for either no navy at all or some form of indigenous service that would meet Canada's needs but prevent the nation's citizens from becoming entangled in European or other overseas conflicts of no relevance to Canada. This last view was strongest in Quebec, which cast a jaundiced eye over any attempt to empty its pockets of cash—or its farms of young men—to serve the distant and, to them, irrelevant needs of Whitehall.

Canada's prime minister, Sir Wilfrid Laurier, was as adept as any politician at holding together the schizophrenic Canadian political structure. Few could disagree with the comment made by the Conservative George Fowler in 1909 that, whatever decision was reached, Canada should "assume a proper share of the responsibility and financial burden incident to the suitable protection of her exposed coastline and great seaports." The problem facing Laurier was how to do that without infuriating imperialists and nationalists alike.

Laurier countered the furor with the Naval Service Act of 1910, which passed after some ferocious argument, and which dragged a reluctant Canada muttering and complaining into the business of defending itself at sea. The Act provided for five branches of activity: a naval force and supporting naval college; fisheries protection; hydrographic surveys; tidal and current surveys; and a wireless telegraph system to tie the whole thing together. The first director of the new Naval Service of Canada was to be Rear Admiral Charles Kingsmill, a native of Guelph, Ontario, who left a successful career in the Royal Navy in 1908 to become head of the Marine Service of the Department of Marine and Fisheries. The first minister for the service was to be the Honourable Louis-Philippe Brodeur.

Recognizing that some form of Canadian commitment to naval defence was better than none at all, the Royal Navy agreed to transfer two light cruisers to the new Canadian service: HMCS *Rainbow*, which came on strength on August 4, 1910, and HMCS *Niobe*, which joined as of September 6, 1910. Joined to vessels transferred from the Department of Marine and Fisheries, their arrival created the beginnings of a true navy, a navy that had been born out of compromise, as so many Canadian institutions were and have been.

When the world drifted into the cataclysm of the First World War, Canada found itself, as part of the British Empire, immediately at war with Germany and the Austro-Hungarian Empire. The Royal Canadian Navy, with 379 officers and men, hardly constituted a major factor in imperial defence, but with *Niobe* and *Rainbow* as the basis it began to assemble a small fleet based on trawlers, drifters and other light craft of an essentially auxiliary nature. Some seven thousand men would eventually serve in the wartime RCN, and the east coast flotilla grew to almost a hundred vessels, mostly of the light trawler variety. HMCS *Niobe* joined the RN squadron in the western Atlantic at the war's beginning, but it was soon revealed to be too worn out and unsafe to remain on active service; *Niobe* returned to Halifax after barely a year of activity. On the west coast, *Rainbow* performed creditably until its withdrawal for similar reasons in 1917, having patrolled as far south as Panama. It was fortunate that *Rainbow* did not in fact encounter any German vessels, for her survival would have been very unlikely.

The small RCN had very little to do until 1917–18, when German submarine activity began to target Canadian fishing vessels and freighters. Unable to mount a serious defence against these attacks, RCN vessels were in the main useful for sounding the alarm to nearby RN vessels—if there were any—which could then pursue the submarine. Ironically, the little RCN owned two submarines of its own, CC1 and CC2, which had been bought from a Seattle shipyard by Sir Richard McBride, premier of British Columbia, who was alarmed at the weak state of Canada's west coast naval defences. The odd little boats made it as far as Halifax by 1917, having been ordered to Europe, but after sober reflection on what the North Atlantic offered in terms of seas and weather, CC1 and CC2 ended their careers at Halifax, paid off and scrapped in 1920. The RCN did suffer casualties in the war: many members served with the parent RN, and 225 lost their lives.

Between 1919 and 1922, the RCN contemplated what its future might hold, but it persistently returned to the idea that a destroyer-based navy seemed to be the most acceptable option for Canada. The British light cruiser *Aurora* was given up, and four ex-RN destroyers formed the basis of the early postwar fleet: HMC ships *Patriot* and *Patrician* and then, some time later, *Champlain* and *Vancouver*. By 1925, however, government interest in the navy had fallen to such an extent that the service struggled to survive with a strength of 70 officers and 446 men. In opposition, the Conservative politician Arthur Meighen would later sneer at Canada's "five-trawler navy," which did little for imperial or Canadian defence, in his mind.

The nadir for the navy came in 1933, even though two years earlier it had taken delivery of the first ships built expressly for the RCN, in British yards: the destroyers *Skeena* and *Saguenay*. Four others, ex–Royal Navy ships, would arrive in 1934–35: the destroyers *Fraser*, *St. Laurent*, *Restigouche* and *Ottawa*. But these ships almost had no navy to join, as in 1933 the influential Major General A.G.L. McNaughton seriously suggested scrapping the RCN altogether and focusing the government's scarce Depression-era funds on the army and fledgling air force.

The little RCN refused to die, however, and unpaid volunteer reservists across the country helped keep a semblance of naval spirit alive through the grim period of the Depression. In 1939 the new and respectable Canadian destroyer force exercised together for the first time, in the Caribbean, a remarkable-enough achievement given that the defence budget in 1939 provided $29.8 million for the air force, $21 million for the army and only $8.8 million for the navy. The flotilla that manoeuvred through the warm waters of the Caribbean while her officers dreamed of a larger, traditional surface navy would have been all but indistinguishable from the Royal Navy except for the accents of its members and some minor uniform touches. It was about to enter a bloody and tumultuous decade that would change the navy forever, and much would vanish, including the dream of a powerful surface fleet and the unquestioned mirroring of the ways and manners of another navy increasingly of little relevance to Canada and Canadian society.

The operational mentality of the interwar Royal Canadian Navy was heavily focused on the lessons most of its officer corps had learned, which were those of the Royal Navy. Their planning and hopes were for the development of a larger surface fleet that would mirror the parent navy, the RN. Some historians have suggested that this caused the RCN's regular officers to be less concerned than they might have been about preparing for anti-submarine warfare, even though that warfare had been ominously a near-run thing in 1917–18. Although the Canadian chief of the naval staff had declared in 1935 that in the event of war "the navy's job would be the protection of trade to and from Canadian ports, and communications in the coastal areas," the threat envisaged seems to have been primarily the surface warship, and less so the submarine. Historian Marc Milner, writing in 1985, quoted Canadian Commodore Percy W. Nelles in saying:

> If international law is complied with, submarine attack should not prove serious. If unrestricted warfare is again resorted to, the means of combating submarines are considered to have so

advanced that by employing a system of convoy and utilizing air forces, losses of submarines would be very heavy and might compel the enemy to give up this form of attack.

Whether, as the naval veteran and writer Jack MacBeth wrote somewhat caustically in 1989, the British-trained regular officers of the RCN dreamed only of big warships and not "the scruffy little buckets and converted yachts that had drearily patrolled Canadian waters in the First World War," or whether they were in fact professionally very aware of the potential war of small escorts against submarines, it could be argued that, again, a kind of "compromise navy" had been arrived at, balancing the needs of an uninterested federal government, an unaware population, an overseas-trained officer cadre and a sober assessment of what Canadians could or could not do at sea. That navy, with which Canada entered the Second World War, owed much of its 1939 character to Commodore Walter Hose who, although trained in the RN, had arguably come, soon after his transfer to the RCN in 1912, to adopt the needs of Canada rather than those of Britain as his principal professional motivation.

Hose recognized that a large permanent navy was out of the question, so he undertook to build up a strong and numerous volunteer reserve force across the country—even though most, as mentioned, were unpaid at times—strengthened the reserve of experienced fishermen and merchant sailors, and doggedly pursued the creation of a fleet that would serve Canadian interests rather than simply dovetail with the RN. Hose recognized that the acquisition of cruisers would raise alarm bells in the press about entanglement in British naval adventures, and that a smaller type of vessel might be of less interest to Canada's closest allies—but more useful to Canada. As the well-researched writing of naval historians W.A.B. Douglas, Roger Sarty and Michael Whitby observed in 2002, "Hose knew from [the U-boat war of 1917–18] and his understanding of naval warfare [that] destroyers were the smallest of the fighting ships that could give the RCN independent striking power against a variety of threats, including submarines and surface raiders."

Despite the efforts of Hose and others, a painful lack of funds had prevented any serious planning for what the RCN would do in the event of a second war with Germany, and indeed defence planning in Canada, if any existed, had only recently ceased naming the United States as the principal threat. The RCN approached the coming of war with little in the way of real preparedness for the storm front that was about to break over it.

When war was declared on September 10, 1939, the RCN's *matériel* consisted of six destroyers, four minesweepers, two training ships and one trawler, with a clutch of smaller vessels, divided between two bases at Halifax, Nova Scotia, and Esquimalt, British Columbia. Its total personnel was 309 officers and 2,967 other ranks, of whom it was observed that only 129 officers and 1,456 other ranks were trained to anything like professional standards. The officers continued to be very much influenced by the training and orientation of the Royal Navy, and the RCN still drew much of its operational methods and service psychology from that organization, simultaneously both of value and problematic in a North American context. On the outbreak of war, the professional officers of the RCN were at once aghast at the scale of the challenge that faced them but also aware that the war was the event that might put the permanent navy on the footing they sought for it—if the war could be won.

When the war began, Germany had 57 U-boats at sea, and the Allies were fortunate that the 400-boat fleet that would confront them three years later was not yet deployed in 1939, or the war at sea might have ended abruptly and catastrophically for Britain. As it was, the vital lifeline of supplies from Canada to Britain was threatened enough by the existing U-boats that the Royal Navy instituted a convoy system to and from North America and asked the RCN to provide escorts out as far as Newfoundland. The RCN did what it could with its small permanent fleet, at the same time entering into a hell-for-leather gathering up of any vessel that might serve as a stopgap until new ships could be built and manned. Within months of the declaration of war, an odd assortment of craft ranging from luxury yachts to odiferous fishing trawlers were coated in navy paint and sent off, bravely if inadequately, to do a navy's job. The fall of France in 1940 opened up Atlantic coastal ports to the U-boat flotillas, and the submarine assault on the vital convoys grew in intensity and lethality.

To face this submarine threat, which evidently was going to be the principal enemy in the open sea rather than the surface raiders so much pre-war planning had focused on, the Allies cast about for ways to produce escorts in large and quickly obtainable numbers. In Britain, the naval architect William Reed had designed a "patrol vessel, whaling type" based on the hunter ships of the whale fishery. They were small ships, barely 200 feet long with a 33-foot beam, and at 15 knots were slower than U-boats. They also were intended for inshore work, not to face the full fury of the open ocean. A desperate Admiralty, led by Winston Churchill, who named the little ships "corvettes" after a small class of French frigate of the eighteenth century, saw them as a cheap and easily built answer to the U-boat challenge. The Admiralty asked if Canada could build them, and Canada agreed: the corvette's small size meant they could be built on the Great Lakes as well as on the coasts, and their construction was simple and "civilian" enough for yards unaccustomed to building naval vessels. In 1940 Canadian shipyards signed contracts to build sixty-four corvettes, and would sign for another forty-three later on. With zeal and energy, if little experience, the Canadian yards roused themselves from the torpor and despair of the Depression and threw themselves into the work.

The RCN's regular officers, trained for and expectant of a surface war of destroyers and larger ships against a traditional naval opponent, now found themselves working against the clock to provide for the acceptance into the RCN of a rush of small sub-hunting whaling ships and of the crowds of volunteers who jammed recruit-

Flower-class corvette of the RCN, Halifax, 1941 *PA 105349*

ing stations, eager to don naval uniform. With a will, and often making things up as they went along, they set to work putting together a navy they had never expected to create.

The corvette would be the mainstay of Canada's sea war in the open Atlantic. Corvette veteran Jack MacBeth, writing in 1989, described the theory of defending a convoy of slow-moving merchant ships with corvettes:

> In the war's earlier days, three or four corvettes would be assigned to act as an escort screen for both eastbound and westbound convoys. This meant they would take up assigned positions on either side, and usually astern, of the convoy. The convoy itself consisted of perhaps thirty or forty ships ranged in rows of five or six. One destroyer (Senior Escort Officer) would station himself ahead of the convoy, and all escorts would follow a precise zigzag pattern in the hope of detecting a U-boat before he could attack, either on the surface or submerged.

The equipment of the little corvettes varied from ship to ship, but it was a constant complaint of Canadian corvettes that they were never as fully equipped or provided with as modern equipment as the Royal Navy corvettes. This had serious and often deadly consequences in the fight with the U-boats. The principal tool of the corvette was asdic, an acronym for a crude sonar device that used the reflection of sound echoes off a submerged body to locate submarines. Once located—if located—the submarine could be engaged on the surface with the corvette's main four-inch gun, a two-pounder "pom-pom" aft, and a variety of machine guns. To attack submerged submarines, the corvette carried depth charges— large, can-like bombs detonated by water pressure and either rolled off the ship's stern or fired to the side by launching mortars. With this relatively crude equipment, the corvette was sent off to engage the boats of a highly trained, supremely motivated and very effective German submarine force.

Pressed into the open-ocean fight, the corvettes soon demonstrated to their appalled crews why they had been intended for inshore work. Their round-bilged hull design was buoyant, but it rolled and pitched sickeningly in anything but a near calm. The bridge was open in all weather including a North Atlantic winter, and very few places in the ship escaped being drenched and sodden during a voyage, including the crowded mess decks, where the men slept in hammocks slung above their mess tables and subsisted on a diet of corned beef sandwiches when the decks were too awash to bring hot food from the small galley. Cold, wet, often numbed by retching seasickness, the young crews of the corvettes also had to struggle with their own ignorance, for in the rush to get the new vessels to sea, newly recruited officers and men alike often joined their ships with perhaps three months of rushed training, and had to struggle with learning their trade on the job. Fortunate was the Canadian corvette in the early days of the war that was commanded by an experienced reserve officer out of the merchant or fishing fleets, who could help keep the ship at least functional and the voyage survivable as young men fresh off farms or out of yacht clubs tried to come to grips with the blow of corvette life, the frightening reality of the North Atlantic and the grim danger of the sea war itself.

At naval headquarters and in the training establishments and dockyards, the regular RCN officers bore the brunt of organizing and training the rapidly growing navy, frequently working themselves and their staff into a somnambulant exhaustion as they tried to do so. They also had to keep in mind a postwar navy, though in their daily overwork that focus was sometimes set aside. Command, too, of the more "traditional" ships, such as destroyers, went to regular officers as a rule of thumb, so it fell to the experienced reservists, and increasingly to the wide-eyed newcomers of the volunteer reserve, to man the corvette flotillas. With their distinctive weave-pattern gold braid on their sleeves, the men of the escort flotillas began to refer to themselves as the Wavy Navy. It would be one of the ironies of the war that the "hostilities-only" men of the escort forces would be the builders of the anti-submarine, ocean-escort tradition upon which the professional postwar navy would come to be focused; the "big gun" surface fleet so desired by the regular force officers, who toiled meanwhile to make the escort force function, would come but briefly at war's end, only to be largely abandoned in the decade following the war.

The green Canadian crews of the corvettes remained driven more by enthusiasm and gritty courage than by knowledge as corvette after corvette rolled out of the yards and men rushed aboard to get them to sea. The "back of the line" place for Canadian corvettes in the reception of, for the most part, British-pattern equipment meant that they were slow to receive vital gear such as new radars, high-frequency direction-finding (HF/DF) devices that could pinpoint U-boat transmissions, and new anti-submarine weapons such as the "hedgehog" mortar. Inexperienced and under-equipped as they may have been, the Canadians were thrown into the convoy fight because they were needed there, not because they were ready for it. As Marc Milner wrote:

The completion of end-to-end [anti-submarine] escort in the North Atlantic was only possible with the commissioning of sufficient numbers of Canadian corvettes. These "cheap and nasties," as Churchill called them, thus assumed a role for which they were never intended. But in May 1941 it was not just the ships themselves that were ill prepared for the rigours of the North Atlantic. The RCN was unable to provide either experienced or properly trained crews for the expansion fleet. . . . They were only sent to sea in this condition on the urgent request of the Admiralty.

At sea, the differences between Canadian and British ships were painfully evident. Canadian corvettes were built without a break-water on the fo'c'sle (forward part of the ship) and were far wetter than their British counterparts; their decks were often not planked over, and were merely treacherous sheets of steel; and in the equipment gap, Canadian attempts to provide their ships with their own detection gear still left the Canadian vessels far below British standards in the early and mid part of the war. The war had to be fought, however, and with the United States Navy focused on the Japanese in the Pacific, Canada could not stand down from the North Atlantic fight. The convoys rolled on: HX convoy numbers sailing from Halifax, SC convoys sailing from Sydney, Cape Breton, and ON convoys sailing from Britain for Canada. By the winter of 1942–43 a hard-pressed and grimly struggling RCN was providing almost half the Atlantic escort force. But the battle was reaching a climax in the North Atlantic, and a grim decision was made by the Allies.

With its poor equipment and its exhausted crews who were unable to benefit from improved training, the RCN's escorted convoys had suffered 80 percent of the U-boats' successful attacks on convoys. Over three hundred U-boats were now at sea, and the valiant Canadian effort against them was proving not to be enough. At the height of the climactic battle, Winston Churchill sent a fateful letter, dated December 17, 1942, to Prime Minister Mackenzie King, as cited by Milner:

> A careful analysis of attacks on our transatlantic convoys has clearly shown that in those cases where heavy losses have occurred lack of training of the escorts, both individually and as a team, has largely been responsible for these disasters. I appreciate the grand contribution of the Royal Canadian Navy to the Battle of the Atlantic, but the expansion of the RCN has created a training problem which must take some time to solve.

The Canadian corvettes found themselves pulled out of the battle and their crews were sent off to be retrained. It would fall to the British to carry the U-boat struggle of 1943 to its climax. From the sidelines, with feelings that can only be imagined, the battle-weary and exhausted Canadians watched the Royal Navy, with its better equipment and aided by VLR (very long range) B-24 Liberator bombers, win the mid-ocean war against the U-boats and turn the tide of the Battle of the Atlantic. The Canadian volunteer reservists and their gritty little ships had given all they could to the fight, and not being in at the moment of triumph could only have been a bitter blow not to be forgotten.

Retrained and re-equipped at last, the Canadian escort groups returned to the fray, and ended the war with an efficiency fully equal to British or American escorts. But it had been a hard and bitter learning experience, one that in training and planning Canada's navy would never forget. What their desperate fight up to 1943 had achieved was clear, as Milner summarizes:

> The significance of the RCN's contribution to the Battle of the Atlantic lay in its successful efforts to hold the line until the Allies could assume the offensive. There can be no doubt that the fleet was inefficient prior to 1943 and that this inefficiency can be measured in lost lives and ships. However, one can only

speculate on the number of lives and ships saved simply because the RCN somehow found the escorts necessary to establish convoy routes and support operations.

The cost to Canada of the overall naval war was high: nineteen warships lost to enemy action, seven to accident, and 2,204 dead out of a total of 106,522 who served. For that price, the RCN had destroyed twenty-nine U-boats outright and helped in the sinking of others.

The war had not only been fought in corvettes. Canadian shipyards produced frigates and minesweepers, and the hasty conversions of the first months of the war had produced useful ships in addition to the short-lived mahogany yachts. Chief among these were the *Prince* class of armed merchant cruisers that were originally three-funnel liners of Canadian National Steamships. They were bought for the navy, converted, and armed as HMC ships *Prince David*, *Prince Robert* and *Prince Henry*, and they served usefully in the Atlantic and the Pacific. At the other end of the scale, Canadians distinguished themselves in small craft operations of MTBs and MGBs (motor torpedo boats and motor gun boats), notably with the Sixty-fifth and Twenty-ninth flotillas. One MGB flotilla commander, Tommy Fuller of Ottawa, carved out such an adventurous career against German shipping and naval forces on the Yugoslavian coast that he earned the title Pirate of the Adriatic for the hell-for-leather way his overgunned, speedy vessels wreaked havoc on German coastal convoys, capturing, it was said, everything from a complete symphony orchestra to three hundred tons of potatoes.

Gradually, the needs of the war brought into the navy's hands the larger ships the regular naval officers had so long sought, notably the excellent light cruisers HMCS *Uganda* (later *Quebec*) and HMCS *Ontario* (ex–HMS *Minotaur*), and Canadians manned light escort carriers such as *Nabob* and *Puncher*. But the most dramatic vessels in Canadian hands were the sleek greyhound shapes of the Tribal-class destroyers, HMC ships *Huron*, *Athabaskan*, *Haida* and *Iro-*

quois. These powerful and fast fleet destroyers operated for five years on the coast of western Europe, gun for gun the equal of any vessel of their class. One of their number was damaged by a German glider bomb, but otherwise they dealt out more than they received in swift strikes along the French coast. In 1944, as part of the Tenth Destroyer Flotilla of the Royal Navy, they were ordered to attack coastal shipping in the English Channel and the Bay of Biscay as a prelude to the D-Day invasion. *Athabaskan* was sunk by German E-boats, but *Iroquois*, under Commander J.C. Hibbard, carved out a typical record for the big destroyers by sinking twenty-two ships and damaging two German destroyers over the course of the war.

Canadian vessels of all types participated in the Normandy landings in 1944, while in the Pacific Canadian colours were carried principally by the *Prince Robert*, which served as an anti-aircraft ship with the British Pacific Fleet. HMCS *Uganda* was taking part in the final days of the war against Japan when a controversial government-authorized vote by the ship's company to return to Canada led the light cruiser to withdraw from the Pacific war.

At the end of the war, the planned transfer of two light aircraft carriers to the RCN was given less priority, and finally a single carrier came to the RCN, HMCS *Magnificent*. This ship and its successor, HMCS *Bonaventure*, would provide an air element to Canada's naval operations until 1968, when *Bonaventure* was scrapped shortly after a costly refit. The light cruisers *Ontario* and *Quebec* would not survive the next decade after 1945, and by 1947 the Royal Canadian Navy was reducing its strength sharply from the 400-ship force that had ended the war.

In 1949, a series of disturbances in the fleet arising from unhappiness with the overall atmosphere in the RCN led to what naval historian Richard Gimblett has aptly termed "a major watershed in the navy's history," the Mainguy Report, named for the senior officer who carried out the study. In essence, the study pointed to failures in the relationship between RCN officers and the other ranks, but specifically to the lack of a "distinguishing Canadian identity" in the RCN. While many naval officers worked well with their men in a style and manner reflective of Canada's social character and values, the legacy of some RN trained officers who artificially cultivated British modes of behaviour, maintained a social distance from the men and even—notoriously—spoke in a transatlantic accent was causing problems in a navy manned by young people who were products of an egalitarian North American society, not a class-based European one. It would take years of change, including the traumatic—and, some would argue, unnecessarily harsh—jettisoning of much of the RN-inherited culture at the time of service unification in the mid-1960s, to open the door to an authentically Canadian character in the navy, one that reflected more accurately the country itself.

With the Korean War and the advent of the Cold War between the West and the Soviet bloc, the RCN began to rebuild itself. The Tribal-class destroyers had a last moment of glory serving with UN forces in Korea, but the Canadian navy began to move deliberately into the anti-submarine role that had been the job of the Wavy Navy of 1939–45. It was a role that Canada selected as an appropriate response to the seaward threat of the Warsaw Pact. Slowly the reliance on British designs and British equipment was replaced with indigenous naval designs, starting with the innovative anti-submarine "destroyer escorts" of the *St. Laurent* class of the 1950s, and increased sharing of equipment and methods with the United States Navy. Until the mid-1960s the RCN uniform was almost indistinguishable from that of the RN, and Canada's navy continued to fly the RN's White Ensign on its ships. But a Canadian character was already transforming the service, to the satisfaction of some and the disgruntlement of others.

The final spike in the coffin of the RN-clone navy was driven home on February 1, 1968, when the Royal Canadian Navy, the Royal Canadian Air Force and the Canadian army were merged to form the Canadian Forces. In the first rush of sweeping change a new army-style uniform and rank structure were introduced, which proved not too difficult for the army and air force to accept.

But there were those in the navy who saw treasured links to a British past being set aside, and who considered them a valid part of Canada's own naval heritage, forged in the corvettes, destroyers and other craft of the Second World War. Unification would remain, but gradually wiser heads prevailed in government over issues of identity, morale and symbols, and by the end of the twentieth century the navy—now called Maritime Command of the Canadian Forces—once more wore navy blue, but of a Canadian design, and used its former naval ranks even as it emerged as a navy at last fully reflective in all aspects of the country it served. There will remain forever the irony that the greatest legacy of tradition for that new navy is a long-ago North Atlantic convoy war that was not the war the old navy had wanted to fight but the war it was *forced* to fight. And in the story of that gritty battle are lessons about character and a deep, enduring strength—lessons that Canadians need to remember now and to reclaim as they face an uncertain future.

18

Darkness and Light: Canada at Sea in the Twentieth Century

THE EXPERIENCE of Canadians in the first half of the twentieth century was of considerable darkness and trauma, as the pressures of two cataclysmic world wars and the grinding misery of the Great Depression set the tone of everyday existence. The century opened on a high point of Victorian and Edwardian certainty that was soon to become a distant memory. Canada's ocean approaches had been a highway of hope for many immigrant Canadians yearning for a new life, but they were as well the setting for tragedies and missed opportunities that displayed the limitations as well as the strengths of Canadian society, its frailty in the face of overwhelming natural forces, and a lack of vision that delayed the achievement of the nation's seaborne potential.

A half-century earlier, in the 1840s, the first great wave of newcomers since the Loyalist migrations had arrived, as the Irish fled famine to seek a fresh start in North America. Of the millions who crossed the ocean to land, often fever-ridden and penniless, on Canada's shores, many passed through to the United States. Thousands stayed, however, and they were the harbingers of thousands of other Europeans who crossed to Canada as the new century

Immigrants in Quarters Below Decks in a Ship, by C.W. Jefferys   C 73435

opened. The British led, followed by continental Europeans,
until in the first decades of the
twentieth century Pier 21 at
Halifax became for Canada what
Ellis Island was for the United
States: the great Beginning Point
for thousands of hopeful, worried newcomers of almost every
origin possible, who were asking
for the chance to make a new beginning with their lives.

For the most part, the insular,
homogenous society of Canada
warily welcomed the newcomers
disgorging from the ships. But there were limits to that welcome,
reflecting the intolerances and prejudices of the day. In May 1914
the Japanese steamship *Komagata Maru* approached the British
Columbia coast with 376 East Indians aboard, who merely sought
what the Irish, the Scots, the Ukrainians and the Germans had
come for: a new life in Canada. But the Canada of 1914 was not
the open, rainbow-hued society it is now. In 1908, Parliament had
passed the Continuous Passage Act, which was intended to prevent
East Indian immigration to Canada. It required a potential Indian
immigrant to travel directly to Canada from India rather than via
another country, a condition few Indians could satisfy. The arrival
of the ship on the British Columbia coast was met with a storm of
protest, and for two months the ship lay at anchor while opponents
of non-European immigration fought to block the landing of its
passengers. They eventually succeeded, and the *Komagata Maru*
sailed away for India, leaving behind only twenty passengers who
had secured legal resident status—and a bitter memory that only
recently saw an apology to the Indo-Canadian community drafted
by the government. It would not be until well after the Second

World War that the immigration policies of Canada became blind to colour or creed.

In the first two decades of the twentieth century, Canadians were repeatedly reminded of the unceasing menace of the sea and of human frailty in the face of it. Three major catastrophes shook the remaining smug assertions of the Victorian-Edwardian era from the Canadian mind. They were the sinking of the great British liner *Titanic* in 1912 off Newfoundland; the loss in 1918 of the Canadian Pacific steamer *Princess Sophia* on Vanderbilt Reef, Alaska, with the cream of Canada's Yukon leadership aboard; and the most appalling of Canada's tragedies at sea, the loss by collision of the Canadian Pacific liner *Empress of Ireland* on a fog-shrouded May morning in 1914 on the lower St. Lawrence River, at a cost of over a thousand lives. To a Canada still to be stunned by the losses and upheavals of the First World War, these events brought home again the reality that the sea is a place of vast and often inscrutable power.

Yet tragedy was not always the product of storm, collision or iceberg; it came as often from a failure of human spirit or imagination. In mid-century, after the long, numbing agony of the Great Depression, there was another war fought against deadly forces, and that was the war for survival on the dark North Atlantic during the Second World War waged by Canadians who went to sea as members of the merchant navy. Civilians who had been hired to operate the vessels of Canada's wartime cargo fleet, they sailed in mostly unarmed ships grouped together in convoys, often carrying dangerous and explosive cargoes, and they were easy targets for the circling packs of U-boats that managed to break through the protective ring of overworked naval escorts. There were many of these ships—Canada had the Allies' fourth-largest merchant service at the end of the war, mostly comprising ships built in Canada—and the ships and their crews suffered a higher loss rate than the naval vessels that escorted them. Viewed by some as civilians and not true combatants, the Canadian merchant seamen considered themselves to be Canada's fourth armed force in the war, a status that was not formally bestowed on them until 1992. Yet by 1948 these same men were seen as "troublemakers" and "dangerous" by a Canadian government that a few years previously had relied gratefully on their services.

Their contribution to the war effort had been enormous. Sailing in Canadian-built, 10,000-ton *Park* ships, a production-line mainstay of Canadian wartime shipping, the men of the merchant navy operated over 170 ships for the Crown-owned Park Steamship Company, with some twelve thousand men shown on the books. These standard-built vessels, very like the American "Liberty" ship program, were turned out in scores by Canadian shipyards. Those busy yards produced some 350 of these 10,000-ton ships, 43 ships of 4,700 tons and six 3,000-ton tankers, in addition to 487 warships for the Royal Canadian Navy. But with the coming of peace in 1945, the possibility that this fleet of Canadian hulls could form the basis of a continuing Canadian merchant navy faded away in the world of profit and loss, high wage demands, and the shadows of anti-Communist and anti-Russian paranoia. As historian Robert Halford, writing in 1995, succinctly put it, many of the Canadian-built wartime ships were sold off and dispersed, leaving a small fleet unable to secure government commitment to its continuation:

> In this way, a much-reduced Canadian fleet remained in being for a few years after the war, though it no longer operated as a single entity . . . Within a few years peacetime ship operating economics, and the Canadian government's draconian union-busting reaction to an industry-wide strike of unlicensed sailors, combined effectively to sink what was left of the war-created Merchant Navy.

It had not only been the cost of Canadian insurance and Canadian wages that caused the collapse of a postwar Canadian merchant navy. With most of the men involved and their union leadership being products of the bitter Depression, the philosophical perceptions of much of that leadership viewed company owners and management in much the same resentful, adversarial way they had in the 1930s; the war had merely been a pause in the struggle. They believed that the poverty and suffering of working citizens were for a grim decade contrasted starkly with the ease and privilege of a wealthy minority largely indifferent to that suffering and prepared to crush social action intended to ease it. Conditioned by the twin traumas of the Depression and the bloody war, and influenced by the effective, if misleading, propaganda of an international Communist movement largely orchestrated by the Soviet Union, many Canadian merchant seamen were embittered and unshakable adversaries of the "bosses" and owners, and ripe for exploitation by a minority cadre of union leadership who were indeed interested in sabotaging the Western capitalist economy and its labour–management relationships. The antagonisms were so great that an alarmed Canadian government reacted by sounding the death knell of a postwar merchant service, laying the blame at the feet of the merchant seamen themselves, fairly or not. As Halford relates,

> Obsessed with the "communists under the bed" syndrome epidemic in the Western world, the Canadian government, with the whole-hearted support of the shipping industry, imported the infamous Hal Banks from the United States to lead the brutal no-holds-barred suppression of the Canadian Seamen's Union, whose leadership, though not its rank and file, was Red-tinged. Having successfully accomplished the destruction of the CSU, the Government then dropped its Canadian registration requirement for the taxpayer-financed ex-Park ships, which the new owners lost no time in transferring to low cost, less stringently regulated foreign registries. With that, whatever awareness still existed of a Canadian merchant navy quickly faded.

The prime minister of the day, Louis St. Laurent, made it clear that market principles rather than any national commitment to the maintenance of a Canadian merchant marine fleet would prevail. On December 9, 1949, he observed: "We have concluded that we are not justified from an economic viewpoint in maintaining a Canadian flag [fleet] by artificial means. It is not the intention of the government to maintain an industry at the expense of the tax-payer." With that, formal government support of a general-cargo merchant navy came to an end. It seemed to mark the end of Canadian public interest as well.

It had not always been so. Shortly after Confederation, the wooden hulls of Maritime shippers had given Canada one of the world's largest merchant fleets. They had gradually faded from the seas, as we have seen, as iron and steel steamers replaced the full-rigged ships and schooners, so that by the beginning of the First World War Canadian-flag merchant vessels were few and far between with the exception of the fishing fleets. The coming of the war, however, led to two major initiatives. Firstly, there was a rush to build a new generation of wooden cargo and trading vessels as a temporary replacement for the steel-hulled steamers that had been called away to the war effort. In this program, a fleet of a dozen or so "timber" schooners was built to carry the lumber of the British Columbia forest industry to its markets. A number of these schooners, notably the *Malahat*, would later have exciting and lucrative careers running alcohol to the prohibitionist United States from 1920 to 1933. Secondly, the Canadian government instituted the creation of a formal, government-supported merchant fleet, known as the Canadian Government Merchant Marine, or CGMM, as a response to the U-boat menace of 1917–18 that threatened to bring Britain to its knees by starvation. Some sixty-three cargo ships were built under this ambitious program, but the hope that the CGMM could remain a large and effective arm of Canadian trade died with the coming of peace in 1918. Many of the CGMM ships were sold off at bargain prices—an apocryphal story holds that Aristotle Onassis's shipping empire began on the basis of six cheaply bought CGMM ships—and just as the Royal Canadian Navy withered to a far smaller size than it wished to be, by 1935 the CGMM was down to ten ships, most of which were trading to Australia and New Zealand. Finally, in 1936, the CGMM was disbanded, and it would not be until the wartime rise of the Park Steamship Company that a Canadian merchant fleet of any size would take form once more.

It was left to private industry, or to Crown agencies better able to function as private enterprises, to keep Canadian hulls at sea after the withdrawal of direct government support. One of the most successful of such efforts was that of the Canadian Pacific Railway, originally formed on February 16, 1881, to build a railway across Canada to meet the terms of Confederation that had lured British Columbia into Canada's grasp ten years earlier. Conceived as a railway company, Canadian Pacific backed into the operation of ships as a necessary support for its railway construction. In 1882–83, the CPR bought ships on the Great Lakes to use in forwarding rail-building supplies westward. By 1884–85 the CPR was operating a regular steamship service from Owen Sound to Port Arthur with a fleet of three modern vessels, the *Alberta*, *Algoma* and *Athabasca*. As the westward rail link moved toward completion, it was not lost on imperial enthusiasts in London, and indeed on pragmatic business-men in Montreal, that the prospect was looming of an all-"British" world communications system, in which Canadian rail—and possibly Canadian shipping—would play a major part. It was a breath-taking vision. In 1885, Sir Andrew Clarke, inspector-general of fortifications in Britain, beamed that "once a regular steamship service with the East by way of Canada and the Pacific is established, the whole empire will be firmly knit together and the chain of communications between British nations will finally girdle the world."

The driving of the last spike of the CPR at Craigellachie in that same year, 1885, completed the cross-Canada link, and the CPR was not slow in developing a shipping service out into the Pacific. By the late 1880s steam and steam-assisted vessels including the *Abyssinia*, *Batavia* and *Parthia* were sailing regularly from Vancouver to the Orient.

The next step in Clarke's dream was the creation of an all–British Empire mail link to the Far East, and Canadian Pacific competed for and won the contract in 1890. The contract provided that "transit time was not to exceed 684 hours from Hong Kong to Quebec between April and November, and 732 hours from Hong Kong to Halifax between December and March." To serve this contract and provide passenger service across the Pacific, Canadian Pacific introduced in the next year the first of the fabled and romantic *Empress* line of steamships. These gracious and well-run ships—the *Empress of India*, *Empress of Japan*, *Empress of China*—executed the mail contract without fault for fifteen years, and the company prided itself on being able to offer an "around the world in eighty days" lifetime adventure voyage for the princely sum of seven hundred dollars.

In 1886, Canadian Pacific began an expansion into the Atlantic Ocean market, building what would become a "Liverpool to Hong Kong" system by buying up the vessels of the Beaver and Allan steamship lines. Establishing regular service over the years 1904 to 1913, Canadian Pacific celebrated the launch of its first Atlantic *Empress*, the *Empress of Britain*, in 1906. Facing the demands of the First World War, the Canadian Pacific Railway applied to the Canadian government in 1915 for permission to run its steamship operations as a separate entity rather than as an adjunct to its rail business. The permission arrived tardily, and in July 1917, Canadian Pacific Ocean Services Limited opened its first office in Waterloo Place, London. Within a year the war had come to an end, and through war reparations from Germany, Canadian Pacific Ocean Services was able to enlarge its fleet with former German vessels. A new era of prosperity beckoned as the 1920s opened, and the company marked the advances on September 8, 1921, by declaring its new title to be Canadian Pacific Steamships.

Until the coming of the Second World War, CP Steamships remained a successful operation in both the Atlantic and Pacific markets. In 1939, however, business altered drastically as some seventeen passenger vessels were provided to the war effort, their white hulls and butterscotch funnels shrouded in naval grey. The cost to the company was high: when peace came in 1945, only five of the seventeen ships returned to Canadian Pacific. Eight had been

CGS *Arctic* beset in ice off Baffin Island, 1925 *PA 102437*

sunk by enemy action; one had burned; two had been purchased by the British Admiralty; and one other had passed to a new owner.

Between 1946 and 1956, Canadian Pacific enjoyed a resurgent business on the Atlantic runs, and in 1956 it optimistically launched a new *Empress of Britain*. In the following year, 1957, four vessels on the North Atlantic service, the *Empress of Britain*, *Empress of England*, *Empress of France* and *Empress of Scotland*, made no fewer than fifty-four transatlantic trips out of Liverpool. But the heyday of liner travel was over, and the cruise industry was still a future dream: in 1957 the number of air travel passengers met and exceeded sea travel passengers for the first time. Between 1958 and 1964 there were three *Empress* ships in service; between 1964 and 1970, only two; and in 1970 the *Empress of England* was sold, leaving only the *Empress of Canada*. This last vessel made thirteen voyages in 1971, but on November 23, 1971, the *Empress of Canada* docked at Liverpool for the last time.

It was the end of a magnificent achievement in passenger shipping. It brought to a close eighty years of *Empress* tradition, sixty-eight years of operation on the North Atlantic, and no fewer than ninety years since the creation of the link from the United Kingdom across the North Atlantic and Canada to the Far East. Canadian

Pacific had also been involved in the inter-island and coastal ferry system in British Columbia, the continuing development of which in the twentieth century rivals as a story the history of shipping on the Great Lakes.

The British Columbia island archipelago and the deep, mountainous fjords that line the coast constitute one of the most beautiful and complex coastal environments on the face of the earth. The British Columbia ferry system, which sprang out of coastal shipping services established in the nineteenth century, developed in the twentieth as one of the most varied and challenging inter-island and intra-coastal ferry systems in the world.

The first regular service of any kind on the coast had been provided by the redoubtable Hudson's Bay Company steamer *Beaver*, which arrived in 1836. Until British Columbia's entry into Confederation in 1871, however, coastal and inter-island shipping remained a matter of private sealing or fishing vessels, HBC fur traders, periodic brief patrols by visiting Royal Navy vessels, and the comings and goings of canoes and boats of the indigenous population.

Then, in 1877, Captain J. Irving started the first regularly scheduled sailing between New Westminster and Yale, B.C. By 1882, Irving had proven efficient enough to be awarded a contract to ferry men and freight in support of the building of the western part of the Canadian Pacific Railway, reaching east for the eventual meeting with the westbound construction at Craigellachie. Irving soon built on his success, negotiating in 1883 the amalgamation of the Hudson's Bay Company flotilla of trading vessels and his own Pioneer Line to form the Canadian Pacific Navigation Company. Despite the name, the CPNC was independent of the CPR.

After fifteen years of operation, the CPNC proved unable to keep up with the increasing demands of inter-island and intra-coastal traffic—particularly on the key Vancouver-to-Victoria route—and negotiations began that saw Canadian Pacific buy the

CPNC fleet in 1903. Canadian Pacific had taken on an Oregonian, Captain J.W. Troup, in 1901 to run its coastal service, and with the CPNC fleet now in hand, Troup began to develop the services linking the province's posts and islands.

Troup's first dramatic move was to bring in the first of the well-appointed *Princess* ferries. Named the *Princess Victoria*—and maligned as "Troup's Folly" by his detractors—this graceful ship arrived in March 1903 and began a career of reliable, twenty-knot service that lasted, incredibly, until 1950. The *Princess Victoria* would be the first of thirty-two such vessels on the British Columbia coast, as well as two others, the *Princess Helene* and *Princess of Acadia*, that operated in the Bay of Fundy between Saint John, New Brunswick, and Digby, Nova Scotia. Troup also instituted the famous Triangle Service ferry link between Vancouver, Seattle and Victoria, which lasted well past Troup's retirement in 1928, on to the Second World War. The postwar period would see the CPR continue with a Victoria-to-Seattle run until 1974.

With postwar population and industry booming in British Columbia, new players appeared to enter the B.C. ferry market. In 1953 the Black Ball Line (Canada) of Puget Sound, Washington, began the operation of car ferries between Departure Bay in Nanaimo, on Vancouver Island, and Horseshoe Bay on the mainland. A devastating 1958 strike in the privately owned ferry system drew the attention of the British Columbia government, and the ferry system left private and corporate ownership to become a provincial agency. In 1960 the British Columbia government built two large ferry terminals at Swartz Bay (Victoria) and Tsawwassen (Vancouver), and began operating spacious car ferries with a 100-car, 900-passenger capacity and the ability to make the passage between the mainland and the Island in 3½ hours. The following year the B.C. government took over the vessels and property of the Black Ball Line (Canada) and also the heterogeneous fleet of inter-island small ferries operated by the Gulf Islands Ferries organization. This set the stage for the creation of the Dogwood

Fleet of the B.C. ferry system through the 1960s, named after the provincial flower, consisting of some forty vessels, of which twenty-four were major ships by any standard. Seven key vessels were the backbone of the fleet established in the 1960s, the largest being the 12,000-ton *Queen of Sidney* and *Queen of Tsawwassen*.

With this extraordinarily diverse and capable fleet, the B.C. ferry system was carrying over 22 million passengers annually as the twentieth century closed, over fifteen major operating routes on the mainland coast, amongst the Gulf Islands and on the key main-land-to-Island route. Few incidents have marred the operation of this fleet, the most serious being a deadly collision with a Soviet freighter in Active Pass in the 1960s and the loss by sinking of the ferry *Queen of the North* in odd circumstances in March 2006.

The growth of B.C. Ferries in the postwar years was a need-driven anomaly in the general picture of Canadian shipping, however. Elsewhere, Canadian-flag vessels were disappearing one by one from the postwar ocean. The Canadian National Steamships Service had given up most of its cargo vessels after the crippling strike of the Seamen's International Union and government policies rendered their operation unprofitable. From 1928 to 1952, the CNSS ran five gracious *Lady* vessels, including *Lady Nelson* and *Lady Rodney*, in trade to the West Indies, but their operations ceased when they became unprofitable, and 1958 saw essentially an end of CNSS cargo and passenger service to the Caribbean from Montreal and Halifax. As has been seen earlier, the cost of registration, insurance and payroll and the bureaucratic impediments placed in the way of owners meant a continuing decline in Canadian ownership. By 1985, a mere 82 Canadian-owned merchant vessels—many of them Great Lakes seasonal vessels and other small coasting ships—were registered in Canada, while fully 114 ocean-going ships owned by Canadian interests were registered offshore under loosely regulated "flags of convenience" such as Panama and Liberia, or oddities like the Cook Islands. Owners insisted that Canadian costs (including stringent environmental controls) and taxes would prove ruinous to their operations, and for that reason much of the business of the remaining major Canadian shipowners was being quietly conducted offshore as the twenty-first century opened.

From a nation that at Confederation provided some one-quarter of the total seagoing merchant tonnage of the British Empire, Canada now maintains virtually no significant merchant fleet, and less than 1 percent of Canadian trade on the seas is carried in Canadian-registry ships. The vessels that do exist and can meet Canadian registration standards find public interest in them lacking as well: the Great Lakes fleet, one of the last remaining clusters of Canadian-owned shipping, estimates that by the second decade of this century 1,500 vacancies for seamen in "lakers" will not be able to be filled. Both in inclination and in actual circumstances, Canada has manifestly turned away from having a hand in the commerce on the sea upon which its welfare so vitally depends.

There is a certain irony in the fact that, even as Canada has lost either the ability or the volition to undertake commerce on the sea, the nation's ability to manage, patrol and regulate its waters has become more developed, although that capability is once again under threat as well. The Canadian Coast Guard is a federal agency that maintains a fleet of many vessels and supporting aircraft divided among five major regions of Canada, and which involves some two thousand personnel. Its vessels range from Arctic-capable icebreakers to British-style motor "lifeboats" intended for small-craft rescue under hazardous conditions, and it is responsible for the non-military provision of a range of marine services to Canadians, among them marine search and rescue, or SAR, conducted in co-operation with other federal agencies, such as the Canadian Forces; the maintenance of aids to navigation; marine pollution response; and the major task of icebreaking. Unlike the United States Coast Guard, the CCG is an unarmed agency with no paramilitary intentions or functions; mirroring Canadian perceptions and values, the application or threat of force is the responsibility of the Canadian navy—Maritime Command of the Canadian Forces—and the Royal Canadian Mounted Police.

Until 1936, coast guard functions were conducted under the umbrella of the Department of Marine and Fisheries, then simply the Department of Marine. In that year the responsibility was handed over to a new Department of Transport. After the hiatus of the Second World War, the sharp increase in foreign-flag activity in Canadian waters and the building of the St. Lawrence Seaway made evident the need for a more identifiable and capable agency, and on January 28, 1962, the Canadian Coast Guard was formally established. For the coast guard and its admirers, the period of the 1960s to the 1980s was a kind of golden age. Government commitment was unstinting, older ships inherited from the Marine Service were replaced, a Coast Guard College was established in Cape Breton in 1965, and Canada was well on the way to taking supervisory responsibility for its vast waterways and coastlines beyond anything that had ever been attempted before. The high-water mark arguably approached in the mid-1980s, when the government proposed a series of world-class icebreakers for the CCG, the Polar 8 class of vessels, in response to American indifference to Canadian claims of sovereignty over the waters of the Northwest Passage.

The Polar 8 vessels never materialized, however, and since those days the coast guard has had to contemplate a far different reality of reduced budgets, an aging fleet with little sign of replacement beyond the purchase of small British or American designs for inshore work, and a not altogether comfortable relationship with the Department of Fisheries and Oceans, to which the CCG was attached in 1995. That relationship has been improved somewhat by the designation of the CCG as a more independent "special operating agency" in 2005, but it also must confront the aging of its workforce, which gives a median age of fifty for its seagoing crews. Government action in response to the coast guard's needs of the twenty-first century and the dawning era of Arctic navigation has been uncertain, and the decision in 2007 to provide the Canadian navy with a flotilla of six to eight ice-strengthened warships—not icebreaking—while welcomed by the navy, has not resolved the civilian agency's increasing anxiety over its own fleet. The opening of the Arctic and the increasing activity—and interest—of foreign nations in Canada's waters and the seabed below them will only increase demands on the coast guard; and Canadian practical supervision of the Northwest Passage is a virtual certainty regardless of American official posturing. All of this suggests that the Canadian government faces a continuing crisis of resource commitment to the Canadian Coast Guard if it is to safeguard Canadian maritime interests and the legitimacy of Canadian sovereignty claims to the waters of the North in the tumultuous era now opening.

Another major issue that Canada has had to grapple with in the transition from the twentieth to the twenty-first century is the precipitous decline and near collapse of the fishery on both coasts.

The west coast fishery, based on the seemingly inexhaustible supplies of salmon, had traditionally been a mainstay of the First Nations societies, and by the 1800s the Hudson's Bay Company saw cured salmon as a trading commodity over which, in 1821, it claimed exclusive rights. By 1850 the HBC post on San Juan Island in the Gulf had a fishing station that prepared thousands of barrels of salted salmon for the use of HBC staff, for local trade and for export to the Hawaiian Islands. This post had to be abandoned when a resolution of the boundary dispute with the United States put the Haro archipelago in American territory. In 1858 the Hudson's Bay Company lost its monopoly over the salmon fishery, and the profit-based pursuit of the salmon by Europeans began in earnest.

The British Columbia gold rush was well under way in 1859, and the hunt for salmon to feed the hordes of miners gave new impetus to the fishery. As historians Joseph and Anne Forester recorded, a local newspaper announced that "the sloop *Leonede* cleared today for the Fraser River carrying a party who intend to engage in salmon fishing at the mouth of the river. We hope to see the time when we shall be able to record the sailing of 300." The

organized fishery evolved to see the precious and apparently limitless salmon used for export, while other fish—cod, sole and halibut—were consumed locally. The pursuit of herring was initially
intended only to secure bait, but then large numbers of Japanese
immigrants created a thriving herring fishery, operating specialized
plants that produced dry salted herring for shipment to Japan and
China. This industry came to an abrupt end with the Second World
War and the disastrous deportation of the British Columbia Japanese inland, along with the confiscation and dispersal of their boats
and property.

The high point of the salmon fishery and its pursuit by a commercial fleet came in 1897. Three years later, the dark clouds of
conflict that would be a continuing feature of the west coast fishery
gathered in a bitter 1900 strike, and in conflict between Japanese
and non-Japanese fishermen. The stocks of salmon remained strong
until the postwar era—many men survived during the Depression
by fishing for salmon from small boats and the shoreline using
"poverty sticks"—but in the 1980s heavy overfishing, population
pressures, the pollution or loss of salmon spawning streams, as well
as conflict between First Nations and non-Native fishermen combined to produce a steady decline in the salmon stocks that threatened, as the new century opened, to bring an end to a fishery once
thought to be inexhaustible. The future of the Pacific salmon fishery is by no means clear.

On Canada's east coast, the stocks of cod and other fish of the
Grand Banks that had astounded the first European explorers five
hundred years earlier were essentially still healthy as the twentieth century opened. An effective but sustainable fishery based on
schooner fleets and dory fishing drew on the teeming stocks of fish
with little danger until the Second World War. Then, in the postwar years, the last of the traditional fishing vessels vanished, to be
replaced by steam- and diesel-powered trawlers. Between 1955 and
1965, a revolution in fishing technology and management occurred,
led by Eastern Europeans and Russians, who were still recovering
from the losses of the war. Joined by Asian operators, these fishing

nations adopted the techniques of whaling to hunt for the catch on the Grand Banks. Trawlers were developed based on the "factory ship" designs that had brought several species of whale to near extinction in Antarctic waters. The trawlers deployed enormous nets that were streamed night and day in all conditions, hauling in enormous catches that were cleaned and frozen in the ship itself. The efficiency of these vessels was such that a single trawler could scoop aboard a catch of two hundred tons in one hour, the equivalent of an *entire season's* catch for a sailing vessel of the discovery period.

In 1968, a record catch of 800,000 tons of fish was lifted from the Grand Banks, but that would mark the end of the steadily increasing plunder of the Atlantic fishery, for catches of this scale were unsustainable. Within ten years the catch had fallen by over one-half, and in the 1970s, alarmed at the uncaring destruction of the fish stocks by the East Europeans and Asians in particular, the Canadian government extended the limits of the fishing zone to two hundred miles off the coast from the previous twelve miles. Unfortunately, the tendency of Canadian fishing companies to then dispatch trawlers to fish in the same destructive manner as the foreign fleets produced large profits for Canadian fishermen in the short term but dealt a possibly irreversible blow to the Grand Banks ecosystem as huge trawl nets plowed the seabed in destructive swaths, the damage caused by them little understood.

That cod and other fish catches by the large trawlers remained steady through the 1980s reflected the efficiency of the technology-assisted catching methods in finding the remaining fish, even while smaller, inshore fishermen were reporting alarming declines in the fish stocks. Warnings by scientists that the stocks were under serious threat went unheeded by government, possibly for political reasons, until finally the outright collapse of the fish stocks in 1992 forced the government's hand. The cod fishery was closed, resulting in unemployment for some thirty thousand industry workers. With new evidence indicating that cod schools and other stocks had been formed of relatively long-lived fish that do not reproduce rapidly, the twenty-first century opened with the fishery still severely reduced, and with no likelihood that stocks would soon recover to historical levels. The scorched-earth fishing plunder of the thirty years that ended in 1992 had virtually destroyed a resource that had once seemed inexhaustible. To this day, foreign fishing fleets continue the pursuit to extinction in the open ocean of other species doomed by indifference, greed or ignorance. The fate of the tuna, being slaughtered in uncontrolled numbers to feed Asian markets, stands as a mournful case in point.

As this century opened, the roles of Canadian seaports and water's edge communities were also changing. The Great Lakes ecosystem remained under threat from sewage and industrial pollution, despite efforts at pollution abatement, and suffered from the introduction of rapacious non-native species of flora and fauna by the irresponsible flushing out of the holds of visiting foreign freighters. Water levels in the Great Lakes have been steadily in decline for some time, and the actual traffic levels of foreign ships up the St. Lawrence Seaway is also in decline, with international cargo traffic moving increasingly to container vessels. These huge craft frequent large, easily reachable and fast-turnaround "roll off, roll on" ports such as Halifax, Saint John and Vancouver. Formerly important ports like Montreal are witnessing a decline in seaborne business and in overall traffic levels as the container ports become the principal ports of entry.

If the whole business of Canadians at sea in their home waters since 1945 seems inexorably to point to missed opportunities, insufficient information, denied resources or a general pattern of dismaying decline, the story of the postwar Canadian navy presents a brighter picture, albeit a checkered one. At the end of the Second World War most of the Wavy Navy reservists who had manned the escorts and other vessels left the Royal Canadian Navy, which had to reduce numbers to peacetime levels. The professional, regular naval officers set about building the multi-role, traditional navy they felt would best suit Canada's needs. With two light cruisers, HMC ships

Ontario and *Quebec*, and the light fleet aircraft carrier *Magnificent*—
later replaced by the *Bonaventure*—Canada had in place the core
of a substantial navy that was, as the previous chapter has discussed,
uncertain within itself as to its identity and, to a degree, its best role
in the shifting postwar world. The latter question was resolved for
a time by the Cold War and the perceived Soviet menace, and by the
establishment of the North Atlantic Treaty Organization (NATO)
in 1949. Ironically, the most appropriate niche for the Royal Canadian Navy in the new alliance's preparations for any new war became
the open-ocean anti-submarine role about which the reservists in the
corvettes had become the most knowledgeable.

Through years of growth, essentially 1950 to 1965, the Royal
Canadian Navy moved away from the idea of a large-ship navy with
multiple roles to focus on becoming an anti-submarine specialist
force. The light cruisers were disposed of, and the carrier's principal
aircraft were anti-submarine hunters designed to allow the carrier
and its escorts to act like the efficient, aircraft-supported escort
groups that had emerged toward the end of the Second World War
and had dealt the final blow to the U-boat adversary. Eventually,
in the mid-1960s, the carrier was disposed of altogether as the
navy pioneered the use of helicopters carried aboard the escort
vessels themselves. Canada had created its own indigenous destroyer
escort design in the 1950s with the advent of HMCS *Saint Laurent*,
and later designs such as the *Restigouche*- and *Mackenzie*-class ships
ended once and for all the long tradition of using Royal Navy vessels or design concepts as the basis for the fleet. Other Canadian
innovations, such as variable-depth sonar, allowed the RCN to grow
in capability as it grew in size, so that by the late 1950s and early
1960s the navy was providing the Western alliance with a 68-ship
fleet that offered a high degree of skill and professionalism. The
fleet that put to sea in October 1962 in response to the Cuban Mis-
sile Crisis was a highly effective and well-trained force; it would not
reach that level of capability again for over thirty years.

Whether occasioned by anti-war feelings caused by the Vietnam
War, the rise of a bureaucratic managerial class in the federal public

service, the anti-military antipathy of ascendant politicians such as Pierre Elliott Trudeau or the motivations of the era's most controversial defence minister, Paul Hellyer, the Royal Canadian Navy fell out of government favour in the mid-1960s. The Royal Canadian Navy itself vanished, being reborn as Maritime Command of the newly unified Canadian Forces in 1968. The inherited uniforms and rank structure of the Royal Navy were dispensed with—the ranks would later return—and a new common green uniform was issued, which lasted for twenty years. The White Ensign was replaced by the new Canadian flag. And with the exception of several Tribal-class destroyers, new ship acquisition for the Canadian navy came to a standstill. Through the Trudeau era, a humiliating period known in navy circles as the great "Rust Out," Maritime Command's ships were kept going by dedicated crews as Canadian warships slowly fell further and further behind their NATO allies in capability and relevance, until they approached national embarrassment status.

In the literal nick of time, wiser heads prevailed in the 1980s, and naval leadership was able to develop a program of new ship construction based on a general-purpose frigate design for a multi-role warship. The result was the Canadian Patrol Frigates (CPF), which formed the principal platform of the Canadian navy as the twenty-first century opened. These vessels gave Canada a fleet of omni-capable warships equal to any in their class in the world as the narrow anti-submarine role of the Soviet era passed and a wide range of potential demands faced the navy. Supported by modernized Tribal-class destroyers and a new fleet of Maritime Coastal Defence Vessels (MCDV), Maritime Command for the moment had rescued itself from irrelevancy and oblivion, and Canada entered the new century with a respected and capable navy that placed in the politicians' hands an effective instrument for the projection of Canadian values and Canadian policy. It wore a new, Canadian-pattern blue uniform, and in their mess deck and wardroom relationships the young men and women of the navy now reflected the views, values and ways of the Canadian society they served.

Yet such navies are not a matter of overnight planning and "off the shelf" purchasing, and in May 2008 Canada's government indicated that it was moving forward on planning for a continuously evolving navy. The common sense was evident of a steady "continuous-build" ship construction program that would provide employment, develop and maintain skills, and prevent another humiliating "Rust Out" just at a time when, looming on the horizon, Arctic warming and emerging geopolitical realities will call for Canada to have the best navy it can afford. The depth of national commitment to securing that navy is yet to be proven.

19

Threat
and Promise:
Canada's Future
at Sea

IN SEPTEMBER 2007, the waters of Canada's Northwest
Passage opened sufficiently to allow the free passage
of a vessel for the first time since the end of the last
great ice age, some ten thousand years before the modern era. No
event encapsulates more starkly both the threats facing Canada and
the promise.

The great environmental issue of the times is global warming—
the precipitous rise in the earth's overall temperature due to the
burning of hydrocarbons in the atmosphere and a litany of other
human activities, including deforestation, that produce the so-called
greenhouse effect. A minority of skeptics argue that such temperature fluctuations are part of a natural cyclical process that would
occur regardless of human activity. A majority point to human
activity and fossil fuel consumption as, in fact, the principal culprit.
The net effect, regardless of cause, will be a dramatic change in the
Canadian environment, with significant implications for Canada's
waters.

The principal effect of the great warming will be the transformation of Canada's vast island archipelago in the north from a largely
icebound fortress of magnificent solitude into a navigable maze of
islands, channels, fjords, waterways and sounds the size of western
Europe, beginning with the historic Northwest Passage itself. This

change will bring dismaying environmental degradation due to shipborne pollution, as well as the altering and in some cases the disappearance of native fauna and flora as the ice pack dissolves and the polynyas become open shipping channels. That the remaining hunting and fishing livelihood of Inuit citizens will be under risk is a given.

The ice is a matrix that holds life together in the Arctic. It is— or was—a relatively stable world of consistent temperature that supported a delicate ecosystem. Diatoms, the minute organisms that form the basis of the food chain, develop on the underside of the multi-year ice in their uncountable millions, and the spring "bloom" of plankton based on these diatoms feeds multi-ton whales and, by extension, the whole constellation of Arctic creatures. The breakup of that stable world puts at risk the entire northern ecosystem, and will affect the world's climatic health as well, from northern hemisphere weather patterns to global warming itself, as the reflective power of the dazzling white ice cap against solar radiation is lost.

The phenomenon of global warming is also causing in North America a discernible northward shift in climatic zones, which at first glance would suggest a more benign face to the weather of Canada's east and west coasts were it not for the concomitant increase in violent and unpredictable storm activity. On the Great Lakes, shifting rainfall and snowfall patterns and volume may accelerate a worrying decline in overall lake water levels, magnified by proposed American drainage schemes and diversions of water southward to replenish their exhausted water tables. The significance of these lowered levels for commercial ship traffic is yet to be determined, as is the degree to which introduced species from other climatic zones, and the decline of indigenous species, will threaten everything from the whitefish industry to the supply of drinking water for Canadian cities along the Great Lakes shores.

On both coasts, a severely restricted fishery still does not have the scientific green light that a significant recovery is under way, particularly in the cod stocks of the Grand Banks. As mentioned earlier,

recent biological studies which show that the schools of cod were
not composed of young, rapidly reproducing fish but rather of a
surprisingly long-lived population that took a substantial amount
of time to regenerate suggests that the fishery survived the 500-year
onslaught only due to the primitive fishing technologies involved.
So far, no new technologies are on the horizon that would allow
a more selective and sustainable fishery. Canada has been slow in
developing viable alternatives to the traditional fishery, such as aquaculture or "fish farming," having been ranked by the United Nations
Food and Agriculture Organization in 2008 as only twenty-second
in the ranks of aquacultural nations. Globally, aquaculture produces
almost 30 percent of the total landed fish catch, but Canada's effort
provides but one-third of 1 percent of that total. With current estimates that the world must somehow find 50 percent more food to
feed itself by 2030, Canada's potential in aquaculture is relatively
limitless, but only if vision and action are combined.

Of concern for the waters outside Canada's jurisdiction is the
indifference foreign and particularly Asian fishing fleets continue to
show to the whole question of restraint and environmental custodi-
anship, even when their national governments voice nominal support for conservation measures and physically attempt to enforce
them. The continuing unlimited destruction of high seas tuna and
the persistent use of huge, miles-long "drift nets" by Taiwanese and
other fishermen off Canada's Pacific coast, which snare virtually
everything in their path including sea mammals, are symptomatic
of a rapacious attitude in certain cultures toward the care of the sea
which shows far too few signs of softening into a more responsible
mentality. The future we face is one in which international forums
for the co-operative regulation of the harvesting of the sea's resources
will continue to be challenged or ignored by self-interested national
governments, unregulated fishing agencies and ruthless corporate
entities.

Canada can expect increasing pressures from these sources on
the waters it controls, their contents and the seabeds that lie beneath
them as international co-operation and voluntary regulation come

up against other nations' "perceived need," cultural indifference to environmental sensitivity, and simple greed. Were Canada's waters to consist of remote archipelagos of limited accessibility and less commercial or exploitable value, the threat might be serious but not immediate. But with Arctic navigation suddenly becoming feasible, with a scramble under way to claim national rights over the seabed, and with many ambitious and sea-capable nations with rapacious primary-resource needs already questioning Canada's rights over and ownership of the waterways amongst Canada's northern islands, the picture is quite clear. The notion of Canada overseeing a leisurely and undisturbed development of the North guided by gradual and considered responses to environmental change is already a forgotten dream.

There is some heartening evidence of a realization amongst nations with an Arctic interest, principally Russia, Canada, Denmark, Norway and the United States, that an uncontrolled competitive environment would benefit no one. In May 2008, this so-called Arctic Group of Five signed the Ilulissat Declaration, in which they pledged co-operative rather than competitive action in the overseeing of polar oil and mineral exploration, maritime security, transportation and environmental regulation. However, such agreements will remain fragile and could swiftly disappear in the face of political change in any of the signatory nations or, equally, unforeseen disaster that undermines the well-meaning commitments to collective responsibility.

Canada's vast ocean littoral is in for a future of pressure, threat and risk that only a country prepared to see itself as a *maritime* nation, with a seaward mentality committed to the defence of vital national interests, will be able to address. It is not too alarmist to state that national survival as a distinct political and social entity could well be put at risk if Canada does not demonstrate *now* a clear perception of the importance of the oceans, backed up by an investment in resources and human capital far beyond what the country has so far been willing to undertake. Both on the "Open Ocean Common" and in the waters that Canada claims as its own, a strong and visible Canadian presence will be necessary if Canada is to leave the twenty-first century as a fully independent entity.

Again, nowhere are these imperatives more immediately apparent than in the Arctic. Recent international efforts to establish in international law, and to have recognized by the United Nations Law of the Sea Commission, that a nation's legitimately held territory can extend as far as 350 miles offshore, provided it forms part of that shoreline's continental shelf, have been actively pursued by Russia. Using the line of the Lomonosov Ridge, which extends 1,100 miles into the Arctic Ocean, the Russians have moved to declare control of those subsea lands, capping their claim with the symbolic placement of a Russian flag at the geographic North Pole. What is occurring is essentially a "sector" argument, in which each nation that controls—or intends to control—continental shelf seabed that extends northward from its territory is now actively supporting that claim of control. Considering that 20 percent of the world's remaining unexplored oil reserves may be located under the Arctic Ocean, the interest is understandable. The great triangle of the northern Canadian archipelago, from Banks and Victoria islands in the southwest to Baffin Island in the southeast and Ellesmere Island in the north, and the attendant continental shelf, is Canada's to claim under such a concept. The argument for Canadian authority in this area, or even regulatory control, is weakened, however, by both insufficient presence and the continuing insistence of the powerful Americans that the waters of Nunavut are "international waterways." Resolution of this issue and the real ability of Canada to exert authority in its Arctic waters will depend on a national commitment that has yet to reach the dimensions it should, the Ilulissat Declaration notwithstanding.

The question of continental shelf claims over where national jurisdictions begin and end—and their implications for resource control—is under examination by the United Nations Commission on the Outer Limits of the Continental Shelf. In 2008 the Commission awarded Australia an additional area of continental shelf equal to one-third of Australia itself, enhancing that nation's prospects for exploiting new undersea oil and gas finds. Canada is scheduled to make an application to the Commission for adjustment of its continental shelf claim in 2013, which could have dramatic consequences in the unending resource hunt and for the state of the northern ecosystem. Canada will need to support its future claims not only within an effectively regulated international environment—something that is by no means a given—but also by arguing from a position of evident strength, both in expressions of national will and demonstrably by national assets.

The decision to scrap the Polar 8 icebreaker program, and indeed the withdrawal of a government proposal in the 1980s to equip Canada's navy with nuclear-powered submarines able to transit under polar sea ice, while defended at the time as required by financial prudence, has crippled the ability of subsequent governments to exert authority in Canada's Arctic. As Chinese research vessels have been known to transit Canadian Arctic waters with little more than token observance of Canadian authority, and as increasing numbers of foreign-flag cruise vessels begin entering the spectacular archipelago, bringing with them attendant pollution control and safe navigation concerns, it is by no means clear that Canada is prepared to respond sufficiently to these warning signs. In 2007 the Canadian government announced the acquisition of six to eight ice-strengthened naval patrol vessels; pledged to establish a year-round deepwater port at Nanisivik, on Baffin Island's northern tip; and undertook the deployment of undersea listening devices on the Arctic Ocean floor as a means of monitoring vessel traffic. Whether these prove to be effective measures of sovereignty protection or are merely "too little too late" remains to be seen. By 2100, when it is estimated that the Arctic Ocean will be fully open to navigation, Canada's actions will have secured its interests—or will be irrelevant, as will notions of real Canadian independence.

On the environmental front, Canadian governments to date have not established Canadian leadership and the attendant moral authority in environmental stewardship that the regulation and ecological survival of Canada's coastal and Arctic waters require.

Canadian commitment to the Kyoto standards of emission reduction by 2012 proved impossible to honour, and successive governments have merely exhorted corporate and private citizens to change their ways while weakly implementing largely voluntary programs of control. Canada's realities do make difficult the country's ability to meet challenging emission reduction goals—a long cold winter and immense transportation distances being among the complicating factors. Nonetheless, until Canadian governments can successfully "walk the talk" of serious emission control, and enlist the strengths of the marketplace and the private sector in the battle rather than acting in punitive opposition to them, Canada will lack the demonstrable clout that will be necessary in the years ahead to fight for the preservation and safe usage of Canadian waters—waters where Canada's national validity may be confirmed or denied.

It is the absolute national dependence on the sea that must somehow be brought to the forefront in Canadian minds, and onto the agenda books and priority lists of Canadian politicians. Whether assuming environmental responsibility or managing its seas and coasts to ensure the economy remains viable, Canada cannot see the oceans as distant borders of a vast land mass; rather, those waters surround a nation that must for its future's sake begin to see itself as, in essence, an island, and understand the importance of the sea to its identity. Canada has the second-largest continental shelf area in the world, and over 7 million Canadians live on its coasts. Canada's coastline is simply the longest of *any* nation's, and it claims an exclusive economic zone off its shores of some 3 million square miles. The sea can no longer be a matter of indifference to Canadians in the age ahead.

The economic dimensions of Canada as a maritime nation are, after all, astonishing. The fishery, as depleted and at risk as it is, still generates over $4 billion worth of annual export income; in international trade with nations other than the United States, 97 percent of Canadian exports and 70 percent of imports are carried by sea; the ports which serve that trade are linked by the sea to over a hundred different world economies; in primary resource terms, more than

50 percent of Canada's total estimated oil and gas reserves lie under the submerged continental shelf. Above that shelf, ships outbound from Canada with export goods carry cargoes valued at over 40 percent of Canada's gross domestic product, which is approaching $10 billion annually. Benefiting from a relationship with the sea, over 11,000 companies with an employee strength of some 145,000 work in the ocean sector, generating almost $20 billion worth of output for Canada's economy. Canada has been increasing by leaps and bounds its dependence on the unrestricted flow of goods over ocean trade routes to and from Canadian ports, part of a worldwide trade pattern that now ships almost 6 *billion* tons of goods by sea each year.

More than we realize, Canada is being shaped by a prosperity— or lack of it—that is linked to the sea, even as the nation's early character was forged on the waters. It follows that Canada is at risk when the safe and regulated usage of the sea is at risk, whether from terrorism or from the more benign but no less worrisome growth in maritime power of established regimes such as the People's Republic of China. The PRC's relationship with Canada at present is not an adversarial one, nor is it in China's interests to threaten the worldwide flow of trade that has set it on the path of extraordinary economic development. Nonetheless, the intention of China to develop a powerful blue-water navy and its unfeigned interest in Canada's resources should be issues of quiet awareness—and prudent preparedness—for Canadians, notwithstanding the tenor of current relations with the one-party Middle Kingdom.

In a worldwide context, it is in Canada's interests that its own waters be seen as subject to Canadian control and regulation, but also that critical ocean trading routes be kept open and world trade stability maintained in the era of globalization, when upset to that stability would severely damage the Canadian economy. Canada must have the resources to ensure that other nations do not use Canadian waters as they please, and that Canadian law is complied with when it should be. Canada must also have the capacity to work with like-minded nations to ensure legality and responsibility in open-ocean use. In the forum of world affairs it is an admitted truth that national capability is as often necessary to earn respect from one's friends as from one's possible adversaries. Canada is already aware of the determination of the Russians and even the Danes to flex their jurisdictional muscles, notwithstanding the civility of the Arctic Group of Five declarations; and Arctic issues remain alive with the United States, such as the legal status of the Northwest Passage, as we have seen, and also where the "high seas" begin that are beyond Canadian jurisdiction. Resolution of these issues must be achieved to allow effective implementation of such measures as Canada's Arctic Waters Pollution Prevention Act, and such resolution will only come to pass when forceful Canadian government action and investment in the active demonstration of sovereignty is witnessed by those with whom Canada has issues. Crudely put, Canada must use it or lose it.

Clearly, government inaction with regard to Canada's three oceans and the Great Lakes is not an option. A majority of Canadians believe that sustained action is necessary to address global warming and threats to the environment in general. The issues of sovereignty and environmental regulation must be brought to the forefront of Canadian minds in equal measure, for to lose control of those waters and lands where Canadians can have an effect is to begin losing the larger battle for the health of the earth itself. Certain steps to be taken are self-evident, difficult to be sure in an uncertain age when oil prices, long departed from their historic levels, will remain unpredictable and render all modern activity difficult.

As a primary, front-line agency, the Canadian Coast Guard must receive a greater share of government resources in order to allow it to replace its aging fleet and its equally senior seagoing staff. It must also have in hand the resources that will enable it to expand as a visible and active presence in the waters of the Arctic as well as on the east and west coasts and the Great Lakes. Understaffed and underfunded at present, the CCG requires a refreshed and *sustained* commitment from government that will allow, possibly through a "continuous-build" ship construction program, for the steady improvement and enlargement of its operational fleet. It must have the funds to recruit new personnel and to incorporate the best in new technologies in navigation, pollution control, search and rescue, and traffic surveillance. And it must have the ability to be *there* on the scene within a reasonable time when circumstances require. The degree to which a nation actually sails the waters it claims as its own often dictates the degree to which other nations respect those claims. The Canadian Coast Guard must see, in the new Arctic being revealed, a frontier of opportunity for which it is properly prepared by government.

Canada's navy, as the century progresses, must receive and continue to receive—with the same "continuous-build" commitment that allows steady fleet replacement, as well as sustained budgetary support—the help it needs to remain capable of conducting surveillance above, on or under the surface of Canada's waters. It must have sufficient ships of appropriate modern types to be able to patrol and, again, be *there* in all Canadian waters, whether the Grand Banks, the Arctic or the fjords of British Columbia. It must be able to respond in any manner Canada's government may require, in any role from search and rescue to disaster relief, from drug interdiction or environmental protection to the simple demonstration of sovereignty, working in close co-operation with its sister agency, the Canadian Coast Guard.

Internationally, the Canadian navy must hold on to its current technical and operational capability in order to retain international respect, to offer the Canadian government the full range of policy options a navy allows, and to make meaningful contributions to Canada's alliance partnerships. It must be able to contribute to the maintenance of international stability in the face of political turmoil, war, terrorism or natural disaster. In all respects, it must continue to carry the face of Canada's values, laws, commitments and national character into participation in the international ocean community from a position of capable self-confidence. Canada's prosperity and eventual survival require no less.

Most importantly, room must somehow be made in the curricula of Canada's schools and in the media world for the inspiration in young Canadians of a knowledge of what the sea has meant for Canada and what it means in the looming future. Somehow, the opening of the ice in the Arctic must be presented as a metaphor for the opening of astonishing new opportunities and a new vision of the possibilities awaiting Canada. Somehow, young Canadians must be encouraged to reach out again to the dark, dramatic seas that surround us, to see the full panorama of what once happened there, and to find a personal destiny and a promise for the country that has faded from view in recent years. It is a promise that sailed with d'Iberville and Angus Walters; with Bernier and McClure; and with Joshua Slocum or the seasick teenagers of the escort corvettes of the Second World War. It is the promise that awaits a Canada that sees itself as an island set in a sea of glittering possibilities, and which embarks on a voyage upon that sea. It is heartening, in the final analysis, to see that there is evidence Canada's young people have been hearing the message of that promise; and in their commitment to a green, sustainable world of international co-operation will lie the greatest guarantee of Canada's survival, and of the health and bounty of the oceans that surround it.

Epilogue

I F THERE is any great obstacle to the claiming by Canada of its maritime rights and heritage in the crowded, changing world that is unfolding, it must surely be the ignorance of its citizens of what Canadians have achieved and experienced on the sea, and of how the sea has affected Canada and is vital to its survival in the future. Ignorance of the past and of the lessons of history is a regrettable feature of current education, wherein so much that arguably is vital for a citizen to know is relegated to an elective process, with national history only one of many choices rather than a core requirement of learning. Writers have quoted far too often the saying attributed to, among others, Santayana that those who are ignorant of history are doomed to repeat it. Perhaps for Canadians it is more a matter that those who are ignorant of history are doomed to lose that history, and the nation out of which it sprang.

As futurists extol the value of an increasingly wired society, which paradoxically provides for instant communication while physically isolating individuals to focus on their desktops or hand-held screens rather than each other's faces, traditionalists wary of the digitized world view with alarm a society that is coming to prefer to see the world in its digitized and electronic depiction rather than in its reality. The capacity of computer-generated imagery to create scenes of staggering verisimilitude is unquestioned. What is disturbing is the degree to which the virtual world as a forum for adventure, achievement, personal validation and growth is overtaking and replacing the real world; and, further, how misconceptions about the nature of the environment or the history of human society, products of a decayed educational process and squeezed through the twin lenses of ideology and the limitations of visual technology, pass for the experiences once garnered in the real world and in real society. To be aware of Canada's astonishing *real* physical environment, now to be augmented by the surge of activity and opportunity in the Arctic, is to gaze upon a canvas of opportunity on which almost any tableau could be painted. Yet there are signs that the interest in, the will to explore, and even the simple caring about all the potential that is out there may go unheeded in generations abandoning the classroom, the playing field and the challenges of the physical world to concentrate on a virtual world of manufactured images. A technology intended to enhance the human capacity to experience the world that surrounds us has, instead, *become* the world, to a dismaying degree at a time when young Canadians' commitment to the real world beyond the front door has never been more needed.

If Canada's astounding coastline, her endless fjords and bays, her stretches of sea-washed beaches and her towering, rocky archipelagos of newly revealed islands are to have the love and commitment of a nation determined to hang on to this heritage—what it meant in the past, means now and will mean in the future—the story must be told and retold of how all this came to be Canada. It must be part of the fabric of Canada's national educational ethos that every young Canadian understands how the sea affected the way in which we came to exist as a people and a society, and how we are dependent on the sea for our continued existence. And that understanding must somehow be imparted so that young Canadian men and women see again with joy the promise that lies outside their door, on the seas that stretch away to the horizon, and have the will to claim that promise.

Islands have the capacity to be places of escape, of refuge or retirement from a hectic or threatening world. The northern island that is Canada offers refuge indeed on an often cruel and tumultuous planet. But it also offers a promise of prosperity and national growth as bright as the shimmering glints of sunlight on the waters that surround it. Canadians have only to reflect on their past and then embrace those waters for that bright promise to become a reality.

SELECT BIBLIOGRAPHY

Abreu-Ferreira, D. *The Cod Trade in Early Modern Portugal*. St. John's: Memorial University of Newfoundland, 1996.

Akrigg, G., and H. Akrigg. *British Columbia Chronicle 1778–1846*. Vancouver: Discovery Press, 1975.

Alberts, R. *The Most Extraordinary Adventures of Major Robert Stobo*. Boston: Houghton Mifflin, 1965.

Armour, C., and T. Lackey. *Sailing Ships of the Maritimes*. Toronto: McGraw-Hill Ryerson, 1975.

Ashe, G. *The Quest for America*. New York: Praeger Publishers, 1971.

Backman, B., and P. Backman. *Bluenose*. Toronto: McClelland and Stewart, 1965.

Bakeless, J. *The Eyes of Discovery*. New York: Dover Publications, 1961.

Bamford, D. *Freshwater Heritage: A History of Sail on the Great Lakes*. Toronto: Dundurn Press, 2007.

Bawlf, S. *The Secret Voyage of Sir Francis Drake, 1577–1580*. New York: Penguin Books, 2003.

Beaglehole, J.C. *The Life of Captain James Cook*. Stanford, CA: Stanford University Press, 1974.

Berton, P. *The Great Lakes*. Toronto: Stoddart Publishers, 1996.

Bourrie, M. *True Canadian Stories of the Great Lakes*. Toronto: Prospero Books, 2004.

Choyce, L. *Nova Scotia: Shaped by the Sea*. Toronto: Penguin Books, 1996.

Coates, R., and W. Morrison. *The Sinking of the Princess Sophia*. Toronto: Oxford University Press, 1990.

Coen, R. *The Voyage of the SS Manhattan*. Minutes, ARCUS 16th Annual Meeting and Arctic Forum, 2004. Fairbanks: University of Alaska, 2004.

Cordingly, D. *Under the Black Flag*. New York: Harcourt Brace, 1995.

Crooker, W. *Pirates of the North Atlantic*. Halifax: Nimbus Publishing, 2004.

Debenham, F. *Discovery and Exploration*. London: Paul Hamlyn, 1960.

Dennis, J. *The Living Great Lakes*. New York: St. Martin's Press, 2003.

Dixon, E. *Bones, Boats and Bison: Archeology and the First Colonization of Western America*. Albuquerque: University of New Mexico Press, 1999.

Douglas, W.A.B., R. Sarty, and M. Whitby. *No Higher Purpose: The Official Operational History of the Royal Canadian Navy in the Second World War, 1939–1943*. Vol. II, Part 1. St. Catharines, ON: Vanwell Publishing, 2002.

———. *A Blue Water Navy: The Official Operational History of the Royal Canadian Navy in the Second World War, 1943–1945*. Vol. II, Part 2. St. Catharines, ON: Vanwell Publishing, 2007.

Elliot, R., and A. McNairn. *Reflections of an Era*. Saint John: New Brunswick Museum, 1987.

Fagan, B. *Ancient North America*. New York: Thames and Hudson, 2005.

Fiske, J. *New France and New England*. Boston: Houghton Mifflin, 1902.

Forester, J., and A. Forester. *Fishing: British Columbia's Commercial Fishing History*. Saanichton, BC: Hancock House, 1975.

Freuchen, P. *Book of the Eskimos*. New York: Bramhall House, 1961.

Froud, J. *On the High Seas*. St. John's: Jesperson Press, 1998.

Gough, B. *Distant Dominion: Britain and the Northwest Coast of America, 1579–1809*. Vancouver: UBC Press, 1980.

———. *Gunboat Frontier: British Maritime Authority and Northwest Coast Indians, 1846–1890*. Vancouver: UBC Press, 1984.

Griffin, G. *Legends of the Evergreen Coast*. Vancouver: Clarke and Stuart, 1934.

Halford, R. *The Unknown Navy*. St. Catharines, ON: Vanwell Publishers, 1995.

Horwood, H., and E. Butts. *Pirates and Outlaws of Canada: 1610 to 1932*. Toronto: Lynx Images, 2003.

Ingstad, H. *Westward to Vinland*. New York: St. Martin's Press, 1969.

Jenness, D. *The People of the Twilight*. Toronto: Macmillan, 1928.

Johnson, E. *Legends of Vancouver*. Toronto: McClelland and Stewart, 1920.

Jones, G. *The Norse Atlantic Saga*. London: Oxford University Press, 1964.

Kert, F. *Prize and Prejudice: Privateering and Naval Prizes in Atlantic Canada in the War of 1812*. St. John's: International Maritime Economic History Association, 1997.

———. *Trimming Yankee Sails: Pirates and Privateers of New Brunswick*. Fredericton: Goose Lane Editions, 2005.

Kimble, G., and D. Good. *Geography of the Northlands*. London: Chapman and Hall, 1955.

Kirwan, L. *A History of Polar Exploration*. Harmondsworth: Penguin Books, 1959.

Koppel, T. *Lost World*. New York: Atria Books, 2003.

Lamb, J. *The Corvette Navy*. Toronto: Macmillan, 1977.

LeBourdais, D. *Stefansson: Ambassador of the North*. Montreal: Harvest House, 1963.

Macbeth, J. *Ready Aye Ready*. Toronto: Key Porter Books, 1989.

Maddison, G., et al. *Leadmark: The Navy's Strategy for 2020*. Ottawa: Queen's Printer, 2001.

Mahan, A. *The Influence of Sea Power upon History, 1660–1783*. London: Methuen Press, 1965. First published 1890 by Little, Brown.

Marsters, R. *Bold Privateers: Terror, Plunder and Profit on Canada's Atlantic Coast*. Halifax: Formac Publishing, 2004.

McCann, F. *English Discovery of America to 1585*. New York: King's Crown Press, Columbia University, 1952.

McInnis, E. *Canada: A Political and Social History*. Toronto: Holt, Rinehart and Winston, 1982.

McLennan, J. *Louisbourg from Its Foundation to Its Fall*. Sydney, NS: Fortress Press, 1969.

McMillan, A., and E. Yellowhorn. *First Peoples in Canada*. Vancouver: Douglas and McIntyre, 2004.

Menzies, G. *1421: The Year China Discovered the World*. London: Bantam Press, 2002.

Miller, D., and S. Hobson. *The Persian Excursion: The Canadian Navy in the Gulf War*. Toronto: Canadian Institute of Strategic Studies, 1995.

Milner, M. *North Atlantic Run: The Royal Canadian Navy and the Battle for the Convoys*. Toronto: University of Toronto Press, 1985.

Molyneaux, G. *British Columbia. An Illustrated History*. Vancouver: Polestar Press, 1992.

Moore, C. *The Loyalists*. Toronto: McClelland and Stewart, 1984.

Mowat, F. *Ordeal by Ice*. Boston: Little, Brown, 1960.

Muhlenbrunch, C., and R. Stuart. *Great Lakes Basin*. Washington: Association for the Advancement of Science, 1962.

Musk, G. *Canadian Pacific: The Story of the Famous Shipping Line*. Toronto: Holt, Rinehart and Winston, 1981.

Neatby, L. *In Quest of the Northwest Passage*. New York: Thomas Y. Crowell, 1958.

Newman, P. *Company of Adventurers*. Markham, ON: Penguin Books, 1985.

Nicholson, G. *Vancouver Island's West Coast, 1762–1962*. Victoria: Morriss Printing, 1962.

Norcross, E., ed. *The Company on the Coast*. Nanaimo, BC: Nanaimo Historical Society, 1983.

Palmer, P. *History of Lake Champlain*. Fleischmanns, NY: Purple Mountain Press, 1997.

Parkman, F. *A Half-Century of Conflict*. New York: Collier Books, 1962.

Parry, J. *The Establishment of the European Hegemony, 1415–1715*. New York: Harper and Row, 1961.

Pyle, H. *Tales of Pirates and Buccaneers*. New York: Random House, 1994.

Raddall, T. *The Path of Destiny*. Toronto: Doubleday, 1957.

Ray, A. *I Have Lived Here Since the World Began*. Toronto: Lester Publishing, 1996.

Rediker, M. *Villains of All Ages: Atlantic Pirates in the Golden Age*. Boston: Beacon Press, 2004.

Roosevelt, T. *The Naval War of 1812*. New York: G.P. Putnam's Sons, n.d.

Rutledge, J. *Century of Conflict*. New York: Doubleday, 1956.

Schull, J. "Masters and Men." In *Canadian Stories of the Sea*, ed. V. Suthren, 116. Toronto: Oxford University Press, 1993.

Seaver, K. *The Frozen Echo: Greenland and the Exploration of North America A.D. 1000–1500*. Stanford, CA: Stanford University Press, 1996.

Seger, E. *Seafaring Labour: The Merchant Marine of Atlantic Canada, 1820–1914.* Kingston, ON: McGill–Queen's University Press, 1989.

Severin, T. *The Brendan Voyage.* New York: McGraw-Hill, 1978.

Slocum, J. *Sailing Alone Around the World.* Montreal: The Reprint Society, 1949.

Snider, C. *Under the Red Jack.* London: Martin Hopkinson, 1928.

———. *Tarry Breeks and Velvet Garters.* Toronto: Ryerson Press, 1958.

Spalding, D., A. Spalding, and L. Pitt. *BC Ferries and the Canadian West Coast.* Vancouver: Attitude Publishing, 1996.

Stefansson, V. *Unsolved Mysteries of the Arctic.* New York: MacMillan, 1938.

Stokesbury, J. *Navy and Empire.* New York: William Morrow, 1983.

Suthren, V., ed. *Canadian Stories of the Sea.* Toronto: Oxford University Press, 1993.

———. *To Go Upon Discovery: James Cook and Canada from 1758 to 1779.* Toronto: Dundurn Press, 2000.

Thomson, G. *The Search for the Northwest Passage.* New York: MacMillan, 1975.

Twigg, A. *First Invaders: The Literary Origins of British Columbia.* Vancouver: Ronsdale Press, 2004.

Voss, J. *The Venturesome Voyages of Captain Voss.* London: Martin Hopkinson, 1913.

White, H. "Nootka Whaling." In *Raincoast Chronicles First Five.* Vancouver: Harbour Publishing, 1975.

Whitehall, W., ed. *New England Blockaded in 1814: The Journal of Henry Edward Napier, Lieutenant in HMS Nymphe.* Salem: Peabody Museum, 1939.

Wright, J: *A History of the Native People of Canada.* Vols. 1 and 2. Ottawa-Hull: Canadian Museum of Civilization, 1995.

Eirik the Red, 40–41, 43
Eiriksdóttir, Freydis, 47
Eiriksson, Leif, 43–45
Eiriksson, Thorvald, 45–46, *46*
Elizabeth I (queen of England), 63, 183
Elliot, Robert, 243, 253
England
    conflict with French, 84–91, 93–120, 131
    exploration of Canadian waters by, 54–56, 63–66, 74. *See also* Northwest Passage
    exploration of Pacific coast, 182–83, 185–86, 188–90, 191
    and North Atlantic fishery, 51–52
    relations with Spanish, 63–64, 183, 185–86, 188–90
    support of French-led fur trade, 76–78
Esquimalt (B.C.), *196*, 289
European exploration, background to, 49–50

Faeroe Islands, 29, 30, 37, 51
Fagundes, Alvarez, 54
Fawson, John, 171
Fenian Raids, 282
Ferrelo, Bartholeme, 66
First Nations
    of Atlantic coast, 13–16, *46*
    and Great Lakes, 220
    of Pacific coast, 12–13, 17–20, 22, 179–81, 183–85, 186, 194–95
    relations with French, 76, 79, 81, 82, 83, 115, 220, 221
    and salmon fishery, 315, 316
    of St. Lawrence River, 16
    War of 1812 and, 153, 157
    See also fur trade; Inuit; Iroquois; Mi'kmaq
Fiske, John, 61

Flinn, Scott, 259
Forbes, Captain James N., 249
Forester, Joseph and Anne, 315
Fort Frontenac, 79, 80, 222, 223. *See also* Cataraqui
Fort Nelson. *See* York Factory
Fort Niagara, 114, 115, 128, 222, 224
Fort Vancouver, 193, 195, 197
Fowler, George, 284
Foxe, Luke, 71, 205
France
    conflict with English, 84–91, 93–120, 131
    exploration of Canadian waters by, 58, 74–75, 79–84
    and First Nations, 75–76, 79, 81, 82, 83, 115, 220, 221
    and fur trade, 75–78, 79–80, 84–91, 121–23, 220, 222
    naval power on Lake Ontario, 79–80, 114–15, 221–22
    and North Atlantic fishery, 51
    on Pacific coast, 187–88
    settlement attempts by, 60–63
    See also New France
Francis I (king of France), 59
Franklin, Sir John, 207, 208, 210, 214
Fraser, Simon, 123, 191
Freuchen, Peter, 21–24
Frobisher, Martin, 63, *64*, 203
Frontenac, Louis de Buade, Comte de, 79, 80, 97–98, 99, 220
Froude, Captain John W., 252
Fuca, Juan de. *See* Valerianos, Apostolos
Fuller, Tommy, 296
fur trade
    Anglo-French conflict over, 84–91, 131
    beginnings of, 72–78
    decline of, 123–24
    First Nations and, 75–76

French and, 75–78, 79–80, 84–91,
121–23, 220, 222
on Pacific coast, 186–96 passim
See also First Nations; Hudson's
Bay Company; North West
Company
Fu-Sang, 33

George V (king of England), 263
Germinus, 28
Gilbert, Humphrey, 63
Gillam, Captain Zacariah, 76, 77
Gimblett, Richard, 297
Gloucester (Mass.), 257, 259, 261,
264, 278
Gnuppson, Bishop Eric, 47
Godfrey, Alexander, 172
Gough, Barry, 181
Grand Banks. *See* Atlantic coast
Grant, Alexander, 154
Gravé, François, Sieur de Pont *dit*
Pontgravé, 60, 62
Great Lakes, 219–40
Anglo-French conflict on, 223–24
canal construction, 232, 235, 236
characteristics of, 219–20
English naval presence on, 127–28,
222–24
and First Nations, 220
formation of, 13
French naval presence on, 79–80,
114–15, 220, 221–22
and fur trade, 79–84, 122
lighthouses of, 236–38, 239
merchant fleet of, 307, 312–13
problems facing, 318, 324
Provincial Marine fleet on, 225–27
sailing fleet on, 230–31
shipbuilding on, 290
steamboats on, 229–30, 231–32,
233–36
traditional freighter of, 223, 233–34

as transportation corridor, 222,
229, 230, 231, 232–33, 235
in War of 1812, 153–61, *155*, *158*
wrecks in, 236, 238–40
See also names of individual lakes
Greenland, 31, 40–43, 47, 52, 70, 74
Griffin, George H., 183
Gulf Islands Ferries, 311
Guzzwell, John, 267

Hakluyt, Richard, 63, 64
Halford, Robert, 304, 305
Halifax
founding of, 243
as port, 302, 318
as Port of Registry, 244
and privateering, 176, 177
as RCN base, 289, *291*
as Royal Navy base, 116, 125–27,
151
and shipping industry, 245
Vice-Admiralty Court at, 164
See also Royal Navy
Hall, Captain George, 154, 156
Hall, Samuel, 146
Harald I (king of Norway), 37, 38, 39
Harbour Grace (Nfld.), 126, 138–39,
141
Haro, Gonzalo López de, 189
Harrison, General William Henry,
157
Hastings, John, 239–40
Hearne, Samuel, 131, 205, 206, 207
Hellyer, Paul, 320
Henday, Anthony, 121
Hennepin, Father Louis, 80–84, 221
Henry IV (king of France), 60, 61
Henry VII (king of England), 56
Herjolfsson, Bjarni, 42–43
Heyerdahl, Thor, 30
Hezeta, Bruno de, 185
Hibbard, Commander J.C., 297

Hill, Brigadier John, 105–7
Holland, Samuel, 116, 124, 125, 126,
127, 243
Hopkins, Francis, 75
Hose, Commodore Walter, 288–89
Hudson, Henry, 65–66, 201, 203
Hudson Bay
Anglo-French conflict on, 84–91,
90, 131
Europeans discover, 65
and fur trade, 76–78, 84–91
lost by French, 108
and search for Northwest Passage,
70, 71, 204–5, 207, 208
Hudson Strait, 65, 70, 71, 76, 77, 204
Hudson's Bay Company
charting of Arctic coast, 209
competition to, 122–24
conflict with French, 85, 87, 131
lack of interest in exploration by,
121–22
and Northwest Passage, 205–6
on Pacific coast, 193–97, 310, 315
predecessor of, 77
See also fur trade; Pacific coast, fur
trade on
Hull, General William, 153

icebreakers, 216, 313, 314, 328
Iceland
English off, 52, 56, 57
Irish in, 30, 31, 38
Norse in, 38, 39–41, 42–43, 47
Île Royale. See Cape Breton Island
Île St-Jean. See Prince Edward Island
Ilulissat Declaration, 326, 327
immigration, 301–3, 302
Imrama, the, 29
Indians. See First Nations
Ingstad, Helge, 45
International Fishermen's Trophy,
258–62, 264

international waters, governance of,
330–31
Inuit, 13
challenges facing, 324
conflicts with Europeans, 65
first encounters with Europeans,
45–47, 206
folk tale of, 24–25
settlement in North America of, 16
traditional way of life of, 20–24
See also Arctic; First Nations
Ireland, early contact with North
America, 29–30, 31
Iroquois
early French encounters with, 58,
59–60
English and, 108
French and, 76, 79, 81, 82, 220
traditional way of life of, 16
See also First Nations
Irving, Captain J., 310

James, Thomas, 71–72, 205
James Bay, 65, 72, 85
James I (king of England), 138, 141–42
Japan Current, 33, 67
Jay, John, 55
Jefferson, Thomas, 152, 191
Jefferys, C.W., 75, 158, 302
João I (king of Portugal), 50
João II (king of Portugal), 51
Johnson, "Pirate" Bill, 148–50
Jones, Gwyn, 38, 40, 44
Jones, John Paul, 171
Jordan, Edward, 147–48
Juan de Fuca Strait, 67, 186, 189
junks, 32–33, 51

Karselfni, Thorfinn, 46
kayaks, 22–23
Kelly, John, 148
Kelsey, Henry, 90–91